Advanced Witchcraft

Go
Deeper,

Reach
Further,

Fly
Higher

Edain McCoy

Llewellyn Publications
Woodbury, Minnesota

FIRST EDITION
Eleventh Printing, 2018

Book design and editing by Rebecca Zins
Cover design by Gavin Dayton Duffy
Interior illustrations by Llewellyn Art Department

Library of Congress Cataloging-in-Publication Data
McCoy, Edain, 1957-
  Advanced witchcraft: go deeper, reach further, fly higher / Edain McCoy.—1st. ed.
        p.   cm.
  Includes bibliographical references and index.
  ISBN 13: 978-0-7387-0513-2
  ISBN 10: ISBN 0-7387-0513-6
  1. Witchcraft. I. Title.

BF1571.M45 2004
133.4'3—dc22

                                                                    2003065805

Llewellyn Worldwide does not participate in, endorse, or have any authority or responsibility concerning private business transactions between our authors and the public.
  All mail addressed to the author is forwarded but the publisher cannot, unless specifically instructed by the author, give out an address or phone number.
  Any Internet references contained in this work are current at publication time, but the publisher cannot guarantee that a specific location will continue to be maintained. Please refer to the publisher's website for links to authors' websites and other sources.

Llewellyn Publications
A Division of Llewellyn Worldwide, Ltd.
2143 Wooddale Drive, Dept. 978-0-7387-0513-2
Woodbury, MN 55125-2989, U.S.A.
www.llewellyn.com
Llewellyn is a registered trademark of Llewellyn Worldwide, Ltd.

Printed in the United States of America
on recycled paper

Advanced Witchcraft

About the Author

Edain McCoy became a self-initiated Witch in 1981 and underwent a formal initiation in 1983 with a large San Antonio coven. She has been researching alternative spiritualities since her teens, when she was first introduced to the Kaballah. Since that time, she has studied a variety of magickal traditions, including Celtic, Appalachian, Curanderismo, Wiccan, Jewitchery, and Irish Wittan, the latter in which she is a priestess of Brighid and an elder. An alumnus of the University of Texas with a bachelor of arts in history, she is affiliated with several professional writer's organizations and is listed in the reference guides *Contemporary Authors* and *Who's Who in America*. Articles by her have appeared in *Fate, Circle, Enlightenments*, and similar periodicals. Edain also worked for ten years as a stockbroker with several large investment firms. This former woodwind player for the Lynchburg (VA) Symphony claims both the infamous feuding McCoy family of Kentucky and Sir Roger Williams, the seventeenth-century religious dissenter, as branches on her diverse family tree. *Advanced Witchcraft* is her seventeenth book.

Other Books by Edain McCoy

Contents

The Earth Chapters: Where Our Powers Live

The Spirit Chapters: Where Our Web Is Woven

Resources & References: Where Our Work Continues

Acknowledgments

There is no way I could hope to thank every individual who contributed to my thoughts, ideas, beliefs, and practices of Witchcraft over the past twenty-plus years. However, for their belief in this project and their invaluable input, I must offer a sincere "couldn't-have-done-it-without-you" thank you to some very special people.

Along with my deepest thanks to each of you for just being who and what you are, I wish you all the blessings of love, success, joy, health, and magick in this life and all those yet to come.

Carl Llewellyn Weschcke
Nancy Mostad
Rebecca Zins
Natalie Harter
Llewellyn's creative staff
Susan
Timothy Roderick
Michele Walker
Sue "Wizzo" Wegman
Dagonet Dewr
Don & Billie Taylor
Lady Cheetah
Rev. Breanna WinDancer
Liban
Jack Sullivan
K. C. Valera
Joanie Neff
María Cervantes

Dorothy Morrison
Nimue
Mollie Síobhan Malone
Avigail MacPhee
Lupita
Kerr Cuhulain
Gail Wood
Zelena Winters
Maggie Shayne
Charlotte Brisbon
Diane Holmes
Barbara
. . . and to all my other cherished sisters at "Witchesinprint" who awe and inspire me with their beauty, talent, and strength

A Special Thank You

I would be remiss not to acknowledge the contribution of one very special man. He was the first to answer my query, "What does advanced Witchcraft mean to you?" His simple, honest answer raised the bar to a level that set the tone for all the responses that followed, and he changed forever many of my own ideas about advanced practice.

In many ways his response stirred within me memories of my father's sense of duty and giving to the community he served. My father, a left-wing Protestant minister, allowed me to explore my interest in the Craft when I was a teenager. He was secure enough in his beliefs that he did not have to force others to accept them in order to feel his path was the right path for him.

Therefore, I must send a special thank you to Dagonet Dewr, Chief of Thalia Clan, membership director of the Pagan Project, founder and activist of the Indianapolis Metro Pagan Allied Coalition. In the recent past he held a leadership role and was an active participant in the Indiana chapter of Witches Against Religious Discrimination (WARD).

Thank you, Dagonet. May your unselfish dedication to giving of yourself to others return those blessings to you three times three. Your words and actions set a high standard for anyone wishing to call themselves an advanced practitioner, one that the rest of us should strive to achieve.

The beginning . . .

Several years ago, when it was first suggested that I write a book on advanced Witchcraft, I refused to even consider such an overwhelming task. First of all, I had no idea how one would define "advanced" within a mystery religion, especially one with so many diverse arts under its umbrella. If that wasn't enough to put me off, I also doubted there was a large enough market for an advanced Craft text. In the third place, I felt a book covering so broad a topic would either be too massive to be manageable or too small to be of any use.

I saw no point in producing a book so esoteric that it would either be unreadable or impractical. I imagined a writer would either find himself trying explain things *ad infinitum* that were not comprehensible to those who had not experienced them, or he would find no words suitable and the few pages he could crank out would be—to quote a trite but true phrase—preaching to the choir.

Yep, I was convinced no mortal could hope to capture between two covers the essence of "that which can never be told."

As most practitioners of the Craft learn within a few years, this old magickal adage about not being able to speak of metaphysical or spiritual mysteries has little or nothing to do with the keeping of an individual's or tradition's Craft secrets, but reminds us that Witchcraft—or Wicca and any other sect of Pagan practice—is an *experiential spiritual path*, one we must undergo alone. No priest or priestess can do it for us, and no one else can step in and score points for us with the deities. Witchcraft is a religion for those with the tenacity of charging bulls, not for flocks of sheep waiting to be led.

When we emerge from our mystical experiences we find, as have those before us, that our deeper mysteries are ones for which no human vocabulary is adequate. You can talk and write and rifle through your thesauruses, but if you've already been there and back, you know as well as I that whatever words you come up with to relate your experiences are just not hitting the bull's-eye. Hence, the mysteries of Witchcraft are packaged as "that which can never be told."

To complicate matters further, we know the experience—though leading us all in the same direction and displaying a certain amount of conformities—will be different for everyone. Our inadequate human vocabulary has created confusion as teachers and writers have tried to distill the essence of the miraculous into descriptions non-initiates can comprehend. This has caused newcomers to expect certain practices to be other than what they are, and many give up in frustration even though they may be on the right path.

A prime example of this problem is the art of astral projection, or sending your consciousness from your physical body to another time period or location. Descriptions of how this is done, how it feels, how it looks, and how your mind perceives the experience have muddled so many minds that I often get letters from readers who I'm certain have been successful and are on their way to becoming skilled in this art, but for some reason they are sure they are not getting anywhere. The reason: "So-and-so said this or that, but what happened to me was different . . . I think."

As you can see by the book you now hold in your hands, I eventually forged ahead and gave my best effort to what I thought was an impossible task. I apologize in advance for any inadequacies in my semantics or other deficiencies in the execution of this book. I can only write from my own experience, and with the limitations of human vocabulary.

Advanced Witchcraft is written for those who feel they are what I term "advanced-intermediate practitioners"—those who are already standing at the threshold of advanced practice and are looking for a guide to help them step through it and on to a new path that will ultimately bring them closer to the deities. Though written from the perspective of Anglo-Celtic Witchcraft and Eclectic Wicca, its concepts and practices should be familiar and/or adaptable to other Pagan spiritual traditions.

This Is Not Wicca 101

Be warned that we will move quickly through many ideas and practices, and we will not stop to explain basic concepts and how-to points to those not ready to comprehend or experience advanced work. This book is targeted to those who are well past the "what's an athame" stage and are ready for a meatier text. There's nothing so frustrating to an advanced-intermediate or advanced practitioner as reading the latest book on the Craft and having to skim every few paragraphs while the author goes on a three-page tangent to explain to beginners the reasons, causes, practices, correspondences, or concepts that are taught in virtually all Witchcraft 101 books. If you want to be a knowledgeable Witch you should seek out and study these books before you embark on this one. There are plenty of excellent primers available. A trip to your local library, bookstore, or online bookseller will help you find what you need. Books on Craft basics have exploded in the last decade, so your problem will be in narrowing down your selections, not in discovering them.

Since Witchcraft boomed to the forefront of religious thought in the 1970s and 1980s, tens of thousands have committed themselves to this path. Many now can boast of being Witches for ten, twenty, or even thirty years or more, and they are seeking advanced teachings or new ways to enhance their current advanced practices.

Though the magickal community now has many experienced teachers, they are not available to everyone as they would have been in the days when humanity lived in tribes or clans (advanced practitioners, please see my request to you in appendix B). In these settings, the tribal or clan elders would have selected those youths whom they believed could master these mysteries, do good for the community, and pass the magick along to the next generation. For the student who excelled, there was no longer a line of demarcation between the worlds of the divine and the mundane. All tasks, all efforts, all work—no matter how menial—served a higher purpose. It still does and we must learn to recognize what that is for each of us.

Advanced Witch What?

A craft is both a noun and a verb. As a noun it refers to an object that has been created, or to a skill or proficiency one possesses. As a verb it means to create with skill or proficiency. Witchcraft, then, must be the art of skillful creation.

There are many skills under the umbrella of the Craft. As you read this book, please let it remain in the forefront of your consciousness that one advanced text will not suit everyone and it should only be used as a starting point for your leaping into the world of the many arenas of advanced Witchcraft. No one of us is proficient in them all.

Some skills no doubt came to you with ease when you first began your year-and-a-day study toward initiation, while other skills that seemed simple may have eluded you for a long time, and may elude you still.

An excellent example of this was seen in a review I read on one of my previous books wherein the reviewer blasted my assertion that remote healing, or the art of astral projecting to someone's sickbed to perform healing, was an advanced art. Therefore, I was just out for the money and she would trust nothing I said ever again.

Regardless of the fact that, like all writers, I've caught factual errors in my work after a book has gone to print, and because of the whopping thirty cents per book the average author in any genre garners in royalties, I'd like to tell this reviewer that I receive letters and e-mails daily from Witches, old and new, who have serious difficulties with astral projection. Again, part of the blame falls on that aforementioned lack of adequate language to relate the process.

Healing is another art at which some Witches are born to excel; others have to work at it over and over. For instance, I found astral projection came to me without too much frustration, while learning to heal others was harder to learn. I still do not consider myself a gifted healer, even though this is one of the Craft's highest callings and most noble arts. Once upon a time it also got a lot of people burned at the stake.

Without digressing further, the idea that others may find it easy to combine both of these arts and work with them simultaneously would dishearten many Witches at all experience levels who give both of these skills their best efforts and still fall short. They would be thrilled to gain some proficiency in just one of these arts, least of all both. I hope that reviewer will one day realize how blessed she is to have these talents born within her, and that she will learn to use those gifts to help others learn rather than belittle them. I'm sure I could learn from her myself. We are all always students in the Craft, and whether we know it or not, we are all also teachers.

Taking Your Next Step, Not Your Last

To advance in any art we must always continue to read, listen, question, practice, and study. Studying Witchcraft is comparable to taking the entire volume of written and oral knowledge, reducing it to sand, and putting it into a huge sifter to see what remains. You'll also find you may have to go through this process several times. As someone once said to me, "Learning is like taking a drink of water from a fire hose. Sure, you get some water in your mouth, but most of it blows right past you."

Take from this book only what is valuable to you and leave the rest. I have tried to cover advanced Witchcraft as I have experienced it, with the full realization that not all of it will apply to every reader. We all have our own inborn talents. Because of this you may find you want to tear out one chapter and cast it into a tar pit while having the urge to frame another in gold.

Think of your advancing in your practice as if you were climbing a huge tree. The higher you climb, the more choices you are presented for exploring different paths, all of which shoot off into dozens of other sub-studies. Some areas may not interest you. Some may be so fascinating that they absorb your entire life. They will cause you to follow what you think are logical sequences of events, and then, to your delight or frustration, will loop you right back to where you began. Others may be familiar friends challenging you to move forward into their deeper mysteries. Others may be harder to grasp as your climb continues, but the effort may well be worth your while. Also know that the many branches, limbs, and twigs on this vast tree hold secrets you may never master, but you can learn something of all of them with study and hard work.

With that said, let's begin our adventure across the threshold into the world of the advanced Witch by finding out what other Witches think and feel about the advanced arts. Be forewarned that the arguments each Witch makes for her feelings and ideas have been gained over time through hard work, and none are wholly right or wholly wrong, but they are expressed in the only language each can find. Know also that some opinions may validate your current beliefs, but many others may have you wanting to pull out your hair. Advanced Witchcraft is not the "God in your pocket" pathway of some churches who present you with an official platinum-plated master's license when you're finished.

Like anything else in the Craft—or in life—embarking on advanced practice is only the beginning of yet another cycle of deaths and rebirths, endings and beginnings. This new course of study and practice is demanding. It requires a mind that can see a full 360 degrees all at one time before you can step very far across the threshold.

It's not an easy task you've set for yourself, as you already know by having come this far. Practicing advanced Witchcraft is the challenge you accept when you know your end goal is to be at one with the deities, the creator force, and all that is, was, or ever will be.

It is hard work, and it will have its moments of frustration, but it's also a joy and sometimes even lots of fun.

As our people have called to one another for generations untold:

Let the rites begin!

the air chapters

❧

Where our thoughts are born

one

The Advanced Witch and the Craft

In the beginning of your journey into the many worlds of Witchcraft, you probably looked upon the Witches who were teaching you with some measure of awe. You were just embarking on a journey they had enjoyed time and again, and everything they said or did fascinated you. Like a sponge in the Sahara, you just couldn't soak up enough water from the well of knowledge they had to offer. You may even have embarrassed a few of your teachers with your adoration because their vast experience made them seem so competent, so knowledgeable, and so holy that you almost confused them with your own spiritual goals.

Then, to your ultimate confusion, you discovered that even the most elder among them still considered himself to be a humble student of the Craft, a servant of his patron deities, and a friend to the elements rather than their master. He might have had more experience than you, but he never claimed to be better. If he was the right kind of teacher, he refused to be idolized and he never talked down to you. No question you wanted to ask was too silly or so simple that he wouldn't give it serious thought and an honest reply—even if that reply was "I don't know."

He may have surprised you even more by referring to you as *his* teacher. What a head rush! It was as if the world had just turned inside out and everyone was now upside down. There was so much information to be filed in your mind, so many myths to hear, so many related areas to explore, so many exciting ideas to dissect, and you wanted to do them all at once. Yet your teacher took you one step at a time, not only sharing and teaching but also listening and learning from you as well.

Chances are about 99.999 percent that not all your first efforts succeeded, at least not at the lightning-fast pace you would have liked. Like the title of one well-known metaphysical book, you may have categorized your initial studies as an experiment in Rick Field's *Carry Water, Chop Wood* (J. P. Tarcher Publishing, 1985). You wanted to know when the "real" magick would begin, still ignorant of the fact that it was already in motion around you and within you. You were learning the essential lessons of patience and self-discipline, enjoying and appreciating the process of the Craft rather than valuing only the end results.

This was maddening to you at first, but if you stuck it out—and you apparently did if you're reading this—you discovered Witchcraft was a religion that required self-discipline and hard work from the individual, a coordination of body, mind, and spirit that can't be taught or learned overnight. Before any lessons would stick in your head, your wise teachers knew two things had to happen. Number one, the swelling of said head had to be brought under your control, and number two, you had to learn the hard lesson that Witchcraft is a *process*, a verb rather than a noun. It might have had a markable beginning, but it has no end. Those who can't learn to carry water, chop wood, cast circles, call quarters, evoke deities, etc., with patience and a love for the process itself would never become or remain a Witch.

In some cases, even that first year and a day was not enough to learn all the basic tenets, concepts, and practices at the journeyman's level, and definitely not long enough to master more than one or—if you were really gifted in a special area—two.

You also discovered that, unlike the religion into which you were probably born, no single leader was going to step forward and do all the ritual and magickal work for you, or even explain to you after showing him your ten blistered fingers from wood chopping, and your thirty-third trip to the well, what all the water and wood were for. If you still didn't get it, you might even have been asked to move the water and wood back where you found them, either literally or metaphorically.

Screwy religion, eh?

At this point you might have questioned your commitment to the Craft. Whether you were aware of it or not, it was expected that you would question just what you were getting yourself into. You were the only one who knew the answers to the questions your teachers were trying to provoke you to probe: Would you have the courage to stick out your entire initial training, or would you decide you knew more than your teachers and the deities and strike out on your own? Or would you realize that you wouldn't be doing all this for no purpose and stick with it even if everything didn't make sense yet? Were you sensing anything spiritual happening in your life, or were all you could see those ten blistered fingers? You might have begun to feel like a lackey, not a student, and suddenly your teachers didn't seem so idyllic anymore.

Things may be starting to seem a little less screwy now. The aforementioned frustrations were signs that you were learning, testing, thinking, feeling, and growing, whether you knew it or not. You were starting to catch on, but there was still much work to be done.

You might also have been frustrated to madness that lessons in magick were not as forthcoming as you'd like. You were anxious to cast spells, light candles, chant, drum until dawn, call out the elementals, and evoke deities. All manner of witchy things were itching to pop like flames from your anxious fingertips (blistered or not). Yet your teachers held this knowledge back until much later in your studies.

Even though you were starting to catch on, there was one important semantic distinction you had to understand: the difference between *wisdom* and *knowledge*. They are not, never have been, nor ever will be the same animal, even though they can appear as identical twins. They are the beginning of our transformation from form into spirit, governed by the cerebral element of air. Within air we learn to connect all parts of our minds to expand our thinking, helping us transfer our thoughts into magickal actions.

Just like Dorothy Gale in *The Wizard of Oz* had to figure out the answer to her own problem, you also had to gain the wisdom, not just the knowledge, that your answers were within you all the time. Finding and recognizing it is the hard part, but the process you take to get there is as important as any end result. You had to attain the wisdom that your commitment to learn was ongoing, the eternal learning curve of an ancient mystery faith.

Knowing is easy, wisdom is hard.

So you kept carrying water and chopping wood as, one by one, bright rays of enlightenment began illuminating your mind and soul.

Baby Steps to the Next Level

As an intermediate student of Witchcraft, you began to appreciate all the hard work your teachers insisted on having you do; well, maybe not the ten blistered fingers, but the other stuff was okay. All your efforts—not theirs, but yours—disciplined not only your body but also your mind and spirit, and your hours of meditation and visualization practice was now paying off. Your broader view of how all these pieces fit together as a whole was making you a stronger Witch, both spiritually and in your magick and ritual practices.

As Nin-Si-Ana, a longtime priestess friend of mine, is fond of saying, "Well, whop me upside the head with the great frying pan of enlightenment."

Boing!

"And, by the way, bring me another bucket of water."

As you continued upon your chosen path, wisdom was replacing knowledge. You began to progress more rapidly. You could see the results of much of your training and so you read, and listened, and spent lots of time contemplating cosmology and eschatology to form your own theories from the thousands of others already hypothesized. You did the same with concepts of reincarnation, the web of being, the deities, and magick.

You blessed the foresight of your teachers for withholding lessons of specific skills until you were ready to handle them responsibly. You understood now that they weren't being dictatorial for the fun of it, but that all life is one and that they, too, would bear the karma your magick created, being as responsible for your errors in judgment as would you because they were showing you the way.

Folk magick is owned by the common people, and it always will be, but when it becomes part of a larger religious practice you must first be well grounded in that faith's ethics and ideology before you can handle the magick with wisdom. Then it not only becomes more powerful, it centers you in the web of being from where you can draw great power. It takes experience to turn knowledge into wisdom, and there's not one of us who can claim not to have singed a fingertip or two in the beginning.

Overall, as an intermediate, you were satisfied with your progress and, as those who have climbed the tree to knowledge before you, you yearned for more. Terms such as mage, elder, adept, sage, crone, avatar, wise woman, cunning man, master, third degree, priest, and priestess danced in your head. You knew they were synonymous with advanced practitioners of the Craft, and you desired to sort them out in your mind and find the path you needed to forge your way ahead.

Which Brings Us to Mystery #1...

You have learned by now that advanced Witchcraft is not synonymous with greater complexity, but with becoming a greater person. To do that requires both bold daring and humility.

Huh?

Where'd that frying pan go? At this point you may feel like giving yourself a few whacks just to enjoy the process.

All Are Students, All Are Teachers

No one's definition of advancement in the Craft is going to be the same as anyone else's, as we shall soon see, but our ideas of the many things that comprise advanced practice may change, expand, or contract over time. This is good. It shows we're still thinking, still questioning, and still growing as both Witches and human beings. When that process stops, life stops.

Take a moment to grab a pencil and write out your definition of an advanced Witch, or what you see as advanced Craft practice. If you need some time to think about it, close this book for a day or two and do just that. Meditate. Look inward. What are you and how did you get here? Where do you want to be and how will you get there? What is an advanced Witch, and why are you, or do you, want to be one?

DATE OF ENTRY: _____

_____

_____

_____

_____

_____

_____

_____

_____

_____

_____

ᛏᚼe Power Within

It's impossible to discuss the art of advanced Witchcraft without first trying to define the advanced Witch, and it's hard to define the advanced Witch without first defining Witchcraft. For those of you standing at the doorway that opens to advanced practice, you already know the word *Witch* is derived from the Old English *wyk*, meaning "to bend or shape," and the Anglo-Saxon *wit*, meaning "to possess wisdom."

You also know Witchcraft is a religion. If you didn't accept and practice that, then you would never have come this far. You'd either have lost interest or found that your Craft practices weren't always working right for you, and you would have left to seek another path to your life's goals.

Being an advanced Witch is not much different than being an advanced person, a wise soul who picks battles with care and knows when the truest display of her wisdom may best be evidenced by her silence. Some battles cannot be won, and there's no point trying. This is why you don't often see real Witches on daytime talk shows arguing moot points with people who are gathering kindling and tying nooses. The producers of these shows don't want to know the truth about what we are and what we do any more than the audience. They want a good old-fashioned knock-down, drag-out war between what they hope their slack-jawed, glaze-eyed viewers will see as a holy war between good and evil.

One of the hallmarks of the advanced Witch is when he reaches a point where he loses the urge to argue minute points *ad infinitum* with both outsiders and with other Witches. Take a look in the letters to the editor in most Pagan periodicals or in online chat rooms. The childish bickering and name-calling will turn your stomach. Some of the writers may sign themselves as "The Great Poobah Grand Guru and Fifth Degree High Priest of the Coven of the One Universal Truth," but the real truth is that they haven't passed all the tests required of the first-year novice. They may display some knowledge but they are clearly lacking in wisdom. They certainly have never developed the inner qualities it takes to be an advanced human being. Perhaps they don't want to. Perhaps the personal power trip is enough for them, or perhaps they just don't know any better. In any case, if one of these gurus reaches out for you, run fast and far.

A Witch's greatest strength can often be found in her silence. Remember that one of our "rules" for successful magick is the admonition to keep silent and not lessen the power by talking about it or risking someone else working to counter our desire. A

Witch exudes a quiet power that commands respect because it does not stand out and scream, "Look at me, I am right." He feels no need to argue every point someone brings up, such as what attributes the color blue possesses.

An advanced Witch also refrains from making value judgments about the spiritual path others choose to take. We are all in our religions to reunite with our creator regardless of how we see him/her/them/it. We have no trouble stepping out of the limelight and retreating to a quiet corner all alone to commune with our deities while the rest of the world battles over the valid uses of a cinnamon stick or who is more powerful, Yahweh or Allah—two deities who are the same. We know both religions have validity, meaning they succeed in keeping in mind their higher purpose. Even worse, we all know no one wins these marathon arguments. All it does is distract us from the greater work we have chosen to do and places us further from, not nearer to, our creator(s).

It has often been said of Witchcraft that "The secret is that there is no secret," or that "The one universal truth is that there is no one universal truth." This mutability of "truth" is impossible for many people to grasp because it topples the foundation upon which their faith is built. If you crack that foundation, the whole building comes crumbling down, like those fabled walls of Jericho. The thought of being cut loose from a group mindset has frightened all of us at one time or another. Standing alone with your faith requires the deep courage of conviction.

What is the only advantage these mainstreamers have over you? No ten blistered fingers.

Witchcraft is the path of the self-responsible. That sounds simple enough but, as many of you already know, it can be a rough road to travel. Our rede of "As it harms none, do what you will" is terrifying to the Powers That Be, whether they are religious institutions, governments, or even that hyper-panicky soccer mom down the street who just knows that you're out to recruit her precious offspring as an agent of Satan. These people's condescending view of the world is born of ignorance, and people fear what they don't understand. Sometimes they are so set in their ways that just the thought of a new idea scares them witless. So they run to others for their marching orders—a way of life that does not allow for individuals to be responsible to themselves without a higher power forcing them to conform.

A Witch knows she doesn't need rules to behave in a way that is ethical and faithful to all beings. The rede to "harm none" and the threefold law that tells us everything we do comes back to us three times over are not threats hung over our heads as a minister holds out the abyss of eternal damnation to sinners. We simply know and accept as fact that we create our own destinies.

All things come in cycles—time, seasons, birth and death, spring and autumn. As a nature religion, we recognize that wheel of existence is with us at all times, ever turning. What we send out on that great wheel makes its way full circle back to us with not only our own energies magnified three times over but those of every other sentient creature in the universe as well. It may come quick or it may not return until another lifetime, but it will return, bringing with it not only all the energy we put onto it but all that it's collected from others along the way.

Humbling, isn't it, to realize how much power there is in just accepting personal responsibility? Sometimes I'm still afraid of making a wrong turn when I come to a fork in the road.

Some Witches prefer to think of this wheel as a web woven by the original spinning Goddess, often personified as a spider woman. We are all joined in some way by the delicate threads she weaves. When one is broken or damaged, the entire web is weakened.

This delicate balance of karma is why many covens stay secret and why many advanced Witches leave covens and return to the solitary practice of their early years in the Craft. We know what we seek and we often realize we won't find it among others not at our level who look only for power or for a reason to drag us back down the evolutionary ladder.

Being a Witch means taking care of yourself. A priestess friend of mine once got so fed up with two years of playing nursemaid to her immature covenmates that she disbanded the group and told them not to come back until they grew opposable thumbs and learned to walk erect like the rest of us.

Facts, Truths, Realities, and 360-Degree Thinking

Being an advanced Witch requires more than knowing advanced magick— that's the least of our worries. Advanced Witchcraft is a lifestyle, the way we look at the universe and how we see ourselves within it. In basic Witchcraft we are thought to perform our rites while standing between all worlds. As an advanced Witch we are expected to live in all of these worlds at once while still retaining some awareness of each, regardless of where our major focus might be at any given time.

These conundrums of time and space cause much debate in the Craft community, not because anyone is wholly right or wholly wrong about them but because they are often saying the same things in words that are inadequate to the task.

As advanced Witches, we don't let ourselves be trampled on like doormats, and we know when it's time to walk away from a pointless confrontation. We pick our battles with care. We do not feel everyone has to know our individual opinions about what someone else thinks or does. We have learned to see all points of view, including the ones we want to dismiss outright, and see all possible harm which could arise from an action. You must view yourself as a vacuum that can be filled with the energies around you at will, with the ability to send out those energies to do whatever task you require of them.

Control of this energy is essential or you risk two unpleasant side effects:

1) You cannot control your intake of energy and you find yourself grounding—therefore wasting—much of it, or

2) It leaves you when it chooses, often in moments of anger, and then it goes toward goals that are not thought out or well chosen, and these will always come back to haunt you.

As you move into the advanced practices, you will realize that power can never be taken from others or given by others. Power comes from within or from the energies surrounding us in the four elements. It has often been described as having "power with" rather than "power over." A Witch enjoys her power, but it also humbles her.

Once this stage of self-concept is reached, there is no turning back. Once the mind expands to see all things at once, you can never return to your boxed-in thinking. You start to look at "truths" and "facts" and suddenly see the lies you've lived with since birth. The Powers That Be indoctrinate us at an early age, and few people at any time in their lives seek to question these.

Witches question.

We learn early on that power is just power, and that it can be drawn upon for good or evil. We do divinations and hope we are on the right path and that our thoughts and actions cause no harm, but we can never be sure. This is the precarious tightrope we walk: wanting to do good for ourselves and others, yet knowing we've sent a great deal of energy onto the wheel of being that will touch everyone and everything until it returns to us.

Another old magical adage that goes hand in hand with this is "The Witch who cannot kill cannot cure." This is not a commandment meant to give us free reign to practice what the seventeenth-century Witchhunters referred to as *malificarum*, or witching someone to death. It only refers to those energies around us. If we truly have the power to draw them into ourselves, then we have also taken on the awesome responsibility to use them wisely and ethically. By the time you reach the advanced stages of the Craft you should be long past the urge to do harm. In fact, finding creative ways to handle your anger, with or without magick, can be a spiritual challenge.

As you pass through this threshold into the advanced Craft, you will discover that your worldview can be disconcerting if you're one of those people who likes their theology tied up in a cute little box to be taken out only to reassure you that everything is as it should be.

The safest assumption to keep in mind from here on is that

EVERYTHING YOU KNOW IS WRONG.

When a writer is asked to make changes it's termed a *revision*, literally meaning "to see again." This is what you have to do if you want to experience growth from knowledge to wisdom. Set aside your prior assumptions about everything and then take another look at everything from that 360-degree perspective and reexamine it. Don't take anything for granted: not gravity, not air, not your magickal tools, not where you stand, not your best friend, not who your parents are, not what you think you want or need, not your favorite piece of jewelry, not your job or school work, not your favorite pastime. Think about the deeper meanings of all these things and more, their place in your life and in your magick and your spirituality. Continuously question. Why do you keep the mementos you keep? Why is a certain rock given a place of honor on your altar? Why can't you get along with your best friend's boyfriend? When you astral project do you see yourself going to inner worlds or outer worlds? How do you feel about reincarnation? Just who are you and why?

These are not comfortable areas to examine. We humans tend to like things tied up in an orderly fashion, but once the threshold into the advanced Craft is crossed you can never return to mundane thinking again. Once you free your conscious, subconscious, and superconscious minds to work in harmony at a higher level, they will not sever their association and they may even seem to gang up on you when they think you're taking a wrong turn. Three against one can be maddening odds at times.

What happens if you decide there are two or more valid and true realities for something you either see or have or do?

(Flash the APPLAUSE sign, please.)

You've now arrived at the mindset needed to practice and live advanced Witchery. Acceptance of multiple realities is hard, especially if one of them is uncomfortable for you, but all realities are part of the web of existence and cannot be forever ignored.

Facing Facts in a Universe of Multiple Realities

Some of you will find this book disappointing in that it will not impart secrets to you to which some others are not privy. As advanced Witches have said for decades, "The secret is that there is no secret, and the only universal truth is that there is no universal truth."

So what about facts? Facts are facts, right? We can rely on those. True?

Some facts are immutable, but most are not. For example, we are taught that William the Conquer took over England in 1066. True to the English, yes, but only by their calendar, and even it underwent eleven years of changes in the eighteenth century. The calendars of China and the Middle East would differ with these accountings of time.

Always keep in mind that facts are simply *a series of events or ideas upon which the majority of people have agreed to accept*—no more and no less. This is why they can be so easily manipulated during political campaigns in which two opponents use the same "facts" to "prove" different conclusions. And when one faction digs a trench for its facts, defending them becomes an exercise in violence, even war, all performed for the pleasure of a supposed god of peace.

I can hear the battle cry of those who are fighting the expansion of their thinking already: "There must be *some* truth upon which I can rely!"

Maybe and maybe not.

But why does it matter so much? People often twist facts in their minds to suit their personal needs, and this becomes as much their reality as the opposite of that fact is yours. This is not always intentional, but is part of a primitive defense mechanism that makes us want to see the world conforming to the way we wish it to be and to our self-concept of our place within it. We see this so often in "implanted memory" experiments, where two people each claim to know the truth about an event, and neither one may be correct. But because these are truths on which each wants to rely to correspond to their self-concept, they are both valid, if inaccurate. Another example of this is seen in wish fulfillments and in how each individual mind perceives or wants to perceive what it sees.

Rotate That Neck, But No Pea Soup, Please

Before you go any further in advanced studies, make it your goal to discard any thinking that is not a 360-degree observation. Toss out that black and white mentality and learn to see in shades of gray, and then in the full spectrum of color. Disregard labels others have put on items, behaviors, or thoughts. Avoid making value judgments whenever possible. Expunge the words *right, wrong, good, bad, love, hate, male, female, yin, yang, negative, positive, liberal, conservative,* and all other supposed opposites from your mind. Try it for just one day and you'll discover how brainwashed we are in our acculturated, narrow channel of allowable thought processes.

Those of you skilled in astral projection may have experienced a real eye-opening 360-degree field of vision. Often we have to mentally pull a hood over our heads because this view can be disorienting. To see semi-omnisciently is scary, and it carries with it a burden to be responsible to what is seen and to act in accordance with it, with harm to none and with the idea that it is for the greater good that we seek ways to change it for the better.

A true Witch cannot feel threatened by the ideas of others. He knows what he thinks and feels and, in most cases, sees no point in arguing details that don't matter in the larger scheme of things. He has worked hard to get to where he is, and he has still greater work to accomplish. There is no room in this kind of life to suffer the angst of self-doubt because someone else uses an ash wand and yours is made of maple. His mind is open to new possibilities and his confidence in all he has experienced so far is strong.

A little knowledge is a dangerous thing (to quote another wise person) and beginning Witches often holler the loudest when the lines of demarcation between the worlds begin to blur. They scream about myths and demand they be adhered to as surely as a televangelist thumps upon his King James Bible.

Every religion changes to meet the needs of its people. It has to in order to survive. And when the religion in question is one that has been the subject of persecution and attempted eradication, the problem is compounded.

Several years ago I saw a wonderful special on public television called *Wiping the Tears of Seven Generations*. It dealt with Native Americans living in the American West who were painstakingly trying to piece together their seven sacred rituals, only three of which have survived intact. Needless to say, there has been a lot of bickering among factions over these. They would all be better off just trying to live their spiritual lives and, if one way doesn't work, be open-minded enough to try another.

Those of us in Euro-based earth religions can learn a lesson from the trials of the Native Americans. If a people can lose that much of their sacred ceremonies in only a little more than a century, think how much we who are trying to revive the indigenous religions of Europe that existed twenty centuries or more ago have lost. None of us were there, and fighting over unprovable details only clouds our vision, taking us away from our spiritual goals while we pursue trivialities that do nothing to bring us closer to our creator(s).

The advanced Witch understands the nature of myths and how they came about, and she can see the deeper secrets rooted in them, as well as in fairy tales and Mother Goose rhymes. She knows we need these archetypes to feel whole, and she takes what works for her and mentally files the rest away to be examined at another time. She is characterized by being comfortable in her own skin and with her spiritual practices.

As you will see, advanced Witchcraft isn't so much a skill level as a state of mind.

Other Witches on Advanced Witchcraft

The true advanced Witch has learned to put aside her arrogance, his need to always be right, her assumptions that she's an expert on everything, his belief that he's learned all he can and no one can teach him anything new, and that it is her right to argue minute micro-points for the sake of others of lesser enlightenment.

As I was writing this book, I sent out a mass e-mailing to some of my friends and colleagues to garner their thoughts on what made one an advanced Witch. This is an excerpt from the e-mail I sent:

> I've been working on a lengthy book on advanced Witchcraft and have hit a few
> snags, most them in defining advanced Witchcraft. . . . I want to emphasize this
> point [that advanced Witchcraft takes many forms] by getting some definitions
> from others on what advanced Craftwork means to you. If you'd like to send a
> line or two, I'll be happy to credit you any way you like. . . . If you do not feel you
> are an advanced Witch at this time, what would make you feel you'd reached that
> stage?

I also asked them not to feel limited. They could comment on magick, practice, thoughts, lifestyle, initiations, thresholds, or anything else that came to mind when the term "advanced Witch" was presented to them. It was their call, their ideas, their own special way of practicing, their self-concept.

I only got about a 25 percent response, but the ones I received were enlightening. The comments ranged across every aspect of Witchcraft, from magick to personal living. The first response I received was a breath of fresh air after reading the bickering letters in Pagan journals on what type of wood makes the best wand and if so-and-so were as enlightened as he claims, this would be obvious. I believe this simple, honest response set the tone for what I felt was not only advanced Witchcraft, but also a shining example of what I would define as an advanced human being. It comes from Dagonet Dewr, Chief of Thalia Clan, who writes:

> To me, advanced Witchcraft is when you take responsibility for teaching, guid-
> ing, and empowering others around you. Of course, my personal vocation is
> towards group work and activism, so someone else's mileage may differ. I'm not
> a "spell" sort of person; I'm more likely to use magick to change minds and pro-
> tect people from intolerance than I am to get myself a new car. I've found the
> activism provides its own rewards.

The theme of service to others, of giving back to a community which gave to you, was echoed somehow in most of the answers I received, but never as succinctly as Dagonet. When you live on a web, reciprocity is the only form of exchange that does not upset its balance.

Think about what that means to your concept of the Craft. Which is more impor-tant—getting that new car or healing a sick neighbor? As Dagonet Dewr stated, "Service has its own rewards." The advanced Witch knows that helping a sick neighbor may result in obtaining the needed car as well.

Another Witch, Nimue, makes no claim to being advanced, but she sees this, too. She credits her teacher and mentor with impressing upon her the lesson of "how to restore dignity in the face of adversity."

Nimue's mentor, Lady Cheetah, is a nurse who also responded to my query.

> Advanced [Witchcraft] to me is having studied for so long that you know your weaknesses and strengths and that you have embraced them both . . . your life becomes a positive example of love, compassion, etc., for those who might otherwise be your foes. Advanced [Witchcraft] is when you know what the Gods' will is and you stand in their Light, Love, Strength, and Courage even if you stand alone.

Lady Cheetah goes on to write about how she knew the gods stood with her as she would look into the eyes of a dying patient. These patients did not know her religion, nor did they care, but this advanced Witch gave them the love they needed to pass over in peace, knowing each one of them felt better in her presence because she brought with her the light, love, strength, and courage of the universal creator.

The theme I see is that the hard work you put in as a novice and an intermediate is now paying off in more ways than just your ability to practice a religion. It's allowing you to reshape your life into what you always wanted it to be—a life that is not only rewarding to you, but to all with whom you come into contact. Isn't this the highest form of magick, short of uniting with our creator? After all, the origins of the word *religion* are from the Greek and mean to "re-link."

Craft author and delightful human being Dorothy Morrison pondered my questions for several days before writing me a two-page response that I wish I had room to quote in its entirety. She starts by saying advanced Witchcraft turns most people's thoughts to magick and "a more ritualized form of the Ancient Arts." Dorothy doesn't view magick as having anything to do with her advancement other than its ability to integrate with her spiritual self. For her it is:

> [T]he ability to live a life so completely saturated with magick that the practitioner not only becomes one with every effort, but that every effort becomes the

practitioner. . . . While this may sound like the workings of ordinary magick, nothing could be further from the truth. Why? Because the advanced practitioner is so accustomed to balancing evenly between the worlds that it's an effortless part of daily living. It is, in fact, as natural as drawing breath, blinking an eye, or moving a finger. That being the case, every simple act—washing a dish, scrubbing a toilet, or even paying a bill—becomes a magickal operation.

Dorothy is also one of the many respondents who confessed to having done away with most of her magickal "props."

We learn to use props and tools, or catalysts, as beginners to help us focus our energy. We learn their affinities and use them with great effect until, one day, we know—not just accept, but *know*—that we are the magick.

Overcoming Acculturation

The skill of being able to see and accept dual, or even multiple, realities is the greatest hurdle most people have to overcome in their spiritual progression. That's the way the Powers That Be want it. As early as kindergarten we are acculturated to accept certain things as incontestable truths and others as blatant falsehoods. The more conservative our education, families, native country, or birth religion, the more we are programmed to fight to keep all things in our lives within the boundaries our society has set for them. When implanted convictions want to wiggle out and put part of their energy in other places, we grow defensive at best.

I was fortunate to grow up in a home with people who embraced learning. My father was a master at coercing people to think for themselves until he could see a metaphoric light bulb pop on over their heads. He did this to me as child when, city girl that I was, I asked where chocolate milk came from. He told me it came from brown cows. At age four this seemed plausible to me. It wasn't until I asked where grape juice came from and he told me it came from purple cows that I was whopped upside the head with the great frying pan of enlightenment.

Advanced Witchcraft accepts nothing at face value. It questions all yet avoids backbiting and petty bickering. There is a distinction between them, and we all know it, so why does it continue? It continues because we each have a vested interest in our self-concept.

Psychologists have long taught us that we will fight any demon that comes along to challenge what we think we are. How many times a day do you hear someone say, "That's just the kind of person I am"? This person will go so far as to act against his or her own best interest to conform to that self-concept. This is why the advanced Witch is an advanced human being: she has overcome the most difficult barrier that blocks the threshold of advancement, the Self; the one that wants it all, but only if it's his way and no one else's.

Barbara, a still-searching Catholic Witch and author, does not consider herself advanced at this time. I've watched her explore with care the labels we call ourselves and why. She writes that exploring "the deeper angles of every small thing" is probably a start along the advanced pathway, and she recognizes that the melding of faiths and ideas have "created the first 'new' religions in thousands of years." She also cautions about Witches falling into the trap of "doctrine," those heresies that turned medieval Europe into a torturing ground for those who did not toe the party line as handed down from Rome.

Rites of Passage and a Witch's Growth Process

Rites of passage are one of the infrastructures we share with people all over the world, and not only with their religions but with all the isolated tribal societies whose communities are still organized around various rites of passage. Some have argued that our epidemic of troubled teens is a result of our doing away with those rites of passage. I tend to agree since, in the end, these rites are public expressions of inner transformations.

A woman I admire is Maggie Shayne, a best-selling author of women's and romantic fiction such as *The Gingerbread Man, Eternity,* and *Destiny.* Maggie is another Witch who has managed to blend all the elements of her life into a single whole. She writes:

> Almost like a new writer who doesn't feel validated until she is published, I needed the degrees and rituals of advancement to assure me that I was progressing. At that time, getting to the Third Degree was my perception of "Advanced." Then I moved from that to what I now perceive as advanced when, with all those degrees out of the way, I let myself look past them, see that they were man-made, and that they were only physical symbols of my inner journey. . . . I think you

have to master the rites, the rote, the tools, before you can grasp that they are unnecessary.

Rev. Breanna WinDancer also sees the first step in advancement as honesty with one's self and with others, including the ability to turn wishes into realities while acknowledging those multiple realities we just talked about. "Once we truly believe in ourselves as having the power to change things, then we really start to see the magickal in the mundane around us."

Are You Living As a Witch?

Yes? No? Yes and no? Perhaps? *Huh?*

Advanced Witchcraft is these things and more. You need no magickal tools, elaborate robes, or witchy jewelry to make this trip. Just bring along your passion and self-discipline, your humility and your courage, your determination and your faith.

Unlike the road of the mainstream religions, where the flock must play "follow the leader" into the realms of higher learning, we Witches must find that path ourselves and walk it alone. This requires the courage of our convictions, faith in our deities, trust in ourselves, and a balance in all areas of our life that allows us to walk the path of self-responsibility to bravely face the wonders of "that which can never be told."

two

The Process of Living As an Advanced Witch

In the beginning your life as a Witch was probably confined to the esbats, sabbats, and your teaching or reading times. Though you may have felt consumed by your new passion and thought about it often, your lifestyle was still very much the same as it was before your self-dedication.

To make yourself feel more witchy it's likely you dressed up your living space with items that made you feel like a Witch. You probably set up a home altar, dedicated a large space on your bookshelves to Pagan-themed books, hung talismans around your home, wore a pentacle or other symbolic jewelry, and set aside as much time as you could for meditation.

As an intermediate you learned where your strengths and weaknesses were, and you were able to feel the deities walking with you in your daily life. The knickknacks around your home felt tired, drained of their power. Your jewelry became more like personal talismans than an expression of your faith intended for the eyes of the world.

You began to do more with magick. Your efforts became easier. You found that the energy around you was always available, and that you could tap into it anytime and do it faster and better than before.

You accepted through experience the cyclic nature of all things, though you may not yet be able to integrate that wisdom into your daily life. But, fortunately, as you have grown, so have your teachers, and they are now ready to escort you over the threshold into the world of advanced Witchery.

With your resolve to continue on, you found that, more and more, your religion wasn't a one-day-a-week commitment, as it is for those we call "Sunday Christians," but

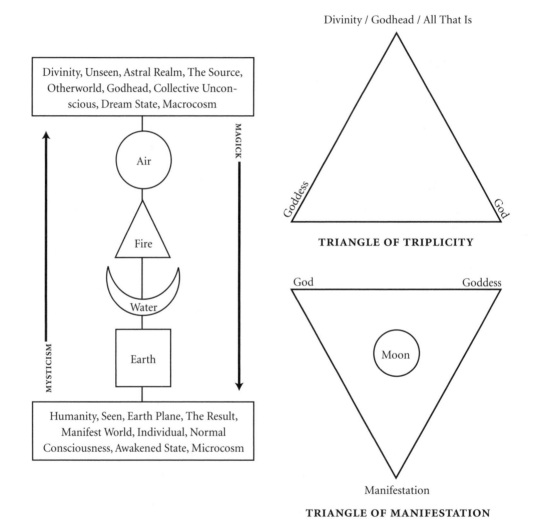

Magick versus mysticism (left), triangle of triplicity (above right),
and triangle of manifestation (bottom right)

it became something that you are. You don't have to think about it. It's not something separate from yourself. It's not an event or a thing, nor is it only one part of your life. As you stand on the threshold of advanced practice, you know that your religion is part of who you are, as impossible to remove as it would be to remove your heart. It's with you for every beat of your life.

Magick versus Mysticism and Advanced Living

Again, it has to be kept in the forefront of the mind that the Craft is an experiential path. Without experiencing the mysteries and internalizing them, they can never be a living part of us.

Living as a Witch is not only knowing that magick surrounds you at every moment, it is knowing you are the magick. It's knowing that All That Is—deities, spirits, nature, past, future—is with you and within you at all times. It's attaining the difficult, and often discomforting, 360-degree vision. It's more an act of fitting yourself into a Witch's life than of fitting the Witch's life into you.

There should also be a certain sense of peace in your life. You may not yet have attained all the material things you want; in fact, you may find you want less material hassles as you progress spiritually. This doesn't mean there aren't days that drive you crazy when work is overwhelming, the car is in the shop, and the kids are out of control. It's knowing that the truth is that there is no "truth," that nothing is supernatural, and that all cause and effect can be explained. We may call it magick, but we know it to be the manipulation of natural energies not yet defined by the sciences. It's a sense of inner calm—what I think of as "soul peace"—that assures you this day will pass and the confidence that praying to your patron deities and doing a little deep breathing to center yourself will put you back on the right place in your cycle of being.

Note in advance that every Witch who responded to my queries in chapter 1 made some mention of living a life they no longer had to think about every day. They are Witches. They do not question their power, but live each day with an assurance that it cycles around them like the wheel of the year, the wheel of life, and the web of All That Is. They simultaneously seek union with the divine and the manifestation of their earthly desires. This is what skilled magickal people have done for thousands of years.

The difference between the two is that one is magick and one is mysticism.

Magick draws energy from the divine and from the elemental energies surrounding us. It can be aroused at will to enhance a spell or to further our journey toward union with the divine. The seeking of union with the divine, or the godhead, as it is sometimes called, is the art of the mystic.

When a Witch learns to live life as an advanced practitioner, he no longer sees these two as being separate events but senses a spiraling around him of energy moving down from deities and up from the earth. It is a personal energy, not one that requires grounding, but one that shields him like the protective shell of an egg as he goes about his daily business confident in who and what he is.

From that divine source in the unseen realms we can cull energy and bring it down through the elements, making it denser and denser until it must manifest in the physical world.

From our place on Mother Earth we can climb into the less dense realms through meditation and pathworking and seek the greater mysteries of the divine.

Witchcraft has been called a "mystery religion," defined as one which must be experienced before greater secrets are revealed to the seeker. Under that definition all religions are, or should be, mystery religions, since we all have the same goals of returning to the great cosmic womb in which we were created.

Go back for a moment to the metaphor of the huge tree in the preface. Tree meditations are one of the first exercises taught to newcomers. They represent the present, with the roots as your ancestors and the branches as your descendants. It also mimics the mythic world tree. In many mythologies, this tree represents the center point around which the entire universe revolves and, when performing acts of magick or mysticism, you are the center point.

In terms of advanced practice, each branch you must work to climb to represents a distraction placed in the path of the spiritual seeker. One reason for this is to divert us from our intended goal so that only the most determined and wise arrive where they want to be. The other purpose is to show us something we may have missed on our journey and to open our eyes to other possibilities. Though we may claim understanding of multiple realities, sometimes the deities want us to experience them before they allow us to further our climb. This may mean going back down a few branches and climbing up by another route. This is why Witchcraft is a lot of work, but the wholeness of being it provides is well worth it in the end.

There's not one of us who hasn't gone off on an inner journey—or meditation, or astral travel—and not been lured off our intended path by a faery or spirit who promises a good time, a diversion, or an easier way to our end point. We've enjoyed most of these unexpected adventures and, more importantly, learned from them.

Some Witches are disturbed by the pentagram, or five-pointed star, the generally accepted symbol of the Wiccan religions when it is turned with its apex down. This is associated with negative magick in many minds, but it is also a symbol of magick.

Each point on the pentagram represents an element, including that of spirit, which is the realm of the divine. When the pentagram is apex upright, it shows we are seeking the divine, which is why it's a fitting symbol for our faith. With the apex down it shows that we are seeking to draw into our lives the power of the divine, taking it from the realm of spirit and moving it through the elements until it reaches the most dense of all—us on the earth plane.

What Is Living As an Advanced Witch?

Living as an advanced Witch requires full integration of your spiritual life with all other areas of your life. It's the point in time when you realize your religion is so much a part of you, you don't think about it anymore; you just live it.

My friend Kerr Cuhulain, fellow Llewellyn author and anti-defamation activist, has been a practicing Wiccan for more than thirty years. He and his wife, author and Wiccan Phoenix McFarland, live in western Canada, where Kerr has been a police officer all his adult life. I once asked him how he reconciles being part of a traditional authority organization with the free-flowing world of his chosen religion. Kerr told me his religion has helped him many times to enter a home in which a domestic disturbance is putting the lives of people in danger. Into this he can bring the peace of love of the deities and defuse an otherwise dangerous situation.

Kerr also learned that much of what he wrote in his early Book of Shadows was of little meaning for him today. The props, the instructions, insights, etc., have all simply become part of his life, which is at one with his spirituality and not merely a part. When I wrote back to him that so many others had mentioned service to others, and I had expected him to do the same, he admitted it didn't even occur to him to mention it. This is how fully integrated service to others is in his life. In case you are unfamiliar with his work, he writes and travels extensively, giving workshops to law enforcement groups about the difference between Witchcraft/Wicca and Satanism and helps them to study, identify, and solve what may appear to be "occult" crimes.

Timothy Roderick, author of *Apprentice to Power* and *Dark Moon Mysteries,* realized he'd moved into the advanced level when he recognized that his spirituality was his life.

> You are in the advanced stages of the Wiccan path when you've integrated your spirituality into your daily life. Mastery begins with a clear vision that spiritual practices do not begin and end in the magick circle. Advanced practices include synthesizing your experience of the Gods, the meaning of the Sabbats, magick, the Wiccan Rede and the threefold law into your everyday living. These practices should result in gaining a new awareness of yourself. You have stepped on the advanced path of the craft when you have truly experienced deity as a manifestation of everything that you do, every person you encounter, every feeling and every breath you take.

Tim has learned that the web of being includes all of us, and that true self-awareness is an expanded awareness that goes beyond the self. In fact, where his self and "everything else" begins and ends obviously blurs in his mind. Yet he retains his integrity by keeping that connection in his consciousness.

A dear friend, priestess Nin-Si-Ana, a tireless teacher, student, and local Wiccan leader, admits to having read Witchcraft 101 books until she was bored crazy. This, she believes, is the turning point for many seekers who finally realize how much hard work it is to be a Witch. "This is when you come to a point where you either move onward, or become uninterested."

Nin-Si-Ana writes:

> The reason we call this the "Craft" is that, like any art or skill, it must be practiced repeatedly in order to be performed successfully. If you practice the basics by observing the esbats and sabbats, you begin to build your skills and learn your own True Will. Then you begin to explore the Mysteries that must be experienced and can't be grasped simply by reading a book.

Even though standing in a sabbat circle doesn't make you a Witch any more than standing in a kitchen makes you a chef, Nin-Si-Ana's words bring us back full circle to the beginning of this chapter. Witchcraft is an experiential path, one where no one can do the work for you, fully explain it to you, or live it in the precise same way. As both the oldest and newest religion in our world, it is also probably the most diverse and easy to mold within our own framework of needs and goals.

Is it wrong to form a religion to our needs instead of finding one that tells us what our needs are? If that were true, no religion would have survived the caveman days.

Our needs are many, but our deepest spiritual impulses remain a constant: we seek union/reunion/oneness with the creative force(s) or divinity that made us and that infused us with a life force and the power to create. This is the point of religion—the re-linking. This is the root of every spiritual impulse and every heroic journey ever undertaken or told. This is also the heart of the Craft, the apogee of what advanced practitioners seek.

Everything Old Is New Again

There are lots of people who love to tell others that their Craft tradition dates in an unbroken line back to the Druids, the Saxons, the Vikings, or any other early Pagan people. In some cases there is some truth in what they say, but for the most part it's a bunch of hooey.

No one would argue that the words *Witchcraft* and *Wicca* have been around for a long time, but early people did not define themselves as Wiccans, or Wittans, or Wicens, or Witches. They might have said they possessed "wicca," or wisdom, and the ability to bend reality to their will. Witchcraft/Wicca as a synonym for Euro-based Witchcraft traditions only became a noun in the early twentieth century, if not later.

No one would argue, either, that some of our roots run deep into the heart of an ancient past, but we have no way of knowing exactly how these spiritual and magickal ways were expressed thousands of years ago. We may find some clues in mythology but, for many of our rites, we have borrowed liberally from other sources. Most of our tools and directional attributes come from ceremonial magick. Many of our modern spirit contact methods and ideas of soul survival were stolen from the Spiritualist churches born in the mid-1800s.

There's nothing wrong with this borrowing if it works for us, nor does it invalidate any other religion. In today's world it can be said without hesitation that all religions are syncretic. In order to survive they have had to adopt and adapt to the laws of the land, often keeping their sacred lore hidden in faery tales and nursery rhymes. Take a critical read of any of them and the Pagan lore is obvious. Snow White, the Three Little Pigs, and even the legends of King Arthur all preserve for us our heritage, and we will look at how these can be practically applied to your advanced Witch life in chapter 6.

And the point of all this?

Witchcraft is both the oldest and the newest religion on the planet. Forget all the haggling and harping you hear about the terms Pagan and Neopagan. No matter how we try to slice them up, they are the same thing. This is a new era. No matter how much we try to work with ancient practices of a specific people or place, these have all been influenced—sometimes for the better and other times for the worse—over many centuries by the world around them. We are all *Neo*, meaning "new" or "reformed" (this of a physical reforming, not a rehabilitation). Paganism will continue to be Neopaganism as we hurl into the future and the world continues to affect our lives and thoughts and spiritual needs.

We all wish we had an unbroken line to our ancestors' beliefs, but they would probably not be as meaningful to us as they were to them. For instance, the emphasis on hunting each autumn to keep the clan alive would bore us after a while. We think "just go to the grocery and buy the damn thing, whether it's in season or not." No matter how hard we try to imagine it, we cannot wholly put ourselves in the position of those who lived 2,000 years ago or more.

Syncretism is not a bad thing. To the contrary, it has saved many religions from annihilation. The Caribbean religion known as Santería preserved the old gods of western Africa within the visage of Catholic saints. Protective icons and candle rituals preserved the pre-Columbian practices of Mexico. Indulgences purchased from medieval priests preserved the concept of talismanic magick, and the conversion of Pagan sacred sites to mainstream ones saved them from destruction so that we can still learn from them today.

Never think that not having an unbroken spiritual line to the past is a bad thing. Granted, many good things may have been lost to us, but we are reconstructing it to be stronger and more meaningful than ever and, as long as we live where freedom of religion is the law of the land, we can pass these practices and ideas freely on to the next generation who will, in time, alter them to fit the needs of their own world. This is how we survive as we continue to seek the divine.

We must ask ourselves again: What is advanced Witchcraft? Have we decided anything; created a common frame of reference? Perhaps—at least enough of one to make this book work.

An advanced Witch:

- Picks his battles with care.

- Knows when to keep silent.

- Knows when to speak up.

- Lives out of the broom closet, but doesn't fly her faith in the face of others.

- Appreciates solitude and its power.

- Appreciates group work and its power.

- Has the courage of his convictions.

- Is confident of her skills, but not arrogant.

- Is confident of his skills, but knows there is always more to learn.

- Knows she is a capable teacher, and that she must always be a willing student.

- Lives by the rede of "harm none."

- Observes the sabbats, esbats, and any other festivals of his chosen tradition and uses them for spiritual growth as well as for fellowship and to honor his deities.

- Knows her place on the web of existence and helps others find their place as well, making all our connections stronger.

- Serves his deities.

- Serves her community.

- Sees the divinity in all life and respects all life for the divine spark that dwells within, even when that being's thoughts and actions are not easily respectable.

- Builds bridges and not walls.

- Asks rather than demands.

- Questions more than he answers.

If you've come away from this discussion feeling a little disoriented, that's good. You need a little off-balanced time in the Craft so you recognize the important state of balance when you find it.

The path lies before you. Raise your lantern high and begin your journey with your first courageous step.

three

The Terror of the Threshold

Sometime during your first weeks of study you began to think of your life as being divided into two broad categories, B.W. and A.W.: Before Witchcraft and After Witchcraft. To help demarcate that turning point, or the spiritual coming of age chapter in your life, you probably devised or, if you were part of a group, went through a self-dedication ceremony to honor and commemorate your commitment to your obligatory year and a day of Witchcraft studies.

During this time of intense learning you were given a few hints about what to expect both before and after your official initiation ritual. You were told you would face doubts and fears, and you soon learned that those fears were your own doubts expressed in concrete emotion. Only you could work through them to overcome these blockages to your goal. You were also told you would be challenged and tested both by your coven and by the deities to whom you were dedicating yourself. You then had to learn how to turn these challengers into allies on your Craft journey.

All of a sudden you found you were relying on your own inner power, confident you could go where you pleased. It was when you passed through this dedication "ceremony" that you first heard the term "terror of the threshold."

As an intermediate student, well after your first initiation, you found new challenges, but for some reason assumed—as we all do—that the terror of the threshold was behind you for good. Yet as you embarked on the second phase of your studies—what some traditions call the Second Degree—you were surprised to learn that there were more thresholds to cross and more terrors to face, each guardian more demanding than the one before. You began to wonder if there might come a time when you could not pass the challenge and what might happen to you if you failed.

Obstacle or Ally?

The terror of the threshold is the magical guardian, or pair of guardians, or obstacle that stands at the gate or the closed door between the place you are now and the place you wish to be. They can take many forms, from the comfortably familiar to the hideously terrifying. In most mental exercises or pathworkings you encounter one or two such guardians. It's their job to make sure you really, really want what you say you want, and that you're worthy of possessing it at this time in your Craft career.

You'll find these guardians at each initiation to a new level of practice and understanding, and you find many of them in your daily life as you work, study, or play. Sometimes they are your teachers, parents, or acquaintances. Other times they are spirits or beings in quasi-animal form. Often they bear weapons that correspond to their challenge. If you're in school the weapon may be a slide rule. In the office it may be a paycheck. In the astral world it may be a spear.

In all worlds you can and will find these guardians blocking your path, coming between you and what can seem to be such simple goals that you wonder why they bother. Sometimes they sit on chests you need to open, or block the elevator to your office, or they lie atop closed books you wish to examine. Often they appear fierce, other times gentle, but they remain steadfast in their purpose: to make sure you really want and are worthy of attaining that which you seek. They appear to you as obstacles, but when you realize they want you to succeed, you make them your allies along your spiritual journey.

There are two important things to remember about these guardians. The first is that you may come back to them again and again to attempt to pass the threshold they guard. There are no limits to how many times you may attempt to advance to a new level of knowledge. The other thing to remember is that you will not be tested beyond your capabilities. We might say that the most terrifying aspect of the threshold terror is that its power grows in relation to your own knowledge and skills. If the guardian wasn't a worthy opponent, it would not make sense to find one protecting the entrance to new levels of thought and being.

The Lesson of Lugh

Often the threshold guardians will ask you questions or challenge you in some other way to test your worth to pass through the threshold and into a new world with yet more challenges.

The only rule?

Never lie, and never say what you don't really feel or think just because you believe that is what the guardian wants to hear from you. There are no trick answers, regardless of what Hollywood and horror novels would have you believe. Usually any sincere answers get you admitted through the next door. There may occasionally be wrong answers or answers given without sincerity, but there are no stupid answers, other than those expressing arrogance.

While it's important to feel pride in your accomplishments and to have confidence in them, it is a grievous infraction of otherworld etiquette to display arrogance for possessing them. Arrogance is the greatest enemy of spiritual growth, and one of the jobs of the threshold terror is to humble as well as empower us, helping us to find our balance between personal power and humbling growth.

Irish mythology tells us the story of Lugh, the hero/god who seeks entrance to Tara, the stronghold of the High Kings and seat of Ireland's magickal powers. When Lugh knocks on the door and asks to enter, the guardian of the gate asks what Lugh can do for them. In other words, why was he worthy of admittance?

Lugh says he is an expert archer.

"We already have an expert archer," the guardian replies.

"I'm also a forger in fire."

"We already have an expert smithy."

"I can foretell the future," Lugh says.

"We have several prophets. We don't need any more."

"I'm an expert hunter."

"We have several of those, too."

Lugh kept trying, speaking honestly about his accomplishments without bragging about any of them, but each time the guardian told him Tara had no need of his skill.

Finally Lugh asked, "Do you have any one person who can do all these things?"

Without another word, the guardian opened the doors to the magickal world of Tara and Lugh crossed the threshold into a new world of learning and teaching.

A Note of Caution

As you embark on advanced practice you should know that the challenges never get any easier and the terrors only grow more terrifying with each step you take. If this has been true of your experience, take it as a sign that you are indeed progressing as a Witch.

I won't insult your intelligence by going into all the many reasons you need have no fear of pathworking, or into the few reasons why you should. Just remember that it's quite easy to fall off your selected path and get lost in adventures that will never get you to your goal. Oh, they're fun, and most of the diversions and diverters are harmless. Just remember that their very existence is meant to distract the uncommitted seeker away from his goal of reunion with divinity. To prove your worthiness of reunion you must know when to leave these playmates behind and forge ahead toward your ultimate goal.

A fine example of the power of distraction can be seen in the popular movie *Harry Potter and the Sorcerer's Stone*. Taken from the book by J. K. Rowling, the scene was so compelling and provided such a perfect distraction for young Harry that it is the one that has stuck in the forefront of my memory since I saw the show on its opening day. In it, eleven-year-old Harry comes across a magick mirror. In its reflection he sees himself with his long-dead mother and father. He spends hours sitting in front of the mirror, watching and yearning for the world he sees inside the looking glass.

When he shows a friend the same mirror, thinking the image would be the same for all, the friend sees himself being elected captain of the school's quidditch (a sport) team. Like Harry, the friend is thrilled with the image in the mirror and would like to keep gazing at it and believe its prophecy.

Later, the wise old professor who runs the school comes to pry Harry away from the hold the mirror's images have over him. He reminds Harry that all the mirror shows is what the person looking into it wants to see, and that many magickal people have wasted their lives pining for these false images rather than working toward real-life goals, both spiritual and physical. He tells Harry the reflection is only an illusion and that "it imparts neither truth nor knowledge."

As you climb the branches of the tree on your way to meet the creator, it's acceptable, even encouraged, that you pause to have some fun along the way, but don't let illusions pass themselves off as truths. It's easy to be distracted by our heart's desire and tempting to remain in a place where we feel we have all we want. The problem is that often times getting all we want prevents us from getting all we need.

At this stage in your practice I don't have to tell you that sometimes it can be difficult to tell the difference between illusions of wish fulfillment and illusions of spiritual progression. If you're unsure, ask yourself what spiritual gain is to be had from the interlude in which you find yourself. If there is none, then enjoy yourself for a while, and move on. There's nothing wrong with enjoying the magick of the astral world as long as you remember what's what, who's who, and where it is you're trying to go.

Improvisational Pathworking

Advanced pathworking can sometimes feel like you've just been selected to appear on *Whose Line Is It, Anyway?*, the British-American television program that showcases comedians who never know what they'll be asked to do from moment to moment. It is in this stage of the pathworking process—there's that "p" word again—where you can grow the most and explore both paths that interest you and the ones leading to reunion with the creator.

If this is not one of the areas in which you feel advanced, you should spend time now practicing, for this will be the basis of many other advanced practices. For those who practice alone, or live in a crowded city or with a large family or noisy roommates, sometimes pathworking is the only way ritual and magick may be enacted. It is a vital skill for the advanced Witch.

Try following these steps to get up to speed:

1) Record and playback, or have read to you, guided meditations or pathworkings already scripted so you can learn how it feels to follow them in and back out (see bibliography for names of books to try). It is wise at this stage to enter and exit by the same route to keep your conscious and subconscious minds in happy harmony.

2) At this stage you may want to allow for longer pauses in areas of the pathworking to allow you to speak to or interact with beings you meet there. Remember that not all beings on your path have your best interests at heart, and few are dangerous, but you are always in control. Tell yourself at the outset that saying the words

"I am home" three times will bring you immediately back to your normal waking consciousness.

3)   You may now want to try entering and exiting by different routes. This is especially desirable if you are working with the Tree of Life model. For example, if you're starting at earth, you might want to enter through a cave or the hole of a burrowing animal. If your goal is the moon sphere, you may wish to exit under a starry sky in a green, fertile valley.

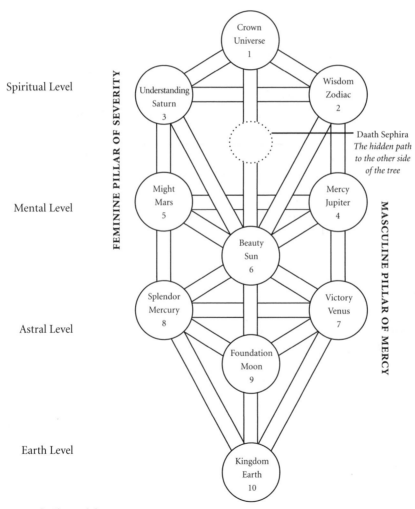

Tree of Life model

COMMON CORRESPONDENCES OF THE 22 PATHS ON THE TREE OF LIFE

PATH: 32. *START #:* 10 Kingdom. *END #:* 9 Foundation. *COLORS:* Indigo, black, deep blue, silver. *TAROT:* Universe. *ANIMALS:* Crocodile, sea creatures. *PLANET:* Saturn. *ELEMENT:* Water.

PATH: 31. *START #:* 10 Kingdom. *END #:* 8 Glory. *COLORS:* Orange, red, gold. *TAROT:* Judgement. *ANIMALS:* Lion, salamander. *PLANET:* None. *ELEMENT:* Fire.

PATH: 30. *START #:* 9 Foundation. *END #:* 8 Glory. *COLORS:* Amber, red, burnt orange. *TAROT:* Sun. *ANIMALS:* Oyster, lion, dolphin, falcon. *PLANET:* Sun. *ELEMENT:* Fire.

PATH: 29. *START #:* 10 Kingdom. *END #:* 7 Victory. *COLORS:* Ecru, white, silver, pink. *TAROT:* Moon. *ANIMALS:* Fish, sea creatures. *PLANET:* Neptune. *ELEMENT:* Water/earth.

PATH: 28. *START #:* 9 Foundation. *END #:* 7 Victory. *COLORS:* Blue, violet, mauve, maroon. *TAROT:* Uranus. *ANIMALS:* Lion, falcon, hawk. *PLANET:* Mercury. *ELEMENT:* Air/water.

PATH: 27. *START #:* 8 Glory. *END #:* 7 Victory. *COLORS:* Red, bright green, crimson. *TAROT:* Mars. *ANIMALS:* Eagle, humans. *PLANET:* Mars. *ELEMENT:* Fire.

PATH: 26. *START #:* 8 Glory. *END #:* 6 Beauty. *COLORS:* Black, indigo, gray. *TAROT:* Saturn. *ANIMALS:* Satyr, goat. *PLANET:* Earth. *ELEMENT:* Earth.

PATH: 25. *START #:* 9 Foundation. *END #:* 6 Beauty. *COLORS:* Yellow, green, sea blue. *TAROT:* Fool. *ANIMALS:* Undine, scorpion, whale. *PLANET:* Neptune. *ELEMENT:* Air/fire.

PATH: 24. *START #:* 7 Victory. *END #:* 6 Beauty. *COLORS:* Brown, indigo, dark blue. *TAROT:* Tower. *ANIMALS:* Burrowing animals, beetle. *PLANET:* Pluto. *ELEMENT:* Water/earth.

PATH: 23. *START #:* 5 Might. *END #:* 8 Glory. *COLORS:* Olive, violet, sea green. *TAROT:* Hanged Man. *ANIMALS:* Eagle, scorpion, serpent. *PLANET:* Neptune. *ELEMENT:* Water.

PATH: 22. *START #:* 6 Beauty. *END #:* 5 Might. *COLORS:* Teal, pale green, blue. *TAROT:* Justice. *ANIMALS:* Sheep, hare, wolf. *PLANET:* None. *ELEMENT:* Air.

PATH: 21. *START #:* 7 Victory. *END #:* 4 Mercy. *COLORS:* Blue, violet, yellow. *TAROT:* Wheel. *ANIMALS:* Spider. *PLANET:* Jupiter. *ELEMENT:* Water/air.

PATH: 20. *START #:* 6 Beauty. *END #:* 4 Mercy. *COLORS:* Olive, brown, gray, ecru. *TAROT:* Hermit. *ANIMALS:* Sylph, eagle. *PLANET:* Mercury. *ELEMENT:* Air/fire.

PATH: 19. *START #:* 5 Might. *END #:* 4 Mercy. *COLORS:* Yellow, green, purple, orange. *TAROT:* Strength. *ANIMALS:* Lioness. *PLANET:* Uranus. *ELEMENT:* Fire.

PATH: 18. *START #:* 5 Might. *END #:* 3 Understanding. *COLORS:* Amber, russet, dark green. *TAROT:* Chariot. *ANIMALS:* Sphinx, horse, crab. *PLANET:* Moon. *ELEMENT:* Earth.

PATH: 17. *START #:* 6 Beauty. *END #:* 3 Understanding. *COLORS:* Orange, mauve, yellow, gray. *TAROT:* Lovers. *ANIMALS:* Magpie, raven, crow. *PLANET:* Mercury. *ELEMENT:* Air.

PATH: 16. *START #:* 4 Mercy. *END #:* 2 Wisdom. *COLORS:* Teal, red-orange, brown. *TAROT:* Magician. *ANIMALS:* Bull, ox, gnome. *PLANET:* None. *ELEMENT:* Earth.

PATH: 15. *START #:* 6 Beauty. *END #:* 2 Wisdom. *COLORS:* All variations of red, yellow. *TAROT:* Emperor. *ANIMALS:* Dragon, salamander, ram. *PLANET:* Mars. *ELEMENT:* Fire.

PATH: 14. *START #:* 3 Understanding. *END #:* 2 Wisdom. *COLORS:* All variations of green, gold. *TAROT:* Empress. *ANIMALS:* Sparrow, dove, lark, boar. *PLANET:* Venus. *ELEMENT:* Air.

PATH: 13. *START #:* 6 Beauty. *END #:* 1 Crown. *COLORS:* Blue, silver, lavendar, violet. *TAROT:* High Priestess. *ANIMALS:* Oyster, camel, llama, cow. *PLANET:* Moon. *ELEMENT:* Water.

PATH: 12. *START #:* 3 Understanding. *END #:* 1 Crown. *COLORS:* Violet, yellow, gray, teal. *TAROT:* Magician. *ANIMALS:* Gazelle, ibis. *PLANET:* Mercury. *ELEMENT:* Water.

PATH: 11. *START #:* 2 Wisdom. *END #:* 1 Crown. *COLORS:* Pale yellow, azure, teal, gold. *TAROT:* Fool. *ANIMALS:* Eagle, unicorn. *PLANET:* None. *ELEMENT:* Air.

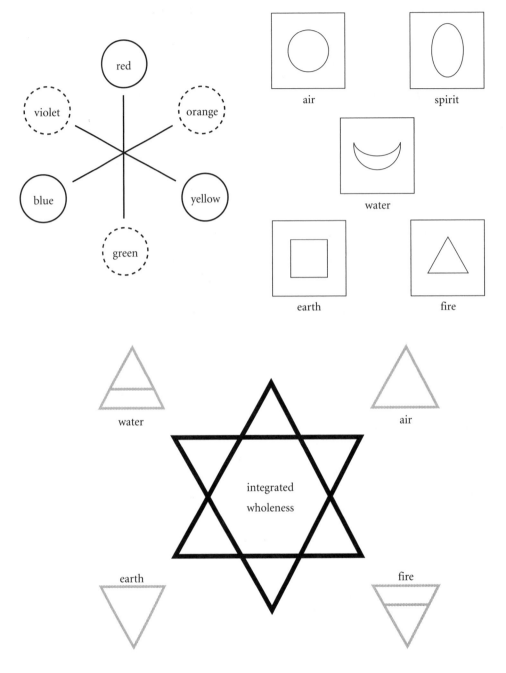

The color wheel (top left), solid circles = primary colors, broken circles = secondary colors; the five basic tattwa symbols (top right); and alchemical symbols/Solomon's Seal (bottom). The Star of David, also known as Solomon's Seal, is one of the oldest symbols of the Creator. The alchemical symbols were extracted from it.

4) Experiment with pathworkings where you enter by using symbols as your gateways. The four alchemical (medieval high magick) symbols and five tattwa (Vedic) symbols for the elements are very popular for this type of exercise and provide a foundation for self-exploration of the otherworlds. There are several ways to enter these:

a) Visualize them becoming thin enough to walk through.

b) Visualize them turning into a curtain that parts so you may enter.

c) For the tattwa symbols, stare at them long enough to create an impression of the symbol in its opposite color when you close your eyes. Walk through into the otherworld where the tattwa will wait for you, often in its original color, to create a closed portal. You don't need or want anything following you in and out of your pathworking. Those experienced in this art can tell you how annoying this can be.

d) Visualize the threshold guardian of the symbol opening the door for you to enter.

e) Visualize the symbol or chosen gateway turning into a liquid pool into which you dive.

f) Visualize any point in nature as your entryway: rabbit holes, caves, trees, woodlands, etc. Mentally mark that point with one of the alchemical symbols to help you find your way back.

g) Find a key in front of you or handed to you that you may use to open the door yourself.

5) Think again of the metaphor of the large tree with many branches and limbs and begin to explore the ones that interest you. You may never get to them all—few of us do—so just calm down and start climbing! Take side trips the various limbs offer and assess them for yourself, keeping in mind that the higher you climb the harder you can fall. You may not reach the top in this lifetime, but you'll be much closer in your next.

6) Be aware of what is valuable for you to learn and what is just a "joy ride." All the branches on the tree have lessons to teach us, even if that lesson is one of staying the course toward our spiritual goal and to not be so often distracted by the lure of pure entertainment.

7) You may call on spirit guides, ancestors, or other helpful spirits to guide you. Be aware that trickster spirits abound. They are there to play and distract you from your goal. Most are harmless. Remember you never have to go off with any being with whom you are not comfortable. You may even ask it to take a different form.

8) Know you're in control of the pathworking and stay in control at all times. If you sense that things are too out of hand and that you've just stepped into Alice in Wonderland's life, awaken yourself and try again later. You should be guiding the meditation and feeling as if you're actually interacting with other beings from other worlds. Many Craft practitioners experience this as lucid dreaming, a hypnogogic state of REM sleep in which the dreamer is aware that he is dreaming but remains in control of his actions and reactions, but not those of other characters.

9) Close all portals and ground yourself well in the physical world upon your return. Never leave an open portal between any two worlds, especially between an other-world and your mundane world.

Astral Nasties and Unmanaged Thoughtforms

Those who forget or who skimp on Step 9 are usually beginners, and they generally find that the energy surrounding their exercise attracts a host of astral nasties, also known as astral junk, astral bogies, unformed thoughtforms, energy vampires, and host of other derisive names. As you can tell from these labels we give them, they are not whole beings, such as elemental spirits or human discarnates, but unwanted energies who have followed us back into our physical or mundane world because we were inexperienced enough or too lazy to make sure the portal was closed behind us.

I had one being in my beginning explorations who hung around my home for weeks. It was hard to call it a "nasty" since it was benign as a newborn pup. I had a vague sense of its appearance and knew it wasn't a "whole being," but it was still a bothersome presence. I could feel it watching me, peeking around corners like a child spying on a parent. I sensed no harmful intent from it, just an overwhelming curiosity about my world. It had an insatiable fascination for my vacuum cleaner and I could feel it "breathing" down my neck as I cleaned the house. Between that and having it peeking in the bathroom while I showered was all I could take. I went and got my best friend, who had begun her Witchcraft studies with me, and together we sought out books and teachers who could help us banish this being back to its own world.

For most astral nasties it's just a matter of commanding them to leave. Say it in a firm voice three times and it should happen. The idea of saying the command three times is an Anglo-Celtic magickal remnant, a sacred number we will explore in chapter 5. If you feel more in command to use a ritual tool such as a wand or athame, then go ahead and use it.

In my case, the astral being ended up *outside* my house instead of inside. I wanted it back in its own world, but somehow I had not made that intention clear when I commanded it to leave. I could hear it scratching at the stone walls of the exterior of my house like a lost puppy wanting back in. With a few more commands, and a clear visualization of where I wanted it to go, it left for good.

The teacher and mentor who helped me learn how to make my command enforceable told me to hold a magickal tool I had faith in and point at the creature as I made my command. This was only a prop, as the magick was in me and not the tool, but pointing my favorite wand at it made me feel as if I would be obeyed. Without it I might not have spoken with the conviction I needed to accomplish the goal. Another teacher taught me to laugh at such creatures. Laughter is empowering and evokes positive emotions that drive away incomplete or negative beings.

She also told me that many times these creatures are no more than thoughtforms that never had a chance to fully develop. They were made up of someone's wishes that were never completed, and they were left in the astral realm to either find more energy to complete themselves or to waste away from lack of fresh energies. Rarely were they harmful at my level of skill at that time, but I was warned that, as I grew as a Witch and learned how to garner and project more magickal power, the beings who would be attracted to me would also be more knowledgeable and powerful.

All of you who have reached this point in your studies probably know this already. Those of you who aren't in the habit of fully closing the portals you create between two worlds should begin to make sure the doors are closed after an astral journey.

Sometimes lessons have to be learned the hard way, and if you are reading this book you probably have your own battle stories to tell around the balefire of your magickal boo-boos. Occasionally, we still make them, and sometimes they are very funny. If you're not an intermediate-advanced or advanced Witch, stop and ask a few advanced Witches of their beginning lessons. Like me, they will have stories that will make you laugh and others that will make you shudder. All will have value to you as you continue to climb that tree.

The essential lesson to learn from this is the same as that of the threshold guardians: you will attract beings of an intelligence and ability just at or just above your current skill level. This means as you advance you will be blocked by beings who can give you greater challenges, and you can bring back to your daily world beings less harmless than my vacuum-loving being.

How Many More Guardians Can There Be?

Consider this subheading to be no more than a rhetorical question. You already know the answer. They are as infinite as the universe.

The terror of the threshold is everywhere, but he is only a terror if you let him be. The secret to getting past him? Honesty. Sincerity. Respect. No harmful intent.

The secret to getting him on your side? Having no fear. The threshold guardian is only a terror if you cower before him, choosing words that aren't from your heart, but from your head—words you think he wants to hear. Nothing outrages a threshold guardian more than doublespeak that is not honest. Such attempts will keep your pathway blocked.

Be ready to be tested by them at any time, but realize they are not playing with you but are offering true spiritual challenges. They'll use riddles, passwords, and tests, but they never play mind games. If you find a being playing with your head, it is not a true guardian, nor is it a positive being who can assist you on your journey. Leave its world as soon as you realize what it is, and make sure the portal is closed tight behind you.

If you follow these steps you will find that, as on the classic hero's journey of our world's mythologies, your enemies and those who test your determination will become your friends and allies as you traverse any world you choose.

New Initiations,
New Invocations

In the beginning you probably stood in your first esbat circle where you witnessed an amazing ceremony called Drawing Down the Moon. The total transformation of the priestess who became the Moon Goddess held you enthralled. You could actually see her aura turn to silver as she became enveloped in the spirit of the lunar deity. Before this moment you probably never really understood the teaching that deity was immanent rather than transcendent. Now, here it was, changing your knowledge to wisdom as you listened to her channel her messages to your group.

As an intermediate it occurred to you—or else that great frying pan of enlightenment was applied to your thick skull—that you, too, had this power to draw into you divine aspects from the natural world or from the ends of the universe.

Before you even approached a teacher about learning the art of Witchcraft, you may have done some reading and been attracted to this spiritual path because it posed no ordained intermediary between you and the divine. *You* could be a vessel for the divine. *You* could be your own priest or priestess. All it took was study and effort, then you, your deities, and your initiatory processes would be unique to you. Elders might have tried to tell you some of what to expect, but, again, words can never convey all of "that which can never be told."

In many ways, that was the most exciting part of all, for someday you knew the deities would be invoked into you and you would become one mind with them as you served their needs and those of your group. More than just being able to connect with deities, you found the initiation process continued on far beyond that first year and a day you so looked forward to completing.

Then it hit you.

The learning process in the Craft continues for a least as long as you live, and probably well after. As you search for knowledge and ask questions, you become more prepared for ritual, have more successful magick, and grow closer to your deities. As each particle of your knowledge becomes a boatload of wisdom, your excitement in Witchcraft is renewed again and again.

The Divine and Its Thousands of Aspects

In our current forms, at this stage in human evolution, we truly cannot know deity in its fullest form: that of full union—body, mind, brain, and soul—with the supreme creator who made all that was, is, and ever shall be. We can, however, connect with success, even with intimacy, with various aspects of deity as we continue to climb the tree of life.

Common esbat and sabbat rituals such as Drawing Down the Moon and Drawing Down the Sun are popular rites. Most do not even specify a particular lunar or solar deity by name. We call into the body of a priest or priestess only the essence of that heavenly body and all its influences and affinities, which we have come to know as the first calendar of the Pagan world.

As we begin to experiment with evoking deities—calling them to our circle to worship with us, honor them, or ask their aid—or as we invoke them, drawing them into our physical and spiritual bodies to speak through us, we learn more about them and about how we relate to each one's unique energy.

After the Drawing Down the Moon and Drawing Down the Sun, we usually begin by experimenting with our own patron deity, one which we have chosen or, more correctly, has chosen us to serve and to be served. Reciprocity between priest/ess and deity is not a prayer promise in exchange for divine favors, but an exchange of love between worlds that enlightens all it touches and urges it to continue to strive to be more. Many times we are not in control of this process, but we recognize it when we have been chosen.

In my tradition, Brighid and Lugh are the principle female and male aspects of deity we worship, so it follows that a great many of the women I knew in my tradition, and even within my own coven, had Brighid as their patron deity. I wanted to be different. I loved Brighid, but I wanted the flamboyant Queen Maeve of Connacht as my patron.

To this day I love Maeve with all the passion that only she can inspire. She's bold, fearless, fiery; a warrior, a leader; beautiful, sexual, arrogant, and smart, and she seemed to me to be a fine match to my own leonine personality. Yet no matter how hard I tried, I could not develop the type of rapport with Maeve I needed to ask her to be my patron. I could evoke her presence but she refused to be invoked into my body. That rejection hurt.

I was just accepting the fact that Queen Maeve did not want me when I realized how many times Brighid had made herself available to me while I went chasing after something else I could never have. Brighid was there in her guise of the flame of inspiration when I had writer's block. She was there as my muse of intellect when I struggled through college classes. She was there in her warrior guise when I was in danger. She was there in her mother-face to smooth tears from my cheeks when I was sad. Like Maeve, Brighid was a personification of fire but, rather than being a fire blazing out of control, Brighid's flame burned like a faithful lighthouse in the night that warmed and led me where I needed to go. In other words, she was offering herself as my patron, giving me the great honor of choosing me as one of her own, and I was too dense to see it for longer than I will ever admit.

When I realized what I was pushing away and gratefully accepted Brighid as my patron, I found I was better off for it. I need Brighid's soothing presence more than I need more tempermentalness. Maeve's erratic energy would not have complimented my own, but instead she would act as an accomplice to keep me forever at war with the internal growth I sought. Maeve would have blended with my worst traits and exacerbated them as she and I chased down all the wrong things for me. Maeve does not stop to make sure of what she wants, she just goes after it with a determination that's unstoppable and, often, detrimental. I still adore Queen Maeve; she'll forever be one of my heroes, but now I recognize that she and I personified the leonine archetype too much when together, and I needed Brighid's soothing fires of inspiration and strength more than I needed Maeve's wild blazes of raw ambition.

After you work with invoking your patron—or patrons, if you have more than one, and you probably do at this stage in your development—you might experiment with deities similar to him or her, seeing what each can teach you. You may even invoke groups of deities, such as all deities of the hearth when you need answers about your home life or all deities of love when you need to give a love spell a boost.

The process for any invocation is the same as for Drawing Down the Moon. Either you or a trusted covenmate will bless and anoint you, then use a magickal tool to pull that energy from the source and then send it into your body. You and all around you will know when success has been achieved, for you will truly not be yourself.

At the end of the ceremony the process is reversed. This is merely a formality and is similar to grounding, because the deities cannot be commanded and would leave when ready anyway.

Are the Deities "Real?"

We can't answer this question without backing up a step and asking others:

Is the word "real" real?

Is reality fixed or mutable?

Do we all have our own reality?

Do I exist or am I a thoughtform in someone else's head?

Can multiple realities coexist?

Did I create my own reality?

Did I allow someone else to dictate my reality to me?

As you found by the time you embarked on your intermediate studies, reality has a funny way of shifting as we watch. It's not the static intangible we were taught to believe it was as children, but an ever-evolving part of the wheel of existence.

Among newer Witches who have not yet experienced direct connection with deity, the question of their existence is a common one. This is common to any religion. At some point all young people or converts will question the existence of the divine and try to decide if, where, and how it exists, and if it's worthy of worship.

As was stated earlier, Witchcraft is an experiential path; it must be experienced to be understood. No one expects you to accept the reality of deities, sometimes referred to as divine archetypes, until you work with them for yourself.

For those who've known the deities, they are real by almost any definition of reality. As you think about your relationship to the deities, remember the old magickal adage:

As above, so below;
As within, so without.

In other words, if the deities lie outside of us, then they also lie within. If they dwell above us, then they dwell on this plain with us and within us. The macrocosm and microcosm reflect and mimic one another, which is one of the reasons our magickal spells work.

If you really think about it, all religions, including our own Pagan traditions, are ultimately monotheistic. You can argue with me later, but for now, please just think about this. We use aspects, or specific arenas, of the divine. We have mother deities, warrior deities, lunar deities, household deities, etc. We can understand and relate to these "pieces" of divinity to find our way to the creator that embodies them all. In other words, we seek union with one life force that is both male and female and contains all divine aspects that ever were, are, or will be.

If you believe the deities are no more than archetypes in your mind, then you still have a lot of "from knowledge to wisdom" work to do before you discover their outside existence as well. You may feel one side of their existence with more strength than another, but you should be able to sense them both within and outside of yourself.

This doesn't mean any deities outside of us with whom we have trouble building a rapport are the transcendent sort of the mainstream faiths. Consider my experience with Maeve as an example. She's as earthy as a woman can be. She lives on the planes both above, below, and upon our own, just as part of us lives in all worlds simultaneously. Yet Maeve is not a transcendent goddess. Some of these mainstream, transcendent deities are so lofty their feet never touch the earth they created, and even worse, they often scorn the earth as "the devil's excrement" rather than as the personification of a benevolent deity. Pagan deities tend to be viewed as transcendent and immanent at the same time: as within, so without. That sounds complex, but it only means that their energies surround us at all times because they are everywhere we need them to be, not on some cloud plucking a harp while the world goes on below them. We only need to recognize them and learn from them to help carry us to the next level in our Craft careers.

Stories of initiations—some unwanted and some sought after with passion—populate our folklore and myths, and it is from these we can learn how to grow so that we know deity on more intimate terms. Like being born or dying, this climb to the top of the divine realms is a solitary adventure. We use ritual, pathworking, and meditation to help us decide where we go next.

Evocation

We won't spend much time on evocation other than to define it, to see how it compares to invocation. Evocation is a lesson of the beginning-intermediate level in many traditions. To evoke something is to call or invite it into your presence. This is done every time you cast a sacred circle when you ask the elements and their representative spirits to come and join you, or when you invite your deities to watch or assist a spell or ritual. In most instances, the being evoked may never enter the boundaries of the circle, but waits just outside its perimeters at its appropriate quarter lending its support.

Most beings you would call on—such as the elements—are sentient spirits, and it is wise in Pagan magick to always *invite* and never to *command* someone's presence. As we've already established, arrogance will get you nowhere; it may even send you in reverse.

Invocation

As its name suggests, invocation is the process of bringing the essence of a divine being into your physical body. We do this routinely in the aforementioned rituals of Drawing Down the Moon and Drawing Down the Sun in which a lunar goddess or solar god are pulled into the body of a priest, priestess, or other person in the circle who is capable of handling the tremendous influx of energy and the responsibility for relaying any messages to the group, if appropriate.

Solitary practitioners also Draw Down the Moon and Draw Down the Sun, which requires a strong sense of one's self so the invoked deity doesn't remain the dominant personality after the ritual is complete.

The term "draw down" causes some confusion because we are not drawing down but drawing *in* the essence of the divine. This is another case where semantics causes those who have not experienced something to think it is what it is not.

The basic process for invocation is to ask the deity for his or her assistance. Candles are usually lit in their honor and a litany of their attributes are chanted as a song of praise. Then a ritual tool, such as a wand, athame, or chalice, is used to collect the energy of the deity and at that point it is transferred by both physical action and visualization into your body.

As an advanced Witch you have other options to try which can yield insights, wisdom, healing, spiritual growth, or help with any magick you wish to do.

Here are four variations on traditional Wiccan invocations you may wish to try.

ADVANCED INVOCATION #1: CHANGING GENDERS

In most instances women tend to invoke feminine deities and men the masculine deities. This tendency feels natural to us, so much so that, even in advanced group work, we tend to stick people in their divine roles based on gender rather than on inner qualities or capabilities. Some more advanced covens have enjoyed reversing these deity gender roles, but many still remain uncomfortable with them.

I admit that, after more than twenty years in the Craft, I still am not at ease with having a male deity invoked in me, nor have I developed as close a relationship with male deities as I would like. Those of us who aren't at ease with these role reversals are usually working through other issues. Our culture and its stereotypes are hardwired in us, and it takes a lot of willpower to rise above them. I know in my case my discomfort stems from childhood when I ended up playing the male parts in most role-playing games because I was tall, and most men are taller than most women. I hated it. Even though I was something of a tomboy until my junior high years, this constant relegation to male roles made me feel unfeminine and somehow of less value than the other girls I played with.

It's no secret that we each have a so-dubbed masculine and feminine part of ourselves. It's almost become a cliché to tell a macho man to get in touch with his feminine half or to tell the high-rolling woman executive to tone down her masculine side. If only it were that easy and human psyches so simplistic!

The feminine-masculine sides we speak of, or the feminine-masculine correspondences we give to plants, herbs, and trees, are labels for—can you guess already?—"that which can never be told." There is nothing inherently masculine about ground cinnamon other than that its magickal energy works as projective rather than receptive, and we have classified projective energy as masculine in nature.

We could just as easily call feminine and masculine energies black and white, or dog and cat, or mammal and reptile. The words don't matter in this case because we don't use these categories to assign a value judgment but to make it easier to understand the energy of something we want to use as a ritual or magickal catalyst. In general, things which are hot, projective, active, or solar-related are masculine, while things that are cool, receptive, passive, or lunar-related are feminine.

If the ancients, whose religions we claim to draw our practices from, had been as rigid in their rites as we are, we'd still be arguing these classifications rather than using them. The preponderance of male lunar deities (see my *Magick and Rituals of the Moon*, Llewellyn, 1995) and feminine sun deities (see Patricia Monaghan's *O Mother Sun*, Crossing Press, 1997) tell us that our ancestors viewed their world more androgynously than we do today.

For the purposes of magick, and in some rituals, it is good to know if the catalyst you've chosen has a projective or receptive nature, though it doesn't make that item female or male in nature. Some of the correspondences we accept are:

MASCULINE	FEMININE
Sun	Moon
Day	Night
Right	Left
Active	Passive
Sends	Receives
Projective	Receptive
Gold	Silver
White	Black
Sabbat	Esbat
Holly	Ivy
Yang	Yin
Odd numbers	Even numbers
Oak	Willow
Fire	Water
Air	Earth

Above	Below
Hot	Cold
Bone	Blood
Blade	Chalice
Wakefulness	Sleeping
Intellectual	Intuitive
Light	Dark

If you've never evoked a deity of the opposite gender, start your experiments the easy way, by taking a lunar or solar deity that is the opposite of the one you usually use. Since we use their archetypes all throughout our wheel of the year, their planetary energies are familiar to us, and to merely change their gender is not a large leap. In other words, if you're a woman who has never Drawn Down the Sun, or a man who has never Drawn Down the Moon, then give it a try.

This exercise shouldn't be made harder than it is. You don't even need to find or give the deities a name* unless you want to look up a few and try to align with one specific deity. Simply change your usual invocation from she to he, or from he to she. If you've already performed this or similar invocations, you might want to try invoking a specific deity of the opposite gender. As a student of the advanced Craft or as an advanced practitioner, you likely are familiar with many opposite-gender deities. One or two may be patrons of yours, also a comfortable place to begin.

Until you are used to handling energies unfamiliar to your usual practice, avoid invoking deities whose energies or areas of influence are different from your normal, everyday, basic personality. The sudden change can upset your conscious-subconscious-superconscious mind links and create incompatible energies inside you that, while they are rarely dangerous unless your mind is highly suggestible, can fit you as poorly as used shoes that are a size too small. This is one case where my Maeve experience is applicable.

As always, ground after you have thanked your invoked deity and told him or her to leave at will.

---

* Three books can give you all the deity information you could ever want: Janet and Stewart Farrar's *The Witches' Goddess* (Phoenix, 1987) and *The Witches' God* (Phoenix, 1989), and Patricia Monaghan's *The Book of Goddesses and Heroines* (Llewellyn, 1998). I feel these, and at least one dictionary of characters in the mythology from your tradition's culture, are an essential part of any Witch's personal library.

ADVANCED INVOCATION #2: USING BOTH GENDERS

Part of being an advanced Craft practitioner is that you have the ability to keep your mind focused on multiple catalysts, concepts, or energies at the same time. This comes in handy for advanced magick spells, as we'll explore in chapter 14, but also for invocation rituals.

If you are a solitary, working alone, and want to do more than merely evoke the God and Goddess—with or without specific names—you can invoke both at once. This is a tricky practice that requires an advanced Witch's visualization and concentration skills and an understanding of the way the brain works.

The feminine side of the body is usually considered the left side; however, because of the way we human beings are wired, it's the right side of the brain that controls the left side of the body. The opposite is also true. In general, in most of the world's metaphysical theory and practices, the right side of the body is considered the masculine side, but we know it is the left side of the brain under which it operates.

Boing!

Suddenly the lines between masculine and feminine begin to blur, but don't duck yet. The frying pan of enlightenment senses that you're grasping this.

The right side of the body was given its masculine attribution because the majority of us are right-handed. In other words, this side dominates and projects. We write with our right hands, toss with our right arms, wave with our right fingers, etc.

The unity of the God and Goddess both invoked in you at the same moment in physical time takes a lot of skill. Most of us are accustomed to having only one invoked energy in us at a time and acting the role becomes second nature to us.

If you perform the Great Rite at any of your rituals, this is an excellent time to try invoking both a god and goddess at one time. The Great Rite is a ritual beginners are exposed to but often not asked to participate in until after their first year and a day of study. It is a symbolic event in which blade and chalice unite to represent the union—sexual and spiritual—of the God and Goddess. Most Witchcraft 101 books will discuss this rite in detail and even provide ritual outlines to follow.

Jean Markale, the French scholar and author who has made it his life's work to study the society and the religion of the Celts, believes that Merlin, being more than a wizard in the Arthurian myths, is a god of nature. He sites the example of he and Vivian, the Goddess representation, dwelling in their clearing in the deep woods in what is sometimes translated as a Castle of Glass or Castle of Air (*Merlin: A Priest of Nature* [Inner Traditions, 1995]). He cites this as a Great Rite, a union of the male and female principles of creation. To find them there is similar to finding the godhead, reuniting with the creative source that brought us all into being.

The easiest way to invoke both God and Goddess—at least in the beginning of your experiments—is to leave them nameless. Focus instead on the general qualities of masculine and feminine deity. If you wish to invoke specific deities you will have to first make sure they want to be in the same vessel—you—at the same time. Drawing warring factions within you can give serious upset to your conscious-subconscious-superconscious mind link and can leave you feeling jittery, ungrounded, and out of sorts for days.

Instead of pulling the divine energy into your body at the usual sites of forehead, navel, or crown area, use the palms of your hands. It's not common knowledge, but there are minor chakra points in both palms, and in both soles of your feet, too. Pull the Goddess or feminine energy in through your left palm and the God or masculine energy in through your right palm. If you feel the need for a magickal or ritual tool to help you, then use one. In fact, to borrow a bad cliché, allow one hand to wash the other. Hold your chalice in your right hand to collect the Goddess energy, and your wand or blade in your left hand to collect the God energy. The one you select first is up to you. Do them in the order most comfortable to you.

As you do this you should be able to feel as if you've been split in two. If you've been using meditative practices or pathworking where you use dual consciousness, you will feel a similar division of focus as you do this. This means that your mind can focus on two separate things or sequences of events at the same time. It often becomes a staple of the advanced Witch's meditation practice because it can be used to escape a physical place where the Witch doesn't want to be while allowing him to be there in active participation, yet be somewhere more fun, all at the same time.

If you are not used to dual consciousness meditation, you may find that the second energy you invoke forces the other out. If this happens, release all the energies and try again at another time. It may be that the deities whom you've chose to work with do not want to inhabit the same space or to work together, or that you're not ready yet to keep your focus on both.

Don't be dismayed if it seems as if you are 70 percent God and 30 percent Goddess, or 40 percent God and 60 percent Goddess. Maintaining a perfect balance is difficult.

Even in dual consciousness most practitioners find their focus shifts throughout the process, one minute giving more weight to one event line or realm, then switching to another moments later. This is perfectly normal and does not mean you are doing the invocation wrong. Judge your success by whether you sense the dual consciousness at all rather than by how much weight each half receives. In the beginning you may find that the gender you are most unused to using will feel like no more than 5 or 10 percent of your invocation. That's fine. It's a start, and your skills will build over time.

You may thank and invite the deities to leave through either your palms or the soles of your feet. Many people like to use the soles of the feet because it also provides a strong sense of grounding for returning to their normal wakeful consciousness, or what we call the beta rate of brain activity.

ADVANCED INVOCATION #3: RITUAL DRAMA

As far as any scholar of the fine arts can determine, ritual drama originated in ancient Greece in the temples of the goddess Kore. Priestesses enacted the myth of Kore's return to the earth from her underworld home on the spring equinox.

Many modern covens are rediscovering ritual drama and the power it has to help us get past knowledge of the deities and their life cycles to giving us their wisdom. It requires familiarity with several myths in the culture in which you work (i.e., Celtic, Teutonic, Greco-Roman, Polynesian, etc.), or of several pantheons if your group or coven is eclectic—that is, it draws from many cultures at once.

In my Irish-based coven in Texas, ritual drama was one of our favorite rites. All traditions and covens have a few secrets they keep to protect the integrity of their rituals and to keep their energies strong. One of the practices we kept secret at the time we were together was how we performed our ritual dramas in a state of invocation.

There are drawbacks to this practice, especially if two or more of the deities don't get along, or if you invoke Mars and Athena, two war deities who would rather battle than cooperate. It took us a while to learn how to best deal with incompatible divine energies. We were a group of twelve, with an occasional student or three, who found it worked best if we allowed one person to remain uninvoked so we would have not only a captive audience but a referee should things go in the wrong direction.

The person chosen to remain out of the drama should not interfere with the direction of the drama unless necessary. Part of this will depend on how much scripting you have done beforehand. There is no right or wrong amount, just whatever your group finds comfortable. However, the uninvoked person needs to possess good arbitration and grounding skills, and must not be afraid to step in and act as a stage director if he sees the need.

As a solitary you can invoke a deity and then evoke, or call to the presence of your circle, many others to interact with you. This, too, can be tricky, but since most evoked deities remain just outside your circle's boundary, you don't risk physical battles with them. Until you're used to having many divine personalities surrounding you, and learn how the various energies interact, it's best not to create a portal for them—or any other being—to come into your circle. Remember your Wicca 101 training. The circle not only contains energy, but protects you from outside energies as well. Use it.

ADVANCED INVOCATION #4: ARCHETYPE GROUPS

Another way an advanced Witch might want to try invocation is by invoking not just a generic god and goddess, or even a god and goddess of a specific name, but *all* gods or *all* goddesses of a specific archetype. In other words, you might want to invoke all wood-land goddesses or all gods of the hunt.

The inner feeling of this type of invocation can be profound, and you will find the deities' thoughts and concerns remain in your head long after you ground the ritual. Sometimes this can cause a magickal boo-boo, or what others refer to as getting what you ask for whether you wanted it or not. For instance, I invoked a deity of the wood-lands who loved animals, and who hunted deer. Now there's nothing unusual about cars and whitetail deer colliding in the Texas Hill Country, but my car had two of its three encounters with deer within a few weeks of this invocation. The lesson?

- Be sure of your goal.

- Don't mix magick with ritual invocation at first.

- Choose your archetypes with care.

- Ground well when you are finished with your ritual.

Some of the more popular archetypes are divided by gender, but most can cross that boundary. The following is a list of common divine archetypes. Not all make good invocation prospects. On the other hand, some may be perfect for your best friend but disastrous for you. As you should already know at this level of practice, we all have our own lessons to learn and wisdoms to attain. No two are the same. We can love and support one another through each lesson, but only the one undergoing the challenge can have any affect on its final outcome.

If you find you've invoked a group of deities that make you feel uncomfortable or afraid, politely invite them to leave but still thank them for working with you. The rules of giving thanks are strict in the otherworlds, and are just plain good manners anywhere.

EXAMPLES OF DIVINE ARCHETYPES

Lunar	Solar
Hunter	Guardian and Defender
Illness and Want	The Horned God
Faery Queen	Warrior
Wasteland	The Fallen or Wounded Warrior
Nurturer	Earth
Grains	Element of Fire
Element of Earth	Element of Water
Element of Air	Element of Spirit
Sexuality	Inspiration and the Muses
Elders and Sages	Communication and Writing
Woodlands and Forests	The Triple Goddess
Virgins	Mothers
Crones	Fathers
The Child God	Animals, General and Specific
Music	Dance
Sky	Stellar, Some Specific
Health and Wellness	Winter
Autumn	Spring
Summer	Dawn or Dusk
Forge or Smithy	Birth or Regeneration

Fertility	Death and Change
Underworld	Otherworld
War and Battle	Warding and Defense
Divine Couples	Planting and Sowing
Harvest	Bestowers of Sovereignty
Kings	Prophets and Seers
Magicians	Priests and Priestesses
Beauty	Prosperity and Abundance
Hearth and Kitchen	The Home
Apprenticeship	Food, General and Specific
Sorrow	Hermits and Wise Recluses
Triumph and Victory	Intellect and Scholarship
Peace	Justice
Boundaries	Hedonism
Shapeshifting	Brewing
Deserts	Trees, General and Specific
Mythical Creatures	Plants, General and Specific
Lakes and Rivers	Flowers, General and Specific
Oceans and Seas	Herbs, General and Specific
Volcanos	Birds, General and Specific
Wine or Ale	Fish, General and Specific
Things Hidden	Mountains
Musicians	Entertainers
Sacred Sites	Stones and Gems

Preparing for the Next Step: A New Initiation

If you've come this far you may wish to make a self-dedication to your study of the advanced Craft. You may even want to start by seeking out initiatory mythic stories, the ones that would have blown past you like a cyclone heading for a trailer park when you were a beginner.

This may be the last or one of the last initiations you undergo, even though your learning and growing will continue as long as you remain in this lifetime and, with luck, it will continue long after your physical body has turned to dust.

Reclaiming the Gingerbread Cottage

Sometimes the resistance to undergo another formal initiation is of our creation. It may come from a fear or other negative emotion or association we harbor for a thing, being, or practice. Sometimes the negative veneer was in place long before this incarnation, one to which we were acculturated to accept since birth. Or we may just be bored with them. Because of this, our lessons about the rigors of initiation can come from surprising teachers. They can spout from the mouths of the uninitiated, whisper to us in the rustle of a leaf, shout at us from behind an office desk, or be heard in a snippet of song lyric or in a story we've listened to many times but to which we've never really heard.

Living as a Witch is more than having ash logs in the hearth, an altar in the bedroom, or a cabinet full of dried herbs waiting to unleash their magickal potential. These accoutrements are nice, and they go a long way to allowing us to feel "witchy," but they are only things.

Living as a Witch requires you to focus on an overall life goal: union with the creator. This is the whole purpose of religion, and Witchcraft is no exception.

By this point in your spiritual progression, you've no doubt learned to see how Pagan concepts and mysteries were hidden in myths, faery tales, and folklore to hide and protect them from the Witchhunters. Usually we are intermediates when we learn to see initiation challenges in mythology. One of the most well known is the Celtic myth of the goddess Cerridwen and her student/servant Gwion. Old Cerridwen has a cauldron in which she brews a potion of wisdom and all-knowledge. When Gwion burns a thumb, he sticks it in his mouth and finds himself gifted with the power of the brew. Knowing Cerridwen will be angry, Gwion flees as his teacher pursues him. As they run they both shapeshift into different creatures; Gwion in an effort to get away, and Cerridwen in an effort to be a better predator. In the end Gwion becomes a piece of grain and Cerridwen the hen who consumes him so he may be reborn to her.

But what about faery tales and stories we often think of as tales for children? Do they also hold insights for the advanced Witch? The answer is a resounding yes, at least for the most popular and enduring of them.

Let's take a look at the imagery in the German faery tale of *Hansel and Gretel*.

In the popular version—so well loved that German composer Engelbert Humperdink (1854–1921) made it into a successful opera in 1893—Hansel and Gretel are the young children of a local woodcutter who loves them, and his shrewish wife, who does not. One day the mother sends the children deep into the dangerous woods, knowing they would not return. In the woods they encounter a house made of gingerbread and other goodies in which an old woman lives alone. She entices the children indoors only to cage the boy to fatten him up to eat and to turn the girl into her personal slave. In the end the children push the "wicked old witch" into her own oven and break the spell. The house turns into the bodies of children captured before, and Hansel and Gretel return to their living father, who is now a widower.

By any standards that's a hideous bedtime tale for any child, but as child psychologist and mythologist Bruno Bettleheim showed us in his famous book *The Uses of Enchantment*, children often have the ability to see through to the deeper meaning of these faery tales in a way that adults have long forgotten.

If we look at this faery tale again with a Witch's eye, what we see is yet another myth of transformation and spiritual growth as we pass through another test and initiation into a higher place of being.

The mother is jealous of her children, particularly her daughter. She is the image of the Mother Goddess who knows that, through the natural cycles of time, her daughter will replace her. Her son will someday replace the father as God, just as our seasonal myths tell us happens each year. They represent a real threat to the mother, who wishes to retain her position of power. Like those in myths before her, she tries in vain to destroy her heirs.

The woods are deep and dark, like kivas, caves, and other secret places of the earth where initiatory and sacred rites have taken place. They represent a new terror to be faced and overcome, and they create a doorway between the world of form and spirit.

The gingerbread cottage is the façade that our imagination places in front of Witchcraft. It's the fantasy element that distracts us from our true path, symbolized by the old woman, or wise crone, who dwells inside.

Fattening up Hansel can be interpreted as a metaphor for his learning. The work Gretel does is the slavish grunt work all initiates must undergo before they can get where they want to go. The Craft is hard work, and any religion that places the responsibility for growth on the individual rather than the leaders is one that many abandon as just too difficult. Yet when we read the autobiographical works of many who have stuck it out, we find they were often made to chop wood, move rocks from one pile to another, tend fires, cook, etc., to learn to appreciate the process. This is a Zen concept as well—that when we learn to focus as much on the process of what we're building as we are on the end goal, we appreciate it for itself and we find joy in the work itself rather than craving only the outcome.

The crone is imparting her wisdom and, when the children learn enough to use it, they push her into her own oven. The oven, like the forge and cauldron, is a symbol of the sacred womb of the great Mother Goddess, the ultimate kiva of transformation. Gods and goddesses throughout history have been sacred to these places of change: Vulcan, Holde, Vesta, Hestia, Luctain, and China's Kitchen God.

In most myths, when the crone "dies" she is replaced by her virgin or younger self, in this case Gretel. She now has the power to break the spell holding in all the other children who did not learn their lessons.

In the end she returns to the father, a metaphor for the God—the God who is the son and lover who always returns to the Goddess in our seasonal myths so that the cycle can continue.

The lesson of *Hansel and Gretel* is not one of defeating the "wicked old witch" at her game of who bakes who first but of learning from her, becoming her, and uniting with the creator in the womb of the Goddess from which we were all born. The story follows the hero's journey model. There is the separation to an otherworld, the harsh lessons of the initiation, and the triumphant return home once the challenges of the initiation have been won.

Questions to Ask Yourself As You Grow

Just as you were tested by a teacher, teachers, or a teaching coven—or a self-testing—before your first initiation, you should do the same intense soul searching as you embark on the commitment to pursue the next step in your never-ending search for knowledge and enlightenment. The questions that appear here have no right or wrong answers; some of them you may want to use as discussion starters with others at your level of experience. They are here to make you think about where you've been, where you are, and where you want to go. They test your ethics, challenge your heart, and help you decide the best route for strengthening your place on the web of existence.

If examined honestly, they should give you a picture of the total person you are, as both a Witch and a human being. Read the questions with care and see if you can see yourself in any of them. If so, decide if this is a good thing or a bad thing. Then think about how you are or are not willing to make changes to your lifestyle or beliefs and practices, and why. Think about how you define advancement and how these questions do or don't relate to your ideal. This is pure self-examination and the only one hurt by your dishonesty is you. Take your time and, once again, I quote from Delphi's Oracle: *Know thyself.*

1) Have you become lazy in your spiritual life, assuming you are so special that you no longer have to work for your rewards?

2) Do you feel satisfaction in practicing alone, or do you always need a coven surrounding you?

3) Do you pray and feel heard? If you don't pray, what do you do?

4) Do you feel constricted by the rede of "harm none," or is it a tenet or ethic that you've always lived by?

5) Do you feel there really is no "harm none"? Do you believe magick can be accomplished without change to anyone but your target subject?

6) How do you feel about hunting? Fishing? Vegetarianism? Animal rights? How does this affect your spiritual thinking and practice?

7) Do you feel compelled to argue minor points with everyone about Witchcraft or magick? Do you write scathing letters to the editors of Pagan magazines blasting their writers and "correcting" their mistakes? Are you still able to be drawn into protracted debates over the powers inherent in the color blue?

8) Do you feel more blessed, more knowledgeable, or more important than your covenmates or other Pagans in your community? Is this good or bad? Do those around you seem to agree with your assessment of your skill level?

9) Do you feel less blessed, less knowledgeable, or less important than your covenmates or other Pagans in your community? Why or why not? Do you feel others share your self-image? Do you want to change it? Why and how?

10) Do you see some traditions as being more valid or having less value than others?

11) Is it important to you to be a leader? Or is it important for you to feel led by someone else?

12) Do you think about your role in group situations? Are you the mediator, the teacher, the organizer, the anchor, the rebel, the seer, the warrior, the priest or priestess, the fool, the shapeshifter, the tender of the sacred fire, the herbalist, the guru, the troublemaker?

13) Can you feel yourself connected to the web of being, even if you've yet to understand your place upon it?

14) How much 360-degree thinking do you feel you've mastered? Are there some subjects on which you are more rigid in your convictions than others? Why or why not? What, if anything, could change your mind?

15) How do you see time and space, and how does this affect your beliefs and spiritual practices?

16) Is magick something you do or something you are? Are the words *magick* and *spell* synonymous? Why or why not?

17) Do you feel capable of teaching a newcomer all by yourself? Do you have a realistic idea of your strengths and weaknesses? How do you feel when another Witch sees a strength or a weakness in you?

18) Can you find some good in all spiritual teachings or do you have specific areas, ideas, traditions, or people you feel compelled to verbally destroy?

19) How do deosil and widdershins affect your practice? Does one bother or frighten you or make you uneasy? Why?

20) Can you sustain an altered state of consciousness for longer than thirty minutes? Do you need to? Want to? Don't know?

21) How many cultures and their pantheons have you taken time to study? Do you feel more drawn to or in tune with some more than others? Are they the same ones your friends or covenmates like? Does it make a difference?

22) How do you feel about psychic self-defense, warding, the cast circle, and other sacred spaces? Are they ritual only or are they actual barriers in time and space?

23) Are you a fit temple for deity? Why or why not? Does your answer change from day to day or is your answer constant?

24) Are there areas of study you have given up progressing in? Are there areas you excel in that you crave to know more and more? Can you accept that no one can know everything within the Craft?

25) What is your household like? You job atmosphere? Does your mundane life reflect your spiritual one? Does your spiritual life reflect your mundane one? Do you want to change this? Why? How?

26) How do you define reality? Can you accept multiple realities? Are you real? How about your deities? What about other worlds? Is there one more real than the others, or merely one of which the bulk of your consciousness is currently aware?

27) Do you find that your magickal wants seem to take care of themselves with greater ease than they did when you were a novice? Is Wishcraft slowly overtaking over your Witchcraft?

28) What examples from your own experience can you cite of "Be careful what you wish for or you might get it"?

29) How do you feel about Craft titles, degrees, clergy, etc.? What are your personal goals in reference to titles?

30) What do you feel is the connection, if any, between ritual and magick? Why is ritual important to spiritual practice? How has it been important for you? How could you make it more important? Why do you want to or not want to?

31) When you separate your astral body from your physical, how do you visualize this happening? Do you see a true act of separation or the power of the super-consciousness at work? Why is your vision of this process essential to your efforts? Why is it not important? Could, would, or should you change practices that have worked well for you for many years?

32) How do you define "wholeness of being"? Do you have it? Have you ever had it? Is it possible to achieve it? To keep it? Is it a constant or something that comes and goes?

33) What special aspects, concepts, practices, or rituals of the Craft can you not give up and why? On what aspects are you willing to compromise or give up altogether?

34) Is one of your greatest joys jumping into arguments with others of your faith who see and do things differently than you? Do they make you feel defensive or threatened? Or do they make you think? Do you enjoy these exchanges of ideas or do you always stomp away in anger if someone doesn't agree with you? Why or why not?

35) Have you ever sensed that your behavior in a group setting has caused others discomfort or that you were on the verge of banishment? Has anyone suggested you might wish to explore solitary practice for a while but you just can't give up the dynamics of the coven setting? Why do you think you act and feel as you do?

36) Do you lie in wait for someone to mention a book or compact disk for which they express passion, saying it has helped them a great deal, just so you can trash it? Do you enjoy tearing apart the spiritual tools that have aided others just because your opinion of them is different, or because you disagreed with a single sentence or lyric and therefore decided to invalidate the entire work?

37) Is it your goal in conversations with other Witches and Pagans to share knowledge, compare ideas, and give each other things to think about, or is your sole objective to make others see that you are right and they are wrong?

38) Does the word "different" imply to you a value judgment? Do you think of *different* as better or worse, or is *different* just different?

39) Can you put up with others' mistakes? Can you laugh when a ritual goes wrong or when your magick yields what you asked for and not what you meant?

40) Is the Craft a joy to you or a forum for self-aggrandization? Can you enjoy your religion if you're not a leader or are not fulfilling other lofty roles to which you feel entitled? Do you insist on being addressed by a title? Why is it or is it not important to you? Do you think you could change your attitude? Do you want to? Why, how, or why not?

Devising Your Dedication to Advanced Study

If you are not part of a teaching coven or working with a teacher or teachers, this should be no hindrance to your continued studies or to your performing a dedication ceremony or self-initiation ritual. At this point you know how these are formatted and what is expected of you.

If you are already part of a hierarchical coven or tradition that oversees the method by which advancement to another degree or title is achieved, one or both of these ceremonies may be planned for you. If you are working on your own you have your choice about when, where, and how you plan these events for yourself. To be honest, even if you're part of a larger group you always remain free to make personal dedications to deities, courses of study, or other cultural traditions. These are personal choices based on your own spiritual goals and needs, and as long as they're not in conflict with any vows or promises you've made to your coven, their details don't have to be shared with anyone else unless you want them to be.

In general, the difference between a dedication and an initiation is that one usually comes at the beginning of a course of study and the other is at the end. Oftentimes newcomers who are working on their first year-and-a-day of study toward their first degree are referred to as dedicants. They have made either personal or public declarations of their intent to work through their year and a day before making that final commitment to initiation, either with a ceremony they do for themselves or one which a coven or other group has planned for them.

You may wish to formalize your embarkation on your study of advanced Witchcraft by undergoing a self-dedication in which you make vows to your spirit self, your deities, your totems, and your familiars of your precise goal. Depending on how far you've already delved into advanced study, this book may be the last one you wish to work with before making that initiation a reality. If this is your first look into advanced practice and thought, I recommend that you study several books and speak or learn from several advanced teachers before making your decision.

At this point in your spiritual career, you know the drill. No one should have to tell you how to cast your circle and make a dedication to the deities, or to explain to you why these initiation ceremonies are so important to the spiritual practices of the Craft. The choice of how you proceed and how you choose to label yourself afterward is up to you unless, again, you are part of a group that oversees these details for you.

From this point on you will find it harder than ever to compare your progress with that of others, as you may have done as a beginner. Back then, there was enough similarity in your emerging skills, even if one person outshone another in one or two areas, to allow you to see where you were all heading. At this point you have fragmented into specialties and discovered your own unique talents that will be unlike anyone else's. You will have to rely on your own instincts, your deities, and perhaps some trusted advanced friends to help you when you get stuck or need a boost of self-confidence.

Witchcraft has always been an experiential spiritual path, one whose greater mysteries cannot be described, taught, transmitted, explained, or understood until you have been immersed within them. This should be true of any religion, and it might have been in the distant past before the central feature of worship became focused on a single, trained leader who assumed responsibility for the spiritual progress of his or her entire congregation. This change made these leaders the sole mediators between humanity and the deities, making theirs a mystery religion for a select few. The other harm caused by this change in focus was that it elevated the male priests and rabbis to having God's ear, and destroyed the memories of the feminine half of the divine by disenfranchising women, who were the traditional healers and counselors.

Fortunately, Witchcraft still is a mystery path that cannot be walked with anyone else. You may have many friends, supporters, and mentors along the way but, like being born and dying, you must seek the creator alone.

However you choose to proceed with your studies and with any dedications and initiations, it's wise to keep in mind what you were told at your first initiation: As there was no true beginning along your pathway into the Craft, there is also no end. Learning, growing, and seeking reunion with the creator(s) is a task we take on not only for this lifetime, but perhaps for many others as well. The deities we have dedicated ourselves to serve will then expect us to honor them by assisting others to find their way up the tree of life, even when the path they've chosen is to another deity. Never fall into the trap of arrogance that deludes us into believing we have all the answers. Until we return to the womb of she who bore us, the greatest of all mysteries will remain just that . . . the greatest of all mysteries.

the fire chapters

❧

Where our
transformations blaze

five

The Three Worlds . . . or Four, or More?

In the beginning you knew there was a world other than the everyday one in which you lived. You may have even heard legends of the otherworld, the astral world, or inner planes before coming to Witchcraft. As your studies progressed you learned there were many more other worlds than you could have imagined, and there were even worlds in which other selves lived—other beings who were part of you—many of them in as blissful a state of ignorance of your existence as you were of theirs.

As an intermediate student you began to study those worlds and were expected to come up with your own conceptualization of where they were, how they operated, how to get in and out of them, and what your connection was to, with, and in each of them. You knew it was important to understand these worlds so you could understand the ways our magick works. You also knew that someday you would be asked or shown how to visit these other worlds and integrate your many selves (see the next chapter for a full discussion of this topic) in order to become a more whole, full, and complete being.

Through your travels to other worlds, you will cull knowledge and, from that, gain wisdom and get closer to your deities.

Why Would There Be Three Worlds?

Three worlds—why, indeed? This is a serious metaphysical question to ask yourself if you are going to form in your own mind an idea of how all other worlds interpenetrate and overlap one another.

So are there three worlds, or perhaps four worlds, as some occultists suggest? Or are there seven, as many Theosophists and other occultists believe? Or are there even more worlds—an infinite variety of parallel universes in which we all dwell simultaneously? Such conundrums are sure to either stimulate your 360-degree sight or just thinking about it may make you crazy.

It's essential to have some personal conceptualization of the various other worlds that overlap and interpenetrate our own if you're going to work successfully as a Witch. These are not only the worlds in which spirits, deities, and elementals live, but they are an intimate part of the tree you to climb to seek divinity.

These worlds are also part of your magick. We many envision that magick going out and coming back on a huge karmic wheel, but magick must first be born as a thought or idea, and thoughts are born of other worlds. They then gain density through our magickal efforts until they are so heavy they must come down through all the other worlds until they end up with us here on the physical plane.

The acculturation and socialization practices of the world's two major religions, Islam and Christianity—who together comprise two-thirds of the world's religious affiliation—have left us with a cosmology of only three worlds, all existing in linear time, a time frame we know cannot and does not exist. Their three worlds are Heaven, Earth, and Hell, and life is a one-shot deal. Make it or break it, and when you leave your earthly life it's either Heaven or Hell. You're offered no chance to visit the world to which God did not assign you, nor can you ever hope to change worlds if you desire or grow in spirit.

It's a sad failing of Western educators that we are not taught the ideologies and divine concepts of other religions as part of our normal course of education. Parental and ecclesiastical fears of indoctrination and, in the United States, separation of church and state laws have blocked all of our young generations from gaining a basic understanding of religions other than their own—information which could help us understand and accept the world we have to deal with as adults when it is much more dangerous and harder to overcome stereotypes.

Former United Nation's Secretary-General, Robert Muller, devised a set of broad blueprints for a worldwide education reform program that was never implemented. In his proposal he included what he believed to be the four "most important aspects of human nature" (from Mark Macy's *Miracles in the Storm* [New York: New American Library, 2001], p. 8):

Spirituality

Socialization

Mental Discipline

Health and Physical Fitness

Mr. Muller was quick to note the greatest shortfall occurred in the two most important areas, spirituality and socialization. This is particularly true in the West, where spirituality and religion are often seen as intertwined, and fear of religious indoctrination or loss of religious freedom prevent spiritual teachings, and where we interact more and more with machines each day than with people and their various motivations, of which religious teaching makes up an important part. We don't know the people with whom we share our homes—how much less are we able to relate to those outside of this sphere? And without knowledge there is no wisdom, which in this case leads to misunderstandings and wars because instead of accepting people as they are, we tend to place value judgments on their beliefs—especially their religious beliefs.

Knowledge is power, it is not indoctrination. This is true regardless of your chosen religious path. Knowledge leads to wisdom, and wisdom is strength—a strength which includes the courage of our own convictions. It gives us the ability to relate to others on an equal playing field, with all parties having similar education and experience. It creates harmony and peace between factions that would otherwise be at war with one another. In fact, they *are* at war with one another, and with themselves. We have Islamic fundamentalists trying to terrorize the West into accepting their view of how the world should operate while, at the same time, intimidating their co-religionists to accept their narrow view of God and the universe or die. Turn on the evening news and we can hear the sabers rattling as the English-speaking West warmongers ready themselves to march off to war, singing "Onward, Christian Soldiers." In Israel the rightist faction is continually elected to the roles of prime minister and Kenesset representatives, despite the fact that the Jewish right is a minority in Israel. Does any of this sound like a scenario in which three diverse groups—three who claim to worship the same God—can communicate?

We may never know all the worlds that exist—indeed, they may be infinite in number—but we can explore many of them and learn how to work in them and interact with the beings who dwell there. This is not just an art of magick, but one of healing, understanding, growing, and of bringing together two sets of beings who otherwise would be fearful of one another. We fear what we do not understand, and fear makes us build walls instead of bridges. Walls beg to be broken down, via violence if nothing else.

True, not all the denizens of every world will be open to your overtures of friendship and power sharing, but as an advanced Witch you've probably developed some sense about who's who and what's what via your astral travel work. Being cautious about who you interact with is a necessity in all worlds, including our everyday physical existence. Like so many other things in life, Witchcraft is mostly just a matter of common sense and self-control.

Mapping the Cosmos Your Way

The reason it's so important for you to have an idea of how the cosmos is ordered, or disordered, around you is because you need a mental map if you are ever to traverse these worlds without guided meditations to use as road maps. You also need to realize that the worlds—however many there may be—are not stacked up neatly from highest to lowest. That's too linear and too simplistic. All worlds interpenetrate and overlap one another.

We can usually accept this concept when we speak about the astral plane because it's the one in which we most often work. But there are numerous other worlds to which we have easy access, and they all have their value, their lessons, and their own brand of magick. What you want to work for in exploring other worlds is the overcoming your cultural programming that one plane is higher than another, or better than another, simply because of the way it's portrayed in an illustration that again is trying to explain in human terms "that which can never be told" about a world that is not the natural dwelling of humanity.

Reaching the Other Worlds

Unless you are in spirit form, the otherworld has to be accessed via guided meditation or astral projection. Guided meditation leads you into and out of other worlds via a script that keeps you on a single path. Sometimes you are given free time to explore, but the reading of the pathworking by another person or a recording will tell you when it's time to go and how to get there.

The preferred method of otherworld exploration for the advanced practitioner is via astral projection.

A great body of literature has been produced on astral projection: what is where, where you go, how you go, how to do it, how to return, personal adventures, etc. All of these are of interest and comparing them will tell you a lot about the many explanations and ideas various practitioners feel about this operation.

Astral projection is an art that is usually introduced to new Witches during their first few months of study. You may have been paired with someone who was skilled at the art but who worked with a method that did not resonate with you. The result was that you found projecting difficult to learn.

I get lots of e-mail and snail mail from readers asking about astral projection. All seem to reach the point where they feel they are about to separate consciousness from the physical body, then their energy peters out and they are back where they began. Yet when I read exactly what they tell me is occurring, I realize they are astral projecting, they just don't know they've gotten the first step right. What they are doing is getting into a light trance state, known as alpha, where they are aware of two worlds at once. The fact that they recognize their corporeal selves at the same time as they recognize the astral world is anything but failure. It means they have made a good beginning, working in a light alpha trance rather than the deeper theta level.

There are four different levels of brain wave activity that psychologists, doctors, and metaphysicians use to measure how aware or unaware we are of our physical surroundings. The four are beta, alpha, theta, and delta. The following chart will give you an idea of the nature of each state if you have not already experienced them.

STATE NAME	BRAIN WAVE CYCLES PER SECOND	MENTAL AND PHYSICAL CHARACTERISTICS
Beta	15–18	Normal wakefulness. Person can carry on a conversation, think, walk, and talk with full awareness of all physical and mental sensations. Conversational level.
Alpha	8–12	Light to medium meditative state in which the subject may for a while shut out the physical world. Daydreaming, reading, watching television, even studying can induce a light alpha state. Brain is more susceptible to suggestions and astral projection is possible but not disassociated completely from your physical state. Alpha is also associated with REM sleep during which dreams occur. Person can be easily jarred back to beta.
Theta	4–6	Deep meditation. This is the ideal state for astral projection, especially into unknown worlds. This meditative state is similar to a medium to deep sleep. Those in theta find it easier to block out all sensations of having a physical self. Waking someone from this state is more difficult; they will awaken groggy and disoriented. This is the ideal state for meditation, magick, and astral projection.
Delta	0.5–2.5	Meditation rarely takes us into the delta state. Brain activity level at this level is equivalent to the deepest sleep and unconsciousness. The person may have no sense of any world but the one on which his mind is focused. He will have no sense of any bodily needs and can only be awakened with difficulty. This is not a desirable state for meditation, astral

projection, or magick. If you are not injured, in a coma, or running a high temperature, it will be difficult for you to remain in a self-induced delta state for more than ten or fifteen minutes. Awakening someone from delta is difficult, and can be impossible in the case of high fever or coma.

If you are an advanced practitioner of the Craft in other areas, but still have trouble with astral projection, you may be suffering one of two problems. First of all, you may be succeeding but you think you aren't because we have no words in our human vocabulary to adequately describe what the process feels like. Be less judgmental with yourself and go with the flow before you decide you've failed. Secondly, you may not have hit upon the method that works best for you to slip easily onto other planes.

There is more than one way to access the astral plane. These include exiting through a chakra, leaping off from a guided meditation, or mentally transferring your consciousness into a mobile vehicle. In my book *Astral Projection for Beginners* (Llewellyn, 1998), I outline six methods in detail. There are more than six methods that will get you where you want to go, and other books can give you even more methods with which to work. Shop around your local bookstore or library to find a book that feels like it contains a method that will work for you. Too much of your advanced work will revolve around astral projection for you to not be proficient. You don't have to be a master at getting to theta every time, but you need to develop consistency in reaching and working in an alpha state of mind.

Of Witches, Broomsticks, and Sacred Hearths

The classic image of a Witch going into another world is the popular Halloween hag with a cackling laugh and a wart on her nose hurtling up through her chimney and into the night sky as she travels to where other Witches will meet her.

It's likely this image came from the fact that brooms were kept where they were needed: near the hearth, which produced ashes that had to be continually cleaned up because the fire was never allowed to go out except for religious festivals, such as Ireland's Bealtaine or Beltane, in which new fires were lit from the sacred communal balefire around which the May festivities occurred.

Because the broom was a normal household tool that no home could be without, Witches of old could use their brooms as wands or other magickal implements without risking being accused of witchery.

The chimney that opens into your hearth has been considered the magickal portal to your home for centuries. Many blessings, protections, and charms surround fireplace lore. In faery tales it's most notably *The Three Little Pigs* who use their chimney to kill the big bad wolf when he falls into their cauldron—a symbol of life, death, and rebirth.

Another telling ditty from the past is this nursery rhyme:

Sweep, sweep, chimney sweep,
From the bottom to the top.
Sweep, sweep, chimney sweep,
From the bottom to the top.

This is nonsense because chimneys are swept or cleaned from the top to the bottom in order to take advantage of gravity. The ash and other collected carbons and dirt are pushed downward where they are collected in a large cloth and removed from the household. Dislodging this stuff and attempting to push it upwards sounds like a monumental task and waste of time. Therefore, it's logical to assume that this was a rhyme meant to preserve for us the fact that the chimney is a sacred portal in and out of your home.

If all other visualizations fail to get you into a state of astral projection, you might try seeing yourself jetting out of a chimney on your broomstick.

Where Do We Go When We Astral Project?

Just where is it we go if we haven't used a guided meditation to get to the astral plane, or did not focus on a specific destination? Do we go anywhere at all? Do we care as long as it works?

My personal concept of astral projection is that no part of your being, such as an astral double, goes anywhere. I believe what is projected outward is your consciousness, and that this is what we perceive as the astral body. Perhaps the term *mental projection* is a more accurate label for the way I see this process working.

Other people see astral doubles of themselves, or transfer their consciousness into another vehicle that will travel for them and bring back information.

Each mind is a universe unto itself, one in which you are, or should be, the supreme ruler. This requires you to know yourself and to have confidence in your abilities and convictions. You should never be afraid of the astral plane. True, there are denizens there who are not open to your presence, and may even harbor malevolent intentions, but you can exit at any time you choose just by wishing yourself home, opening your eyes, and then grounding to close the portal between the worlds.

Many of you will argue with me that a spirit part of you does indeed travel out of the body and into the otherworld because people report seeing you out and about. I counter that argument by asserting that it is the power of your mind that projects your image where others can see it, though it may be far away from your physical self. We use less than 10 percent of our brains over our lifetimes. Whether you accept my concept or not—and there's no reason why you should or shouldn't—if you don't believe in the infinite power of your mind to create, then why are you bothering with Witchcraft, which teaches that thought becomes action on the astral or otherworld planes? This is one of the basic explanations of how our magick is born and how it comes into manifestation. We can't have one without the other.

The Three-World Concept

The three-world concept came to Witchcraft via Anglo-Celtic Pagan practices. Three was a sacred number to the Celts; therefore, there were three major worlds: an upperworld that corresponds to the world of the divine and the dead, a middle world that corresponds to our physical world, and an underworld that is the home to certain faeries, mythical beasts, and some deities. They believed that within each of these worlds one of our other selves dwelled (see next chapter).

The *Eddas* of Norse mythology tell of their worlds, which are accessed through Yggdrasil. Yggdrasil is name given to the world tree, the centerpoint of the universe on whose axis it spins. If you could get past the serpent who guards the threshold to the tree, you could follow its roots to any world you chose. The root word, *Yggr*, was one of the many names of Odin, one of the more powerful and well-known of the Teutonic deities. He ruled over many other gods and was a patron of war, magick, writing, and the dead. Odin rules the underworld of Teutonic mythology, and seeking him there is similar to climbing the tree of life to seek the godhead.

Another way in which the Norse accessed the otherworld was by crossing Bifrost, the rainbow bridge that took fallen warriors to their eternal feast in Valhalla.

The Four-World Concept

You might think four worlds correspond only to the four elements. While this can be the case for some practitioners, the usual four-world concept includes:

The Spiritual World

The Mental World

The Astral World

The Physical World

Plotted on the tree of life, the physical world corresponds to the bottom sephira, and the spiritual world to the top three sephiroth. The other six are divided equally between the mental and astral worlds. Plotted on the body, the astral body is the one we see when we talk about seeing someone's aura. Its color, symbols, and spaciousness can tell us a lot about a person at any given moment in time.

Aura reading is another basic magick skill taught to newcomers and lots of books are available to teach you what is actually a process of learning to use your own vision in a different way. It's not psychic vision and anyone can learn to do it. I recommend Mark Smith's *Auras: See Them In Only 60 Seconds* (Llewellyn, 1996) because it approaches auric viewing as normal vision and not as psychic manifestation.

The astral and mental worlds are the worlds in which our magick is crafted, where thoughts are born, and where they become an action which eventually creates manifest reality. In fact, I prefer to call the mental plane the plane of thought or of thoughtforms. This is to avoid confusing it with the physical brain, which is what "mental" suggests to me. The brain and the mind are connected, but they are two different things. The brain is your physical self, and your mind the part of it that connects you to a higher self or other worlds and beings.

Anyone who is a regular traveler to the astral plane will also understand that the astral plane seems much larger than other realms of existence. This may not be a truth, just our perception. Navigating is easier in the astral world than in other realms, and most of us can find all the worlds we want to explore on this vast plane.

We also know that there is a realm known as the "lower astral" in which baneful spirits, ghosts who cannot move on to the spiritual plane, and other negative beings dwell. This place is to be avoided, but this should be no problem if you enter your otherworld adventures in a positive state of mind, heed the rede of "harm none," and remember that you are always in control of where you go and with whom you interact.

Other Worlds and Parallel Universes

There have been other spiritual thinkers and explorers who have come up with a myriad of multiworld concepts, and who's to say any of them are right or wrong? Perhaps the world we enter upon physical death depends upon what we believe in life.

This myriad of worlds has no one world that is higher, lower, greater, lesser, better, or worse than any other. Like the astral plane, they all overlap and interpenetrate our own world. Each world intersects with our own physical world and interlocks with many others. Though the illustration here that conceptualizes this idea is finite, the worlds that can be plotted onto it are infinite.

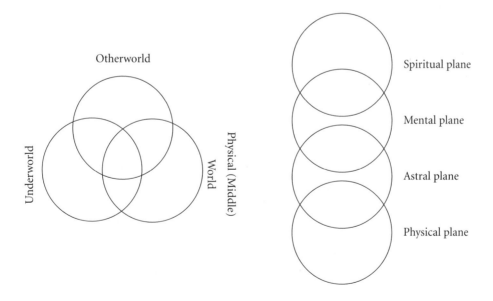

Three- and four-world conceptualizations

This brings us into the realm of disorder and chaos; situations as important to our understanding of the universe as order and beauty.

We tend to think of disorder being born from order, when other philosophers see it as just the opposite. Hesiod, a Greek poet who lived in the eighth century BCE, writes, "First of all Chaos came into being, and then Gaia, the broad Earth . . ." This is a common idea, that chaos or disorder existed before it was molded into manifestation. That idea of order being born from chaos is not so different from the Judeo-Christian Bible version of Creation where their God created "out of the void."

The following is a list of worlds I've heard of, been to, or read about. Remember that it is not necessary to pass through one to reach another. They all overlap our physical world in some way so that a safe route in and out of them can be plotted. Some of the worlds may only be subsets of other worlds listed here, while others are worlds unto themselves. All are real and can be accessed if you want to seek them out. You may even be able to add others to the list:

The Unknowable Realm

The Penultimate Realm

The Ultimate Realm

World of the Divine or Godhead

The Highest of the Knowable Realms

World of Spirit Guides

World of Higher Human Discarnates

The Plane of Triumph and Success

The Spiritual Plane

World of the Akashic Records or Collective Unconscious

Mental or Thought Plane

World of Animal Discarnates

The Plane of Joy

The Upper Astral Realm

World of Wishes

The Lower Astral Realm

World of Collective Consciousness

World of Lower Human Discarnates

World of Faery

Elemental Plane

The Castle of Glass

The World of Sleep

Superconscious World

Subconscious World

The Plane of Sorrow

The Dream World

Meditative World

Land of the Ever Young

Physical World

Again, please note that these worlds are not ranked from lowest to highest because it's just not possible to plot two overlapping worlds into a higher or lower system. I did try to make the worlds with a higher or faster vibrational rate—corresponding to planes on which higher beings live—nearer the top. Still, don't take this list as perfect or even as complete.

Seek and Ye Shall Find

It's vital to your advanced practice that you have a map in your mind of the cosmos and how it's put together. As you advance in your practice, you'll find more reasons to work in other worlds and less to work in the physical with your usual tools. You must be the one to explore all the worlds for yourself and decide how to conceptualize them in your mind. Your faeryland might be my world of thoughtforms, and my world of divinity may be your world of the unknowable. My Summerland, or world of the dead, may be your upper astral world.

Each of these places may harbor sub-areas for us to explore. The universe is endless and is expanding at this very moment. With practice, there is nothing you cannot learn and nowhere you cannot go.

Your concept of how the universe is organized is all yours, and you should not allow anyone to talk you out of any positive experience you have had in the astral and to get you to accept their conceptualization instead. Yours is as valid as any, and you will need that mental map well fixed in your mind as you move on in your advanced Craft work.

The Akashic Records

The term *akashic* is from a Sanskrit word meaning "etheric" or "of the spirit." Beginning in the late nineteenth century, modern occultists adopted the term for the body of knowledge that is found on the astral plane. Later, in the early twentieth century, psychologist Carl Gustav Jung related the akashic records to his concept of the collective unconscious.

For Jung this was a realm beyond our higher selves or soul selves in which all actions, thoughts, ideas, and works that ever were, are, or will be were kept. To see them, all you have to do is will yourself to where they are kept. For some, this is a huge library full of many books. Others see their records as projected on a giant movie screen. The images will appear to you in the format in which your spirit guides deem will be most comfortable for you. If you'd rather view your records in a different manner, simply ask. Most of the time the request will be honored.

Many students of the occult have accessed their own records to help them to understand their spiritual path. In them you can find recordings of past lives, past failings, and past successes. You can also see a glimpse of your future based on actions currently in motion. However, the future remains yours to change.

You may ask how this is possible in a world where time does not exist and the past, present, and future are all occurring at once. Perhaps in our perception of linear time we only think we're on one path that cannot be altered. Perhaps change is occurring at every second but we are only perceiving one timeline at once and remain unaware of the lightning-fast changes taking place.

We'll explore time concept in the next chapter, where we will look at the many selves that are us and how learning to know and work with our other selves can bring us a wholeness of being, a sense of peace and accomplishment, and bring us closer to the deities.

six

How Many Selves Have I?

In the beginning of your year and a day of Craft study, the only self that really concerned you was your physical self and how you were going to make it do all the things your teachers, coven, or textbooks asked you to do. In time, you grew more intuitive about the various aspects that make you you. It was then that you learned about the astral plane and accepted that you had an astral body that could travel through that other world.

Your first efforts may have been arduous, or you may have been one of those Witches born with an innate talent for this art. In either case, astral projection probably consumed a good portion of your Craft practice time.

As an intermediate you began to delve deeper into otherworlds and began to notice that some form or essence of yourself was in each of them. As you spent more time thinking about time concepts and reincarnation, you probably wondered just how many of you there were.

My favorite poet, Indiana's James Whitcomb Riley (1848–1916), wrote this around 1890:

> How many of my selves are dead?
> The ghosts of many haunt me . . .

Mr. Riley was writing about the selves of a single lifetime—the baby in the crib, the child at play, the boy growing to manhood—but his question is one that those of us who seek to unravel the mysteries of our inner or other selves and peer through the illusion of linear time always seek to answer. Questions posed by poets are comparable to those once asked by the bards of Europe. Neither the question nor the answer is what it seems at first.

But is there an answer for that question? If so, is there one answer, several answers, or many?

Perhaps we should rephrase and expand the poetic question and ask: How many of my selves are alive and well and living in other worlds and times? Do they haunt me? Do I haunt them? Will we ever be joined? Can and do we learn from one another? Can we better communicate? Are we on the same spiritual path? Are there any of my other selves who could be a danger to me? Can I be harmed by exploring other selves less spiritually advanced than me? Can I be helped by experiencing the lives of those more spiritually advanced than me?

Those are just some of the questions that will keep you awake all night if you like discussions in which there are no clear-cut answers and in which the truth comes in many guises. Tie on your seat belt, for this chapter will be fast and fantastic, asking you to broaden your mind to its limits. Witchcraft is not a "God in a box" religion. The ever-changing universe requires us and our concepts of being to change right along with it, whether we're sure of what we're doing or not, or who we are or are not.

One Theory, Four Selves

There is a school of thought that teaches we have four selves, all connected to our physical bodies. Of course, the physical self is the first body and it links us to Mother Earth. It is the vehicle in which we go through this lifetime.

Nearest to our physical body is our astral self, or what we see when we look for our auras. This is the body that can travel out from the physical body and travel through space and time at our will. It can gather information, keep an eye on loved ones, and break the space-time barrier.

Just beyond the astral body is the mental body, or what we might think of as the body on the plane of thought. This is an area corresponding to the upper astral world, one closer to the divine plane, where thought is action and where the magick we create in our visualizations first starts to take shape.

Beyond the mental body is the spiritual body, or what many refer to as the higher self. The spiritual body is often thought of as residing in the crown chakra and is able to link us to the divine during prayer, magick, or ritual.

Witches and the Many Views of the Afterlife

We all have our own hard-won ideas about the afterlife, and they may all have validity and all may be our personal truths. Who's to say there's only one way the afterlife operates?

One of my favorite metaphysical writers is researcher Dick Sutphen (see Resources). While attending one of his popular seminars in Sedona, Arizona, there were about a half dozen of the nearly three hundred people in the room who didn't seem to want Mr. Sutphen to teach and share his experiences as much as they wanted him to verbally validate the way they saw *their* souls, past lives, inner worlds, spirit guides, etc. He would listen politely to all of them while nodding his head, but his reply was always the same, "That's absolutely true—unless, of course, it isn't." Keeping that simple phrase in mind has helped me many times when struggling with new ideas and practices that challenge my worldview. Try it for yourself when you find yourself desperately guarding your own spiritual concepts and theories.

Before we begin this discussion, we all have to have some similar starting point. So, for the purposes of this book only, we'll assume there is one of you in every world that is, was, or ever will be. We will further assume you have archetypal selves that make up your wholeness, such as your warrior self, your priest/ess self, your spirit self, etc. These can all be exhibited in this and/or in other lifetimes. And we'll also assume you are living past lives as well, and perhaps future ones, at this very moment in time.

Since this is not a book about the worlds of the many selves, but of advancing in the Craft, we'll focus our attention on the three most imposing "other self" figures: the co-walker, the fetch, and the all-important shadow self.

The Co-Walker

When Witches think of the co-walker, the fetch, and the shadow self, they often tend to lump the three together as if it were one being instead of three distinct beings linked to your physical self.

The term "co-walker" was coined over three hundred years ago by Scottish minister Robert Kirk, who saw his co-walker as a faery or otherworld ally and helper. In an age that still believed in Witchcraft as a Satanic cult, and all spirits as Satan's minions, Rev. Kirk took a huge chance on making his belief in the co-walker known to his congregation.

The co-walker can be found in the astral world just beyond the sight of your physical world. It usually appears as your etheric double and, like your conscience, helps direct your path and keep you from harm. Many people who claim to have a guardian angel near them are sensing their co-walker self.

The Fetch

The fetch is another etheric double, one that dwells in the Land of the Dead. It appears only within the fortnight of your death. Germanic culture terms this the "doppleganger," and the English came up with the name "fetch" because of its function of warning you of deadly danger or, if the danger cannot be avoided, of escorting you to the otherworld where newly discarnate spirits go.

The fetch is usually seen standing just behind you as you gaze into a mirror or other reflective surface. When you turn to look at it, it vanishes. Appearances of the fetch are said to increase during the last week of one's life.

The fetch belongs to the world of the dead, but the co-walker is a spirit ally whom I have encountered when traversing the world of the fey or faeries. We will explore that world further in chapter 18.

The Shadow Self

Your shadow self is one of the most important selves for you to meet. It dwells deep in the otherworld or, by some cultures, the underworld. To look at it is to see an exact duplicate of your physical self, but it is the inner shadow that is of spiritual value.

Famous early twentieth-century occultist Dion Fortune emphasized that this is not the Shadow Self of Jungian psychology, which is your personal dark side, nor is it another threshold terror to be challenged by and passed along (from *Applied Magic*, a collection of her articles on magick written from 1927–1940 [Samuel Weiser, 2000], p. 88). It is a journey into your deepest level of consciousness to your true personality.

Meeting your shadow self requires you to let go of your ego and take a look at your true self. Jewish mystics who are asked why God doesn't speak to people as the Bible tells us he once did answer by saying that today humans cannot bend low enough to hear what he says. It's hard to listen to our deities. Even in deep meditation we may be anxious to be elsewhere or wish to have our questions answered only in a way that does not challenge our current ideology. Indeed, we can't always hear the voice of the divine when it speaks because our ego is in the way.

Throughout history writers, philosophers, and visionaries have sought to define the shadow that follows us like a puppy through this lifetime, dogging us with our true self that may challenge our self-concept. Carl Jung felt his Shadow Self thwarted his best intentions, perhaps testing his resolve or commitment to his field of study. He encouraged us to bring the Shadow Self into our conscious world so that we could control it, otherwise he feared it would appear as "fate" and gain control over us.

William Shakespeare acknowledged that the shadow had to be discovered, embraced, and cherished to become something of use to us. In the early seventeenth century he wrote:

> The web of our life is a mingled
> yarn, good and ill together: our
> virtues would be proud, if our
> faults whipped them not; and our
> crimes would despair, if they
> were not cherished by our virtues.

Many Witches make the mistake of thinking of the shadow self as a negative being. Others think of it as being bad where the physical self is good, and good where the physical self is lacking. Neither of these concepts are correct.

The shadow self is a frightful specter, that is true, not because of what it hides but because of what it shows. The shadow self is your true reflection. It is you as you really are, with all your faults and all your good points laid bare for you to see. It is your chance to look at and into yourself as others do and as the deities see you. This is your chance—if you dare—to probe the deepest secrets of your soul and make positive change in your physical life based on the meeting.

No one will argue that the meeting of self and shadow self can be a daunting prospect; it's rare that we find in our shadow self what we expect to see. No one comes back from the encounter content with the vision, for none of us is perfect, the shadow self just shows us how imperfect we really are. The good part is that it is also an opportunity to make positive changes in ourselves that others and our deities will note and accept with pleasure.

Entering the Shadow's World

In meditation you will want to access the otherworld as your Craft tradition sees it. It may be an island, part of the Land of the Dead, a place where deities or heroes dwell, or it can be part of an underworld. Access this place as you do with any otherworld exploration. You may cross a bridge, ride a horse, take a boat, walk over a rainbow, fly, or spiral in or down. All the while focus on being taken to the place where you will find your shadow self.

When I found mine, I sensed what part of the otherworld it would be in, and I deliberately visited the other three quarters of that place first so I could approach my shadow self with a feeling of balance. As I sought my other self, I found my spirit traveling through a dense and dark forest.

I met with with my shadow self more than once. At our first meeting we faced one another and I sensed a primitive form of mental communication taking place. I admit that I didn't hear many expressions that I could have put into words. Yet the experience left me with many new insights into my life. I saw my faults in clarity and my virtues in darkness. Then one of us turned around. I can't remember now if it was me or my shadow self. We then merged into one another for only a moment, then the shadow self passed on through me. After that we touched palms, shared our energy and blessings, and then I left for home.

Not everyone finds their shadow self in a dark place. My friend Liban found her shadow self in a sunny meadow in what she felt was part of the Wiccan Summerland, or Land of the Dead. Her shadow, though, appeared in black and white, as if she was watching a color television in which only one image remained in the shades of gray from the black and white television days.

Liban sat down beside her shadow self and they began playing together in what looked like a sandbox. Her shadow did not speak to her, but communicated with symbols drawn in the sand. As their session went on, Liban was able to see parts of her black and white shadow self gaining spots of color. She felt this was happening as she recognized her negative aspects. These, she believed, were the negative traits of herself she needed to work on most. Her belief was that she would attain soul perfection on the day she went to visit that shadow self to find it in full color. According to her that has not yet happened, and she's pretty sure it won't occur in this lifetime, but she is hopeful for the next.

The Many Selves of Reincarnation

If you thought discussing a myriad of worlds caused your mind to do summersaults, just wait until you encounter the mental gymnastics of contemplating the many selves you are via reincarnation. Just thinking about it can make you crazy. Take the classic paradox that says you go back in time and meet your grandfather. While there, you argue and kill him before he has had the time to have a family. How, then, can you exist to go back into time and kill him?

When I was in school at the University of Texas there was a popular night spot where many of the left-wing students hung out at night to study and talk. We envisioned ourselves as being on the cutting edge of the modern intellegencia when, in truth, nothing we were discussing was new. Time theories, reincarnation, and the role of the working class—many had been there and done that, over and over. It was only new to us.

Reincarnation is a basic tenet of Witchcraft, though not a requirement. It's safe to say most Witches have formed in their own minds some idea of how the process works. For many of us that's all we want to know, but the advanced Craft student wants to dig deeper. So to the concept of reincarnation we add the mind-spinning theories of omnipresent time, which creates conundrums and paradoxes that can drive you mad.

Reincarnation is the belief that we get more than one shot at an earthly life. Some say the reason for returning over and over to an earthy body is to learn and grow, some say it's to perfect the soul, some say it's to make amends for past wrongs, and others say it's because life is meant to be lived, so that's what we do.

Is there a purpose for reincarnation, and just how does the process work in a world in which science has proven—and our Wiccan magick has proven—that time does not exist? We live in one omnipresent now where all things are happening at once and all lives are being lived at once.

How can that be when we know only one past? There are two probable reasons. One is that we do not perceive the changes in the circular timeline as they occur. Two is that there are an infinite number of worlds in which each new choice creates a new reality that another you is living.

Just like a novel, life is a series of conflicts followed by actions that lead to resolutions. Some of our choices are bad, some good, but the choices are always our own. The lesson of self-responsibility is never more easy to see than in our concepts of reincarnation.

There is no codified theology that demands Pagans accept the tenet of reincarnation, but the majority appears to believe that it occurs in some form. We can accept this for the same reason our ancestors did: because of the eternal cycles of life, death, and rebirth they saw in the cycles of nature and in the lives of their deities. The wheel of the year turned and all things came, went, and came again, an endless cycle of new lives.

No one knows for sure exactly how reincarnation works, especially since we must accept the omnipresence of time, but it can be broken down into three categories:

1)   Transmutation or transmigration of the soul

2)   Genetic memory within kin groups

3)   Earthly reincarnation by one of six means

Transmutation and transmigration of the soul is no more than the immediate transfer of a spirit into another concrete form. For example, the spirit of someone newly deceased might wander for a while, eventually taking up residence in a plant, animal, or newborn child. Some Witches accept that transmigration can occur with human adults if the spirit can inhabit the body before a death is discovered.

The trouble with this theory is that it ignores the basic Wiccan belief in the Summerland, or the otherworld Land of the Dead, which our many mythologies tell us awaits us at the end of this life. We are also told that we do not have to immediately go to the Land of the Dead, so perhaps these two theories can coexist.

Genetic memory is the belief that instead of living numerous lives in numerous physical bodies, we tap into past lives through genetic memory. Each clan, kin group, and family has these memories, which many Witches believe can be accessed through guided meditation. Since we all can trace our ancestry back to the same single female at the dawn of humanity, this means we can all be or have been anyone in any time period.

I have given genetic memory a lot of thought because too many people whose intelligence I respect have given it credence. Believing in this theory of reincarnation does not negate either of the others, but allows us to lock onto the lifetime which can most help us to understand our current problems and issues. Genetic memory is also in line with Kabalistic teachings, which say that your children are your *kaddish*, or "those who will remember."

The Six Reincarnation Theories

If you've ever struggled through all the paradoxes and time conundrums of a how-does-it-work conversation, you know there are no easy answers to that question. There are six viable theories, all of which are possible—and, who knows, maybe they are all at work somewhere, for someone.

These six theories are:

1) A sequential succession of individual lifetimes based on an individual's personal karma.

2) A succession or variety of lifetimes conducted by an oversoul or master being to whom the individual souls ultimately belong.

3) Concurrent lifetimes lived separately from an oversoul.

4) A repetition of earthly lives for an individual soul meant to teach that soul a specific lesson.

5) Concurrent or sequential lives lived with the support of a kin-soul group who support and assist once another to grow spiritually.

6) All lifetimes lived all at once in omnipresent time.

The first five of these theories avoid the idea of unity of all souls. They emphasize the spiritual growth of an individual throughout successive lifetimes until some lesson is learned or some plateau of knowledge is achieved. Because we often recognize people who are in our current lifetime in a past-life regression session, many believe that we come back together as groups of related souls to assist each other on a spiritual level that remains unknown to our physical selves.

An oversoul is a being who is believed to be able to split itself into many smaller parts so it can send smaller souls into a variety of bodies to gain the experience of a wide variety of races, time periods, genders, and cultures.

Only theory six recognizes the unity of all souls. This is the theory I accept because it makes sense to me in terms of what science knows about the universe. It can be seen to be expanding at a rapid rate, giving credence to the "Big Bang" theory in which a single atom exploded into smaller particles, each expanding exponentially and giving birth to the universe as we know it.

Scientists believe that someday the universe will begin to contract. Some hypothesize this has happened many times before. Because of this, I accept that we are all one soul, part of an ever-expanding universe, and someday we will all be reunited again as that single atom before the cycle begins again.

Though we think of this as the cutting edge of modern quantum science, the concept of cycles of life, death, and regeneration have been accepted and written about for thousands of years. In the sixteenth century, Sir Walter Raleigh expressed the concept with these words from his "Liberty of Conscious Thesis" (January 1655):

> Whoso desireth to know what will be hereafter,
> let him think of what is past, for the world
> hath ever been in a circular revolution:
> whatsoever is now, was heretofore; and things
> past or present, are no other than such as shall be again.

Exploring Your Past Lives

Your personal beliefs about how the process works do not impede your ability to experience past-life regression and to gain something from the experience. Learning to access your past lives via guided meditation is not an advanced art. What is advanced is trying to discern whether the information being presented is psychodrama, an actual scene from the past, or a mixture of past scenes, perhaps with a bit of psychodrama tossed in just to make it difficult.

Psychologists and therapists have been using past-life therapy for nearly thirty years, and it continues to gain acceptance as a valid tool to help patients overcome issues in the present. Neither the therapist nor the patient has to believe in the reality of the visions experienced in a regression session, but the results have won over lots of doubters. If a woman who overeats believes it's because she starved to death in a past life, or a man who is afraid of the woods believes he was accosted and murdered in a wooded area in another life, and accessing those memories—"real" or not—helps them overcome their problems, then that is all that's really important.

Many Witches are taken through their first regressions as advanced beginners in the Craft. Until you are advanced it's better to have someone else with experience guide you through the process so if things become frightening, your guide can remind you to pull back and watch, to divorce your emotions from the visual experience. A guide can also bring you out of the trance should you become overemotional and can ask the questions needed to establish both veracity of the lifetime and the things you need to learn and remember—or not remember—from the experience.

Those of you who are advanced can take yourselves into past lives by going into a deep meditative state. Reaching and maintaining a theta level is essential. As you do this focus on a question about a past life you want answered or just ask to be shown something which will help you in your life right now.

First of all, give yourself a mental trigger for a quick release from the vision if it gets to be too much for you. I like to use the words "I am home." This allows me to immediately open my eyes and ground myself in the physical world, closing the portal between worlds with the surety of a bank vault.

As you travel back in time, allow your spirit to feel as if it is falling backwards through a deep void. Feel the breeze as you move. Some people need to imagine pages of a calendar being torn away as they pass by; others like to see images of people and things in other times flash past them. Use the imagery you are most used to using or the one which feels right to you.

Eventually you will see a light growing larger, as if you were approaching the end of a long tunnel. When you reach the light, open your eyes and look down at yourself first. Note how you are dressed. Notice your gender. Then look around you. Note whether you are inside or outside. Think about where you are in both place and time. Note your occupation and note what others around you are wearing and doing. You may recognize some as souls who are with you in your current life.

You may explore this life for as long as you like, or you may let go of this one and return to the void to seek another life.

Remember that even though past-life exploration can be entertaining, its purpose is to give you insights into your growth as a spiritual being. If you see yourself doing wrong, try to think of ways to make amends in your current life. For example, if you stole money you might want to donate a similar amount to a favorite charity.

This is another hard lesson to learn, one in which the shadow looms large: karma. Karma is a Hindustani word that may have come into modern Hindu dialects from Sanskrit. It refers to the belief that what we do to others we get back fullfold. Contrary to popular belief, karma does not have to occur in a different lifetime from the one in which the wrong was first done; it can be balanced in the same lifetime. Recognizing a wrong and making amends, as in the aforementioned stealing versus charity example, is one way to overcome karmic retribution. The more you understand your transgressions, the more you can try to make up for them, and this will allow you to grow in spirit and overcome karma.

When you are ready to stop your past-life exploration, visualize yourself coming back from the void until your soul and body are again one. Open your eyes, ground yourself, then make as many notes as you can about what you experienced. Just like dreams, past-life memories tend to fade fast and you will have the best chance of recalling the most information if you don't wait to record the experience.

seven

Advanced Warding and Psychic Self-Defense

In the beginning you learned that your magick and rituals could attract other beings to you who want to feed off the energies you raise. You also learned there were people who fed off them, too. They were referred to as "psychic vampires" who could suck out your energy faster than the neighborhood thief could siphon your gas tank dry.

You learned how to erect simple defenses against these intrusions. You learned to place yourself in an egg of light, to cross your arms over your solar plexus area, and to envision yourself as a large mirror to reflect back negative intentions.

As an intermediate practitioner of the Craft, your methods of self-defense became more sophisticated. You could make a witch bottle to protect your home, draw mugwort or basil pentagrams on windows and doors, and do simple or complex house blessings with salt and frankincense to ward off astral beings who might have followed you home from your otherworld adventures.

It was all fairly simple until your skills continued to grow. At that point the beings who were attracted to your energy were stronger, and psychic vampires could smell you in the next town. Those who wished you harm or ill had grown in knowledge and strength, too.

Fortunately, true psychic attacks are rare, but the wise Witch always keeps his defenses in place just in case. Never leave an opening for the local bully if you want to play in the world of magick.

Locating Portals Between Worlds

The most common problem facing a Witch is having pesky astral beings or spirits from other realms following you home from a jaunt into their world, or with having spirits passing in and out of your home somewhere where a natural portal between the worlds exists.

Such portals are common if you live in an older home, in particular if you live in one that has been updated so the doors and windows aren't in the same place they were a century or so ago. These now-hidden passageways make excellent entry points for ghosts or other earth-bound discarnates to come into your home.

One of the keys to finding these is seeing a spirit who doesn't appear to be using the current layout of your home correctly. For example, I remember reading an account of a home in England in which a ghost was often seen going up and down the same hall night after night, but the spirit was unusually short in stature. At first it was assumed to be the spirit of a child until a closer look showed that the spirit was only seen from the waist up and that the waist was always at floor level. An architectural look into the old building determined that, several hundred years before, the floor on that hallway had been several feet lower. The ghost was walking the floor as it had been at the time he lived in the house.

Pets who are disturbed by or drawn to a specific area of your home, or who appear to be watching the movements of someone walking through your home at specific times, are other clues to portals. If you're psychically sensitive you might sense a place in your home that's vulnerable to becoming a portal or through which spirits are already passing.

Other times you might see a spirit pass through a specific wall, or antique mirror, or other piece of furniture. Though we'll take a closer look at handling human discarnates in chapter 19, for now your immediate need is to clear your home of unwanted spirits and close down the portal, putting in its place defenses that uninvited guests cannot pass through. This includes the uninvited energy of that mean Witch down the block who often sends you a shot of unpleasant negativity your way out of pure jealousy.

A portal is no more than a thinning between the world of spirit and our physical world through which bodies more etheric than our own can pass with ease. Your first line of defense is always closing portals after you do magick or rituals, and remembering to ground yourself to avoid carrying around the bright psychic energy to which many astral beings are attracted.

What to Do When You Find a Portal

Before you take any action to close the portal, make sure all astral beings and unwanted spirits are on their own side of the gateway. Trapping a spirit in this world will cause you more trouble that allowing it free passage through your home ever could. The angry spirit can shake your home, attack pets and children, and make whatever threatening gestures it's able to toward you. The amount of havoc a spirit can wreak depends upon how much energy it possesses and how much coherent consciousness it has. Some astral thoughtforms have little consciousness and may eventually fade away on their own, or they can be banished with a simple command to leave your home. Ghosts and other fully integrated spirit beings can get nasty when their route "home" is closed off.

When you locate a portal, and you are sure that your home is clear of unwanted entities, you should either wash the area with an infusion of mugwort and rosemary, or smudge the area with sage or frankincense. As you do this, visualize the portal area becoming thicker, closing off the gateway between worlds.

Raise your hands to your forehead and and press your thumbs and forefingers together so they make an upright triangle. This is called the triangle of creation. By placing it against this strong chakra of psychic energy, you can project protective energy exactly where you want it to go. This is a common technique in most all schools of magickal practice, Witchcraft included.

Visualize your energy collecting there at your third eye and, when you've gathered as much there as you can, mentally send it blazing forth in the form of a fiery pentagram that sears shut the portal forever, then remains on guard to prevent it from being opened again. Remember to feed your ward some fresh energy once a month to keep it working for you at optimum strength.

Though I can think of no reason why you would ever want to reopen the portal, it can be done by taking back the flaming pentagram and visualizing the thinning between the worlds. Please note that when you open a portal, especially when you're not enclosed in sacred space, you are opening yourself to anyone and anything that wants to come through. This is never a safe or smart practice. Chapter 19 on handling human discarnates will go into this in more detail.

sSolar Plexus Armor

The solar plexus region of the body seems to be the most vulnerable to psychic interference. Sometimes we who are psychically sensitive can see the fine threads of psychic energy attached to it after astral projecting, communing with spirits, or being in contact with psychic vampires. These can be removed through simple visualization that severs and burns them.

For magickal purposes, the best defense is a good offense. You want a plate of armor over your solar plexus region whenever you feel someone or something could be trying to attach itself to your energy field. Often times you'll be clued into this by having the urge to cross your arms over that area as if to block the attachment. Psychologists have told us over and over that this body language should always be read as defensive, indicating that the person performing the gesture feels hostile or unwelcoming toward whomever they are interacting with. If you find yourself constantly adopting this posture with a person or in a specific place, take it as a warning that there are negative or harmful energies there that need cleaning out.

A flaming pentagram in the solar plexus area works as well as it does on a portal. Another good visualization is to picture lots of small mirrored surfaces reflecting back any energy that comes into contact with that area. Strong visualization is the key to putting your defenses in place, keeping them there, and keeping them strong.

The Checkered Box

Your home or other sacred space may also need protection from psychic attack. Again, those flaming pentagrams can work wonders, but you want to use all the elements to seal any area larger than your own body.

As you make your pentagram, see it flowing with the essence of all the elements: fire, water, air, and earth. I do this ritual anytime I leave my home, even if I'll only be out to run a quick errand. I make the sign of the invoking pentagram and state aloud:

> Protected be and blessed be this dwelling, by the elements, from the elements, from intruders astral, spectral, and physical I do not invite. Make it a comforting, compelling place for (state names of family members, pets, etc.) to come and stay. By my will, so mote it be.

When I sense that something more than this ward is needed, I fall back on a trick learned from ceremonial magicians and evoke the checkered box.

The black-and-white checkered pattern has been used to adorn the floors of ceremonial temples, and is used today, as it has been for centuries, in Masonic rites. The alternative squares that show the absence and profusion of all light rays make a natural area of energy tension that can be drawn on for magick similar to the way we draw up energy from Mother Earth in our outdoor rites.

Start by standing and facing the direction you or your Craft tradition sees as being that natural home of the deities. For me and most Celtic traditions, this is the west, but none of the four cardinal directions are a wrong place to start. You may even want to start and stop the ritual in the direction of your front door, or patio, or wherever you feel your home or personal space is most vulnerable.

I stand facing west, with both my hands before me and palms facing outward. I mentally project a wall of black that covers the entire west side of my home from basement floor to attic ceiling. As I see it appear before me I say aloud, "To the west, black."

I then turn one full quarter turn to the right so that I'm moving clockwise. I keep my hands in front of me and use them to project a wall of white. As I see it appear I say, "To the north, white."

I repeat this process with the other two directions, saying, "To the east, black. To the south, white."

I then turn to face the west again and raise my arms, stating, "Above me black as dark as night."

Then I put my hands to my sides, palms down, and say, "The floor below me white with light."

I remain standing still while I make sure my visualization and energy projection have put the checkered box into place the way it should be.

As I leave my home, I use my common sense and close my drapes, set my intrusion alarm, and lock my door. If I'm feeling especially distrustful of the world that day I will draw an invoking pentagram of protection on the front door as I leave. Crime statistics tell us that over 65 percent of home intrusions are via doors.

The Witches' Foot

Contrary to popular misconception, creating a witches' foot is not malificarum and, when created for defensive and not offensive purposes, it does not constitute negative magick. A witches' foot is a talisman that was supposed to have been used by one Witch to kill another. In the Middle Ages this was dubbed *malificarum*, or murder by witchery.

A witches' foot works similar to a witch bottle, but carries a greater impact because it is often aimed at protecting you from someone or something specific rather than being a general deflector of negativity, as is a witch bottle.

To make a witches' foot you will need some wire and some briars, thorns, or other naturally occurring prickly substances. Bind them together while focusing on protecting yourself from harm. Visualize the witches' foot tripping the feet of those skulking around your home in both astral and physical forms. Place the foot near your front porch or another vulnerable area of your home, but make sure that it's not in a place where it can cause any real physical harm to a pet, child, or innocent person who might be on your property. Visualize the bare feet of an unwanted intruder stepping on the witches' foot and see him running away in pain and fear.

Is There Such an Animal as Advanced Warding?

As I prepared my outline for this book I considered several times taking this chapter out. Warding is usually nothing more than using washings, incenses, or intense visualization, all things taught the beginning Craft student to ensure his magickal integrity as his skills grow.

However, all these techniques that are taught are defensive in nature. Sometimes it's necessary to go on the offensive if we are going to protect ourselves and our loved ones from harm, both psychic and physical.

As you can see, I decided to leave in this chapter. For those of you who already know the value of offensive magick and can distinguish between defense and offense, and who know when to stop before the "harm none" rule is broken, please feel free to skip the chapter. Those of you just starting on the advanced path may want to stick around.

Is There a World in Which We Truly Harm None?

I've known many intermediate and advanced Witches who question if there is any action on any plane of existence in which our actions do no harm. We learn in high-school physics that for every action there is an equal and opposite reaction. Therefore, can anything we do, no matter how positive our intent or how pleasant our pre-spell divination looks, *really* be free from harm, since in some way the impact of the action—even the coherent thought—will be felt by someone, somewhere, at some time?

Naturally, we can't live our lives in fear of causing chain reactions of harm. Just going to work or school each morning puts us out in the world interacting with others in ways that could cause potential harm. You could distract a driver and cause an accident. You could get asked to run an errand meant for someone else who depended upon it for income or self-esteem. You could say something that hurts someone's feelings and, even if the hurt was unintentional, you could start a war of psychic energies.

In truth, there probably is no way to exist without harming someone at some point. The act of living in a society sees to that. What we can do as responsible Witches is to see to it that any harm is minimized and assume responsibly for that harm.

We also have the right to move freely about our world without fear of being harmed by others. In order to do that sometimes we need offensive rather than defensive magick. It's in that distinction that we blur the lines of the rede. In the advanced Craft you'll often find the worlds of black and white colliding and shattering into millions of shades of gray we have to sort through and work with if we wish to continue upon our positive path.

The Warrior Witch

There's no gentle New Age nonsense in the Craft when it comes to self-defense. It's foolish to assume anything that happens to us is the result of some karma we incurred thousands of years ago. To fall into this trap of thinking is to fall into a blame-the-victim mindset. Logic should tell us that if every bad thing that happened was the result of karma from a past life that we'd all only have lived once, been nauseatingly happy, and harmed no one, therefore incurring no negative karma. What would be the point?

We all have the divine gift of free will and we can choose to behave ethically or not. Those of us who do live ethically are not obligated to tolerate the tortures of those who do not. We all have the right to defend ourselves against harm. The world is too dangerous to let our defenses grow weak. We have terrorists, pedophiles, rapists, politicians, and televangelists all screaming their demands so loud that no one can be heard. There is even greater danger when one lives a lifestyle or practices a faith others do not understand. To be a warrior Witch is to be aware of the power of one's own body and spirit to deflect or prevent physical and psychic attacks on ourselves, our covens, our families, and others we love. This is not negative magick. You have the right to defend yourself. Leave turning the other cheek to anyone you can find who would actually react that way in the face of a personal attack.

More is being written about the warrior archetype in the Craft. My own *Celtic Women's Spirituality* (Llewellyn, 1997) and Kerr Cuhulain's *The Wiccan Warrior* (Llewellyn, 1998) are two examples of popular books that teach readers it's not only right to defend yourself, it's your duty.

In the case of a psychic attack, you should feel free to send the negative energy back to the sender. If you don't know from whom this little gift came, just put the energy back out into the cosmos and trust it will find its own way home. The beginning Craft student is often shown several spells for returning negative energy.

But what happens when you're in physical danger?

Why should you react any different than you do if under psychic attack?

There are two things you need to do to bring out your Wiccan warrior self. The first is defensive. Mentally construct a shield around yourself. Maybe you'd even like to draw it out on paper first. Cover it with symbols of personal strength and protection. Give it color and depth. Make it real. Make it strong. You want to be sure you can call it to mind, charge it, and have it in front of you in only a second of thought if you feel the need.

I recommend using a charging word or a symbol you mentally project onto the shield that activates its defensive energies. You may choose any word or symbol that has meaning for you. When you feel the need for defense, call up your shield, activate it, and then take all commonsense efforts to disengage yourself from whatever situation is causing you to feel anxious.

The other thing you have the right to do is offensive magick if you are being threatened. When I lived in southern Texas I used to go walking late at night, in part due to the heat of the day, and in part because I was a night person who was most energetic at night. One evening I noticed the glowing ember of a cigarette from the shadows between two houses in the block facing the one on which I lived. I knew someone was watching me, gauging his chances of accosting me before I could react.

My first reaction was to send out a mental warning to my would-be attacker, letting him know I would not be an easy target. I tuned in to him and could sense his hesitation begin to stir.

I kept circling my street, but the man remained where he was, thinking himself hidden. Obviously he was not put off enough by my warning to go away. I then called up my defensive magick from Mother Earth. I surrounded myself with mental light, light being a good crime deterrent in any realm.

Next I tried to think of what type of weapon would best work against someone contemplating a sex crime. I visualized a huge labrys, the double-headed axe that represents feminine power, and I envisioned it being hoisted above this pervert's head and smashing down upon it, splitting his skull.

I continued walking in my circle up and down my own street and soon realized the man was gone and the danger had passed. I never felt his presence again.

Don't be afraid to be offensive in your magick when you feel threatened. Visualizing something like I just described does not mean you're wishing that type of harm on anyone. You're sending only a mental version of that harm, one that warns and wards. Never be afraid to use magick rather than be someone's victim.

You can use these same techniques to help a friend who asks you or gives you permission to help her if she's living in a violent situation in her home. You should also be trying to get her, and any children or elderly people who depend on her, out of that house and into a shelter where they can be helped. Though I used the pronoun "she" in this example, women can also turn violent. Don't let a man you know and care about endure abuse any more than you would expect a woman to endure it. In situations of violence, always seek outside help to support your magick.

Binding for Self-Defense

Binding spells are often lumped together with negative magick regardless of the reason for the spell. It's true that a Witch must be cautious about this type of magick because in this case it walks that murky gray line between being defensive and offensive.

There is an old Witches' adage that tells us to be cautious with binding spells: *As ye bind, so are ye bound.* We don't want to tie someone up so tightly that we tangle ourselves in the process. And we *never* want to tie someone's hands against their will unless that person is using those hands to harm others. A burglar, a rapist, a sniper, a terrorist, or anyone else who intends harm to others has lost their right to free will in this case. They seek to impede the free will of all of us because we live in fear of their actions and are forced to spend money and time protecting ourselves from their acts. We most certainly have the right to be freed from that obligation.

Binding spells can be found in a variety of books on magick and basic Witchcraft. The easiest way to construct the spell is to write on a piece of paper what negative action you seek to stop, then bind it up with black, white, or gold thread. Circle the thread around the paper over and over until it is a small tight ball. Pour your energy into this effort while visualizing the criminal's hands being bound each time he or she wants to strike out at someone innocent. Keep this as a talisman of protection until the danger passes. Burn the talisman and make a new one when needed.

Creating Your Personal Body Guards and Home Guardians

The most advanced method of warding and self-defense is to create an elemental being you control and who takes instruction only from you. The technique for doing this will be discussed in detail in chapter 18 on faeries, aliens, and other elemental beings.

eight

Wiccan Shamanism

In the beginning you probably did not associate Witchcraft with shamanism, if you even knew what shamanism was all about. You certainly didn't connect it with Europe or with Europe's indigenous religious practices. Even today, well-educated people think of shamanism as being the provence of Native American or Polynesian tribes rather than an aspect of human spirituality that was once universal in scope. Even worse, many brush off shamanism as a sham, a hocus-pocus sleight of hand to amuse the masses rather than as a powerful link to the deities that takes not only some innate talent but also many years of intense practice to master.

As an intermediate Witch your understanding of shamanism as an integral part of the Old Religion grew. You understood that it has been a worldwide practice of indigenous people to have a healer of individuals and the community who can appear to walk among the deities and bring back healing and information on where the herds were moving and where the best place would be to set up camp for winter. You could see for yourself how the threads of those ancient practices left their mark on the magickal lore of various cultures.

The word *shaman* is Tungunese in origin and has been loosely translated into English for years as referring to a "walker between the worlds." Others translate it as meaning "too see" or "to know." Other etymologists have tried to link the roots of the words to verbs meaning "to heat up" or "to burn," thus the popular phrase for an ecstatic shamanic trance as "fire in the head."

Regardless of how long shamanism has been practiced, evidence of its existence in tribal and clan groups dates back to the Paleolithic period, nearly 50,000 years ago (Rutherford, Leo, *Principles of Shamanism* [Thorsons, 1996]). Unlike Wicca and other

Witchcraft traditions, shamanism is not a religion in its own right, nor is it even a codified set of beliefs or a unified set of practices. Shamanism is a path to the wisdom of the divine taken on by visionaries who feel called to pursue this path of leadership and service to their coven or Pagan community.

In the distant past, older shamans probably watched youngsters for signs that they could interpret their dreams, communicate with animals, have an affinity for healing plants, or were able to see or sense disembodied souls moving among the tribe. These young people were taken on as apprentices to learn all they could to be the next shamans for the clan.

Noted American anthropologist Dr. Michael Harner wrote a book for the layperson from his studies of indigenous cultures—*The Way of the Shaman* (Harper and Row, 1980)—and wrote of the dominate trait he saw among societies still relying on their shamans: the ability to commune with or be possessed by various spirit beings, or to be able to be in multiple realities concurrently. This is a common hallmark of the advanced Witch, the dual acceptance and involvement in two sets of concurrent realities.

More famous is the scholarly work of French anthropologist and researcher Mircea Eliade, whose *Shamanism: Archaic Techniques of Ecstasy* (Princeton University Press, 1971) sought to uncover the methods used and value brought to communities through the ecstatic trances of the mysterious shaman across several variant cultures. Often the future shamans of the tribe were chosen through the dreams of the current shaman or by contact initiated by the spirit world.

Male shaman apprentices often dreamed of a goddess or female spirit coming to them and anointing or offering them the gifts of the shaman. Modern Witches quickly see how this offering parallels the myths of male rulers in Celtic societies whose kings were granted the right to rule by the feminine spirit of the land, personified as the Goddess of Sovereignty. For instance, this is similar to the Lady of the Lake offering the sword known as Excalibur to a young King Arthur, or of the warrior woman and battle teacher Scathach offering a similar invincible weapon dubbed Gae Bolg to Ireland's young Red Branch warrior known as Cuchulain.

The fact that these tools were gifts from the divine realm is not as interesting as the fact that they were given names. In most older cultures people sought a person or object's "true name," for in the utterance of that name was the gift of having power over that which bore the name.

Even in today's tribal cultures, it is not uncommon for young people to seek visions in which they are bestowed with an adult name or given a sacred object whose name is revealed only to the one receiving the gift.

The Tremendous Scope of World Shamanism

Today's Wiccans often make the choice for themselves to study this path. In the few indigenous societies still in existence, the choosing of shamans has changed little over the last century. However, there are marked differences in the choosing of shamans in the setting of modern Wicca.

We may either hear the call for ourselves, or we may choose to investigate the shamanic world to see how it fits in our overall plan for spiritual growth. Often a dream, a book, or a meditative vision will spark an interest in shamanic practices. Some Wiccan traditions consider themselves shamanic in nature and expect the traditional practices of the shaman to be magickal techniques learned and used by the entire coven or tradition.

Shamanism, even when paired down to methods and practices common to Wicca, is a huge subject with dozens of books devoted to its theory and practice. This is one of those areas of the Craft that, if you're really interested in pursuing it, you should make your specialty. There's more than enough material for a lifetime's worth of study. I keep discovering new books on the subject I think are wonderful all the time, and I still would not say this is my area of greatest expertise. My favorite books are listed in the bibliography in the back of this book, but don't limit yourself to those. There are lots of good ideas in other books, and no doubt new ones will appear that will offer further insights and practices for the serious student.

This book will cover Wiccan shamanism from the viewpoint of someone who already understands the basics, can perform the prerequisite skills such as astral projection and remote healing, and is ready for going deeper into the self and assisting others in need in the Pagan community.

Shamanism and the Use of Psychotropic Drugs

In many cases, psychotropic plants or hallucinogenic substances derived from plants are used to induce the ecstatic trances of the shaman. That they do work to some extent is a given, but over the long term they can destroy all you've worked to build.

My college anthropology class did a detailed study of one South American tribe in which the majority of adult males used hallucinogens. Documentary film footage showed the results of dependence on psychotropic drugs for the men in the tribe who used them initially for shamanic practice, then it became a daily habit. The men became useless shells of their former selves; ill, listless, and unable to contribute in any positive way to their families or their tribe.

Face it, we all know there are times when we're not at our psychic best and using something to "get us over the hump" is tempting. Occasionally, our visionary sight just won't come into focus no matter how hard we try. To the contrary, the harder we try, the more aware of our physical bodies we become, and the process of seeing into or traveling to other worlds is impossible for periods of time from a few hours to several weeks, depending on what physical or emotional issues are blocking our way.

Using hallucinogenics is not the best answer to the problem. Though I would defend to the death someone's right to do what they please in their own home, I also feel that to turn my back on the practice without a cautionary word is in conflict with my promise to "harm none." The fact is that these drugs cause harm to one using them. It's all too easy to become dependent on them for daily magickal operations rather than to rely on one's own well-developed skills. When the time comes that you need a boost to help you create your shamanic vision, try one of the following instead. These remedies are gentler and have little chance of becoming habit-forming:

1)   Use a gentle herbal tea that helps relax you into your meditative state rather than forces one on you. Catnip, chamomile, valerian, and hyssop all help you relax.

2)   Going without food, sleep, or using the sweat lodge technique can help push you into a meditative state of mind. Since most of us don't have sweat lodges or saunas handy, a steamy bathroom makes a perfect substitute. Just please remember to get out of the tub before attempting meditation. This is a commonsense

measure to prevent drowning accidents. And, yes, your mother was telling you the truth: human beings can drown in as little as two inches of standing water.

3)   Rhythmic drumming can induce an altered state of consciousness. You don't need a partner to do the drumming for you either. Many CDs and tapes are commercially available that use different rhythms, and even different woods, to help you produce the desired level of altered consciousness you seek. If working within a particular culture is important to you, it's possible now to find rhythmic recordings using the indigenous instruments from West Africa, South Africa, Aboriginal Australia, Native North America, Native Canada, Peru, Siberia, and Polynesia.

True power is power to control all aspects of the self. Forget your failures—they happen to all of us once in a while—and note the successes that you attained using nothing other than your own will. The ability to perform feats of magick, divination, or ritual using your own body, mind, and spirit as your only tools is the best indication that you have reached the plateau of advanced Craft practice.

Dream Incubation and Interpretation

All things brought into being must first be born as an idea, an unformed thought that begins to take shape as a dream in the depths of the mind. From this germ of an idea, realities are incubated and, with care and nurturing, are born into being.

In many tribal societies it is an everyday morning ritual to share dreams with your kin group. Those deemed by elders to be of importance to the community as a whole are taken to the local shaman or priest/ess for further interpretation.

The concept of dream incubation as a method of making magick is common to shamans around the globe. In modern Witchcraft we tend to use the term *dream alchemy* to refer to a similar process. This is when the practitioner first gets what he feels is a prophetic or important message in the dream state. He then takes that awareness with him on guided journeys he deliberately induces, or goes into a similar state known as lucid dreaming, to help get a clearer picture of the meaning of the dream idea and, if need be, will continue to use the dream state to craft the concept into manifestation in the physical world. This is magick on a truly advanced level.

The tribal shaman is expected to have the wisdom to know when a dream should not be followed, or when one's awareness of an idea that popped into his head in the night should be channeled elsewhere. This can be accomplished by replacing the old dream with a new one through guided meditations, or by performing a divination to help show the dreamer another pathway to the same goal or to another goal which is better suited to the desired outcome.

The "Gift" of Prophecy

The shaman is in a unique position to perform divinations for her community. She works her magick almost without error for her community and not for herself, therefore it is difficult for her to get an accurate divination reading for her personal questions or to make magick for her personal needs.

We Witches have similar trials in divination. How many times have you found that a reading done by a friend works better to answer your questions than one you do yourself? Yet, at the same time, you seem gifted at performing divinations for others. What's the deal? In some circles this may simply be the price you pay for serving your coven or community rather than your own needs. It's also sometimes difficult to do accurate divinations for yourself because often we really don't want to know the answers to questions of our own fate. To this end we block our own energy, leaving us wondering about the future but also feeling relieved that no clear answer appeared.

Unlike the average Wiccan, those working with shamanic energies will often use time travel techniques in conjunction with astral projection to see a coven's, community's, or friend's future. They may also use this technique to travel into someone's past to attempt to make positive changes in their present, or to find at what point a wrong spiritual turn was taken so that it can be corrected by the querent.

In the book *Psychonavigation: Techniques for Travel Beyond Time* (Destiny Books, 1990), author John Perkins talks about indigenous communities in South America whose shamans foretold the devastating effects of the Amazon rainforest's deforestation twenty years before the first logging company moved in and took out the first tree.

As a student of history—it was my college major—I always had a wild craving to view the past as more than black and white snapshots from an antique camera but, as with most magickal operations, overdesire can block the effort as efficiently as underdesire.

The ceremonial magician Aleister Crowley once described the perfect state for magickal work as one of "will-less will"; actively and persistently seeking your goal, but not pushing too hard or becoming so anxious you overforce the process when you begin to see it manifest.

Most of you who are ready for advanced work learned this lesson the same way I did: by finding your consciousness right back in your mundane little head every time you got too excited that something was working for you. We learned that we best progressed with rhythmic breathing and a relaxed attitude rather than with a racing heartbeat and go-get-it-now attitude.

Another occult researcher and writer, J. H. Brennan, who has done some excellent studies on astral projection, wrote a book on metaphysical time travel called *Time Travel: A New Perspective* (Llewellyn, 1997). He describes a trip into another time frame not as a sense of traveling there, but as if he were dropping "into an air pocket" where suddenly you know you are not where you were, but are viewing another scene in another time. "The acid test of reality," he writes (p. 86), "is no longer common sense, but whether or not you can find a viewpoint in the physical universe from which your ideas are possible." In other words, if you can see it, it is real.

I actively sought the possibility of metaphysical time travel after a friend of mine described passing by her front window, just as she had hundred of times before, and seeing a small group of people in circa-1900 clothing standing at the edge of her yard. She thought it was odd, and thought about questioning their presence, but when she looked outside a minute later they were gone. In the weeks that followed she did some research on the property and found that the old road on which she lived once contained the main trolley track that took the new suburbanites to and from the city center. The nearest trolley stop happened to be at the foot of her property where she'd seen the small group standing.

Years later I found an impractical but beautiful circa-1900 home in a small town outside Indianapolis known for its turn of the century architecture. The house was for sale, but it was too small, too expensive, required too much upkeep, and was totally unsuited to my needs. Nonetheless, I obsessed on that house for several days. Then one night, as I was falling into the hypnogogic state just before sleep, I found myself floating, as if in astral projection, near the ceiling of the living room of that home. To my surprise the back wall became transparent, and I could see through it into a kitchen I had not seen when touring the house with the realtor. The original kitchen had been remodeled in the 1930s, and what I was seeing were several women wearing a style of clothing fashionable about 1904–1906 working in a kitchen that was the height of modernity at that time.

As soon as I realized I was seeing the past superimposed on the present, I lost my will-less will and snapped back into my mundane consciousness. I never went into the house again, but some questions aimed at the right people and some time spent at the local library confirmed that the wall that I had watched become transparent had been erected during the 1930s kitchen remodeling project.

A Deeper Connection with the Spirit World

The primary trait of the shaman is a connection with the world of spirit that seems more a gift than a talent. This includes the spirits of ancestors, animals, elementals, and those of the deities of both the upperworld and the underworld.

The concept of the world tree that we discussed in chapter 5 is a shamanic staple. It is the axis on which the universe turns and it is used by the shaman to reach the upperworld of deities and ancestor spirits, and also the underworld of deities and ancestor spirits.

As you may have figured out on your own by this point in your studies, the Pagan underworld bears little resemblance to the Christian Hell, though many clerics and sidewalk salesman would have us think otherwise. The underworld is neither lesser nor greater than the upperworld, which many beginning Witches mistakenly equate with the Christian Heaven. They are simply two different areas of the otherworld, each offering us their own special aspects of knowledge and gifts of the spirit. Like our magick, we take from them what we put into them. Those who enter with negative intent will take away a negative experience, and those who enter with positive intent will take away a positive experience.

Oftentimes a familiar spirit or animal figure will come to the tree to help guide the shaman to where he will find his answers. Other times he may meet with a council of ancestors, past leaders or elders of the tribe who have messages or warnings for those still living. This communal link to the world of spirits is an important function of shamans still living in indigenous societies. The information he or she obtains in this manner will be discussed at length with current tribal elders, and dream incubation will be tried to gather further knowledge before decisions affecting the entire tribe are made.

Those following Scandinavian, Saxon, or Anglo-Celtic traditions tend to see their deities and ancestors as lying beyond or beneath the western sea rather then in trees. You are probably familiar with otherworldly voyages of heroic proportions called *immrama* in the old Irish language. One such epic is the "Voyage of Maelduin," an Irish hero who takes his legion of boats to sea and visits thirty-three different islands, with thirty-three different threshold guardians and thirty-three different species of residents, and from each receives a total of thirty-three special gifts to take back to the people of Ireland. Bran, whose voyage was Christianized as the Voyage of St. Brendan, underwent an identical experience.

Celtic writer and researcher Caitlín Matthews translated the tale of the voyage of Maelduin and put it into an easy to understand book she titled *The Celtic Book of the Dead* (St. Martin's Press, 1992). It comes with a set of divination cards for each island Maelduin's ships visited, and instructions on using them to garner your own information from the otherworld and to attain its specific powers for yourself.

I find that just reading about the voyages to the various otherworld islands just before going to sleep can induce a type of dream incubation that can carry me into the otherworld. For me this technique has offered the greatest spiritual help at any given time. Tales of the voyage of Maelduin, the voyage of Bran, and similar ones about the mythic journeys of the fighting corps known as the Fianna (under Finn McCool) and the Red Branch warriors (under Cuchulain) work well, too.

If you are interested in exploring the thirty-three isles of the otherworld, you can get Matthews' book, or a copy of *The Voyage of Bran*, and begin to work through the energies and challenges just as you worked through the thirty-two paths on the tree of life in chapter 5. A bilingual Gaelic-English version with detailed footnotes is still available through Llanerch, a Welsh publisher that has a facsimile edition of the 1895 translation by Keno Meyer still in print.

NAME OF THE ISLE	GUARDIAN SPIRIT	INHABITANTS
1: Giant Ants	Ants in swarms	Giant ants
2: Birds	Twins of discontent	Many birds
3: Dog-Footed Horse	A questioning dog	One dog-horse hybrid
4: Invisible Riders	Unseen riders who challenge a race	Horses ridden by unseen specters

NAME OF THE ISLE	GUARDIAN SPIRIT	INHABITANTS
5: Many Salmon	Gifts of hospitality	Plentiful food & drink
6: Trees	Twin apple trees	Plentiful fruit trees
7: The Hideous Beast	A shapeshifter	A creature of illusion or many facets
8: Cannibal Horses	Two beings who cannot come to terms with what they are to do with you	Horses who fight to the death, then the winner consumes the loser
9: Fiery Pigs	Twin birds	Pigs who were in sole possession of the Celtic deities before being gifted to humans
10: Cats	Twin black cats with gold eyes	Many cats of all shapes, sizes, and colors who are able to catch you by surprise
11: Black and White	A shepherd and his flocks	Beings, plants, and animals of all kinds; all are either black or white
12: Giant Cattle	A cowherd	The cowherd and his herd of giant cattle
13: The Mill	A miller	A goddess of sovereignty
14: Sorrow	Two stone pillars	Lamenting human discarnates
15: Four Fences	A gateway of gold	Kings, queens, warriors, and maidens
16: Glass Castle	A warrior goddess	The Goddess and the animals who symbolize her powers: boars, birds, horses, and bees.

NAME OF THE ISLE	GUARDIAN SPIRIT	INHABITANTS
17: Singing Birds	Twin Druids	Many birds singing in a harmonic chorus
18: The Ancestor Spirits	One's own ancestors' power or totem animal	Ancestors
19: The Hermit	A hermit	A hermit with the gift of prophecy
20: The Forge	Fire	A blacksmith
21: Glass	Pillars of silver	An area of glass that appears as if it were a part of the sea, but in it all one's fears are reflected back
22: Mist	A carnivorous tree	Cattle and oxen
23: Wisdom	A goddess of plenty	Celtic symbols of wisdom
24: Abundance	A salmon	Food and drink, peopled by those without sin or negative karma
25: Faery Knoll	A faery or trickster spirit	The fey folk or sidhe of Celtic myth and folklore who are also deities from the days when the Tuatha de Danann ruled Ireland
26: Closed Portal	A door bearing symbols of meaning to the traveler	Knowledge
27: Woman	A queen or goddess of regeneration	Many women and priestesses

NAME OF THE ISLE	GUARDIAN SPIRIT	INHABITANTS
28: Fruit Trees	None visible	Trees bearing all types of vegetation, especially those of the twin specters of knowledge and forgetfulness, or regret and gladness
29: The Eagle	A hermit	The eagle of peace and regeneration
30: Happiness	None visible	People celebrating and feasting while inviting all comers to join them
31: The Round of Fire	A wall of fire	People feasting and celebrating but who will allow no one else to join them
32: The Otters	Fish and bread	Otters and other water mammals
33: The Falcons	Twin peregrines	All manner of livestock, people, trees, and plants

Soul Healing and Wholeness

Healing is another function of the shaman, but rather than dealing with herbs and ointments, the healing of the shaman is likely to occur at the soul level. While in trance, the shaman will astral project to your soul or any parts of your soul that have broken off from you and gone astray. He will collect them and bring them back to your astral body so he can reconnect them and make you whole once more.

Anyone in a coma, with a concussion, or with a high fever was thought to have had part of his soul leave his body due to the trauma. Some modern shamans and Witches still see it this way. However, in no way does this advocate forsaking the lifesaving measures known to modern medicine to rely only on shamanic or Witchcraft healing techniques. The two work best hand in hand, and each year more members of the medical profession are taking a second look at so-called "traditional" healing methods and allowing them to be used in conjunction with modern treatments. Never give anything to, or apply anything to, a patient under a doctor's care without consulting a physician, pharmacist, or botanist who can give you some idea of the type of interaction you could expect.

This is where soul healing, or soul retrieval as it is more often called, comes in handy, for it does not require dosing the patient with anything. The shaman does not even have to be in the same physical location to do his work. The shaman will go out into the astral world and seek out the missing part of the soul, and return them astrally to the person from whom they have been lost or stolen.

The belief that a piece of one's soul can be stolen or bound through use of negative magick is a popular indigenous belief. In Witchcraft we see the same concept at work in the idea of faeries leaving their babies, or changelings, in the place of human babies, or of another Witch blocking our pathway to something we need or want that is of no harm to others.

If a person is dying, the shaman may chase down the entire soul as it floats aimlessly, deciding if, when, or where it wishes to go. Here is where it's difficult to allow someone their free will. If someone is obviously very sick, in pain, or has little chance of being able to live a life of quality, and that spirit tells you it does not want to return to the physical body, most shamans allow it to wander on and make its own decision. In cases where the prognosis for recovery are good, the soul can be coerced back to the body, but be aware of forcing it to go back against its will. Some people know when the Goddess is calling them to the Isles of the Blest and this may be their time to go. Others genuinely don't know what to do, or may not even know where they are or what has happened to them. In these cases the shaman's skill of leading a soul back to its vessel are priceless.

All these considerations are, of course, void in any emergency situation. A true emergency where a life is at stake transcends all other laws during the time in which the injured person cannot speak or act for himself. When tragedy strikes suddenly, and the injured party is unable to give permission for your healing efforts, you should take it upon yourself to do everything in your power to save that life. If you know CPR (cardiopulmonary resuscitation) or have access to a phone to call for emergency help, you should do those things immediately and worry about soul healing as a last resort.

CPR literally breathes life back into a body that cannot breathe for itself. That makes it an interesting correlation to many old clan-based societies, including those of western Europe from which most of our Witch lore derives. They saw the breath as being part of the soul. In Celtic warrior society it was common to give a dying warrior a "death kiss," one in which you inhaled the dying breath of the warrior. This was so that a part of his soul would remain within the clan, better ensuring his next reincarnation experience back into the same tribe.

The other place the Celts saw the soul was in the head. Heroic legends are still told of the heads of severed warriors kept mounted at gateways and signposts as oracles and talismans of defense.

The Role of Sacrifice and Suicide in Shamanic Cultures

There is no culture today in which suicide is acceptable, with the possible exception of cultures in which a person feels they have "lost face" or "dishonored" themselves, their family, or their country. Oftentimes the spirits of suicides are thought to return as demons to haunt the living, mourning forever the thoughtless act of taking their own lives.

In the case of suicide, or even death from natural causes, great pains are taken in shamanic societies to make sure the spirits of the dead do not come back to haunt the living. Burying bodies facedown or with herbs and religious symbols over them are the most common ways in which the roaming spirits are suppressed. In some cultures the name of the dead person is never spoken for fear of evoking him. By contrast, other cultures will name their children after deceased loved ones in hopes that the beloved spirit will make a reappearance in the youngster.

In many indigenous cultures, ancestor spirits are on the same plane as the deities and are worshiped as such. This is most common in southeast Asia and the South Pacific islands. In these cultures, the shaman will often attempt to contact the dead or to appear before a council of ancestors to attain their foreknowledge concerning the community. However, this is never done in the case of a suicide.

About fifteen years ago I read a newspaper account of two young women in China who committed suicide in hopes of being reborn into lives in which their basic circumstances would be better. The coven I was part of at the time debated the wisdom of their action. One side believed the two girls had not allowed themselves to learn the lessons of the life they were born into, and by cutting those lives short, they were doomed to repeat them through another life with similar disadvantages. Our organizer insisted life was a gift, and it was up to us to make what we could out of what we were given. She refused to comment on what she believed lay ahead for the souls of the two girls. Another faction saw nothing wrong with the girls' efforts to improve their position in life and felt that, if this was their focus at death, then their will would carry over into the world beyond and they would indeed find something better in their next lifetimes.

All I saw was waste. These girls were too young to know what might lie ahead for them, or what they might have made of their lives. No indigenous society I can find condones suicide as a method of self-improvement, nor are the souls of suicides sought for spiritual knowledge and guidance. In most cases, their bodies are not disposed of in the usual tribal manner, and their ghosts are feared above all others. Is this a control measure for these societies or do these fears have merit? We may never know but until we do, I tend to side with the indigenous people who believe that the tortured spirits of suicides are incapable of helping us grow spiritually until they resolve their own issues in life.

Human sacrifice has disappeared from the global spiritual scene as well. Symbolic sacrifices, or sacrifices of animals or important personal items, are still commonplace in some parts of the world. In modern Witchcraft we know that we must harm none, animals and spirits included, when we make a sacrifice. Our sacrifices are usually of service, time, money, or perhaps some token item, such as a coin, gemstone, or special herb.

Animal Allies and Helpers

Another function of the shaman is working with animal allies, totems, and animal spirit helpers to seek answers from the natural world. This working in close contact with the animal spirits also allowed the shaman to know where the herds were moving so that the tribe's hunters could find them. This was crucial in the late fall months, when meat had to be salted and stored for winter.

Another important skill of the shaman was the ability to become the animal from whose energy she sought to learn or whose favor she wished to garner. We will look into this aspect of the Craft in the next chapter, in which we delve into the world of the animals, animal spirits, and the advanced shamanic art of shapeshifting.

The Animals and the Shapeshifters

In the beginning of your Craft career, you may have had trouble distinguishing between animals as omens and as allies or familiars. The vocabulary of Witchcraft was a whole new language back then, and as much as you wanted to know it all right now, it just wasn't possible to absorb everything at once.

As an intermediate Craft student you began to understand that the animal lore of any given culture was quite ancient, harking back to its most primitive beginnings as a society.

However, you were probably cautioned by your teachers not to attempt shapeshifting other than through dance or in group ritual situations where the shift was more an acting out of a shift than an actual change on any level of the self. But as you practiced the rudimentary forms of becoming your power animals, they revealed their secrets to you and you could sense that a full shapeshift or merging of energies was looming in your near future.

You also learned many animals had a well-honed psychic sensitivity, one we humans must have also possessed early in our development but which was bred out of most of us centuries ago. The proliferation of television programs about animals and their amazing skill, and popular books such as *The Psychic Power of Animals* by Bill Schul (Ballantine, 1977), chronicled verifiable accounts of the psychic potency of the animal kingdom.

Children naturally love animals and have a great curiosity about how they live. Fear of a creature is rarely expressed unless that fear is transmitted from a trusted adult. The uncanny and smooth communication between a child and its pet needs no words to be expressed, as many parents have observed to their amazement.

Somewhere in your intermediate-level studies of the Craft you realized your child-self knew more about helper spirits than you did after years of struggle. You stopped thinking of the animals as being on a lesser plane of existence than you, or on a lower scale of reincarnation cycle, but as being on a level that was different—neither higher nor lower, just different. And it is from that difference that we can learn if we allow ourselves to develop our shapeshifting skills.

Animal Totems, Allies, and Familiars

By the time you began intermediate Craft studies, you were probably getting a good grasp on the energies of different animals and what their appearance meant in folklore, myths, dreams, or inner-world journeys. The archetypical meaning of animals remains consistent throughout most of the world, though you will still have your own alliance with special animals whose meanings you will understand in ways that may be different from those of the masses.

This close connection between Witches and their power animals made it dangerous to own a pet during the Burning Times. Toads were supposed Witch favorites because their sweat contains bufotenin, a potent hallucinogen reputedly used in the some types of flying ointments, or astral projection ointments, of the Middle Ages.

Nocturnal creatures, such as cats, were also marked as Witch familiars. Some scholars believe the mass killing of cats during the beginning of the Witch hysteria in the late twelfth and early thirteenth century helped contribute to the increase of the rat population, which in turn caused the devastating Black Plague that swept across Europe, taking two-thirds of its lives in less than a single generation's time.

Some animals may become your "familiar" or animal ally, the familiar spirit that helps us access deeper areas of our spiritual selves or can provide omens concerning our future. Animals also appear to us in the wild as omens. (A list of some of the more common animal omens appears in chapter 13 with other auguries.)

Connecting with Your Power Animals

Many intermediate students of Witchcraft learn or are taught techniques for meeting with a power animal. The power animal doesn't always remain the same or, if it does, you may find it appears only long enough to take you into the presence of another animal whose wisdom or guidance you can draw from as needed.

If you have not yet tried to meet with a power animal, follow these steps:

1) Go into a meditative state, or astral project, while focusing your mind on meeting with an animal that can help you answer a specific question or give you spiritual guidance. If you have no specific question at this time, ask for the best animal to appear to teach you something you need to learn right now.

2) In your meditative state, you want to create a place to go that will remain consistent throughout all your animal encounters. The best place is a spot where many different environments meet. This keeps the path open for the largest number of different animals to appear to you in their natural habitat. The best spot I've found is outside the mouth of a cave over which hangs a high cliff. I keep this to my left. Behind me is a rich open meadow beside a stream-fed lake. Beyond that is a small marsh, and beyond that is a veld or plain. To my right is a forest, verdant in its summer glory, but as you peer deeper into it, you see that it is also a jungle or tropical rainforest. In front of me is a saltwater sea with one area of beach made of sand, the other of smooth, water-washed stones.

3) Keep your mind on your goal as you wait patiently for an animal to appear to you. When it does, greet it as a friend and ally who is your equal. To not condescend to it, pet it, play with it, or engage in any behavior with it not initiated by the animal itself. These are actions you take with your pets over which you exercise ownership and control, and they are inappropriate for meeting with a power animal who is at least your equal in spiritual status and who is autonomous and not owned by anyone.

4) Do not immediately judge the fitness of the animal who appears to you in relation to what you think you need from it. Many Witches who are just beginning to work with power animals have a preconceived idea of what their power animals ought to be. They want big and predatory creatures: wolves, bears, lions, etc., are the ones most often sought.

   This animal who comes to you may be a familiar who will always appear in your inner-world journeys to take you to meet another animal who can help you, or it may be trying to teach you something all on its own. Don't dismiss it or you could cheat yourself out of a learning experience and a spiritually beneficial long-term relationship.

The creature who appeared to me on my first animal quest was the type of lizard known as a gecko. While living in Texas, geckos lived in the crevices of my stone home. I made no effort to remove the geckos from the exterior of my home, and my dog enjoyed chasing them, but made no attempt to harm them.

I was both disappointed and a little put off that I'd been greeted by a power animal so small, and of an order of being with which I have no affinity, but I knew not to show that disappointment and to just see what transpired. That gecko who came to greet me at the entrance to the cave gave me my first lesson in shapeshifting by teaching me to make myself small enough to ride on its back while it took me inside a geode with a cavernous crystal formation inside. It also taught me how to get there on my own to absorb healing energy.

Chapter 13 contains a listing of animal auguries, or archetypical meanings. These should help you make sense of a message being sent to you from the animal kingdom when you encounter one on a hike or on an inner-world journey.

5) The animal may speak to you verbally, mentally, or it may communicate with gestures. Its meaning will almost always be clear. It may ask you to follow it, ride it, or change your own shape and run with it. Do whatever it asks of you. If you have trouble accomplishing the task it desires, ask for its help. You will not be challenged by the animal to do more than you are capable of doing at any stage in your magickal development.

6) No matter where the animal takes you, either it or another animal in whose care the first one has left you should escort you back to your starting point. If not, wait patiently again until an animal appears to lead you back to where you began. If you go back on your own, you may miss out on something your animal allies wish to teach you, or you could offend that animal's spirit.

7) You should always thank each animal who assists you when it is clear that its task is complete. Again, refrain from petting or playing with the animal unless it initiates such contact. As you get to know your power animals better, and learn to

shift with ease into their shapes, you will get many opportunities to play and enjoy your new allies.

8) Try to get a sense if the animal will allow you to call upon it for further guidance in your next meditation or journey. Sometimes you can sense that its goodbye to you is final, other times you may sense you've met one of your major totem animals who will be your spirit friend for life.

9) Once you are out of your meditative state, or your consciousness is back in your physical body, immediately make detailed notes of your experience while it's fresh in your mind. Something that isn't clear now may make perfect sense when you look back on it a week or a month later.

Again, look to chapter 13 on advanced divination for guidance interpreting animal omens.

The Magick of the Shapeshifters

Shapeshifting of any kind is the very soul of magick. We're taught from day one that "When you change, everything around you changes." The opposite is also true: "When things around you change, you also change, either in contrast to or in harmony with the outside change, depending upon which of the two realities appears dominant to you at that moment."

Beginning students of Witchcraft often come across the concept of shapeshifting when they learn to astral project. At this time they are usually cautioned not to try to take on the shape of another being. It can be too jarring to take on the traits and personality of another creature before you've fully assimilated all the nuances of a magickal art in your own form first.

By the intermediate stage of your studies you are encouraged to try some simple shifts in shape in your inner journeys or astral projections. The shapeshifting is done for one or more of the following five reasons:

1) To see the world or an experience through the eyes of another species.

2) To accomplish things in the otherworld that you cannot do in your human guise, such as fly or burrow.

3)   To protect yourself or to flee with ease if threatened or attacked.

4)   To know the true name of something that will allow you to harness its power. Animals have a natural sense of the true name of beings and plants of the elemental world and they can often transmit these to your consciousness during a shapeshifting experience.

5)   To have your resourcefulness and shapeshifting skills tested during an otherworld journey in which a deity is attempting to initiate you into a higher state of spiritual awareness.

The last point, number five, is the only reason not really self-explanatory. The testing of your skills goes back to the initiation tests we discussed in chapter 4. A deity or other being pursuing you may force you into a decision to change your own shape to combat it (for example, the myth of Cerridwen and her son).

The concept of a second birth is a common theme in most religions, ours included. Once we are in recognition of our initiation at the hands of the Goddess, we are well past the beginning stages, worthy of the challenges of the deities, and shapeshifting becomes a natural part of our practice.

Remember your beginning teachings, when you were told "Thought is action on the astral plane"?

Things happen on any of the otherworld planes at the speed of thought, almost as if in a dream world. It requires more than just drifting along and allowing things to happen to you to meet divine challenges. Quick thinking as you will yourself into another physical/astral shape and frame of mind will be required for you to learn these new lessons.

The Many Faces of the Shapeshifter

There was no pun intended in creating this subsection of this chapter. Many Witches differentiate between types of shapeshifts, some which occur spontaneously and others that must be thought out or planned.

The greatest controversy is over whether an actual shift in shape and being can overcome us in the physical world. There are people who believe they become "werefolk" in their daily lives, or at night while they sleep. The etymology of the word *were* is Germanic and is a form of the verb "to be." The most common of the animals prefixed with "were" is the wolf, meaning simply to be a wolf. Conversion of a human being into the body of a wolf is also known as lycanthropy.

I found several interesting websites while using the search terms "shapeshift" and "lycanthropy." If you wish to continue a serious discussion of psychical world shapeshifting, I suggest you check out these sites, read what they have to say, and join the discussion on the sites that have them. Whether you accept their beliefs or not, the possibilities are fascinating and the well-thought-out arguments for them deserve our respect.

Obviously we cannot change our inherent DNA structure. This is what makes us not only human but gives us the precise human form we possess. This is where I have problems with claims of full-body shapeshifting in the physical world. On the other hand, I also respect the infinite power of the mind. The reality it perceives becomes your reality; you change and the world changes to conform to your new perception. So I find myself torn between the two sides. The debate will no doubt continue, and you will have to decide the question for yourself, just as I will eventually.

Another form of physical-world shapeshifting is the auric or etheric shift. This is when the aura, or energy field, that is projected from your physical body is that of a particular animal. This often happens when you're in a dangerous situation and your power animal merges with you to help protect you. The menacing air you project, consciously or not, may thwart those who seek to harm you. The animal essence who enters you might also be one who can best help you escape a bad situation or overcome a problem. For instance, a rabbit might enter you to help you make a quick escape, and a wise old owl may merge with you during an exam or mental trial.

Aside from a full shift in the physical body, Witches recognize other types of shapeshifts that can take place both in the physical world and in the astral. These are:

THE FULL ASTRAL SHIFT

This is when the vehicle in which your consciousness moves through the astral world takes on all the characteristics of a particular animal or mythic being. You have its body, senses, and thought processes.

THE SPIRIT BODY SHIFT

This occurs when the essence of a power animal in service to or representative of a specific deity enters you to help you learn a lesson or grow closer to that deity.

THE MENTAL BODY SHIFT

This occurs when your five natural senses take on the ability of a special animal. This can occur in either the physical or the astral world.

BILOCATION SHAPESHIFTING

This is when your animal self is outside of your consciousness or physical body while using the animal guise to observe something occurring in another place or time. This is similar to an astral projection technique taught to beginning Craft students called "the watcher," a ball of light in which the consciousness is placed for its travels but which does not take on the form of an animal or any other being, including that of the Witch who sent it out.

After some time has passed, the animal is recalled from its remote locale or it returns on its own to give you a report or sense of what it is you needed or wanted to know about the place and time the animal self went.

THE DREAM WORLD SHIFT

You may unexpectedly dream or astral project into an animal form. This may be to teach you, to protect you, or to help you out of a difficult situation.

Most times these shapeshifts occur spontaneously in the physical world, often when a specific animal's unique sense is needed for protection or learning. At this point you will feel you are the animal whose shape you have taken on. No one else may see the change, though sensitive people will notice the change in your aura and personality.

In the astral we can will these shapes to take place, though you're likely to find with shapeshifting, as with any other Witch skill, you'll naturally be better at some types of shifts than at others. Practice, patience, recording your experiences, and reflecting on them as you try to develop them is the only way to learn some of these advanced techniques. Persistence will also allow you to explore a wider variety of animal allies and helpers.

the water chapters

Where our mysteries wait

ten

Dark Witchery

In the beginning you probably had some misconceptions of the dark aspect of Witchcraft. You'd no doubt heard the terms "black magick" and "white magick," and you didn't want to be lured down the dark side, or what you thought of as the eternal damnation of the left-handed path. So strong was this repulsion in you that you may even have had some qualms about working the Crone aspect of the Goddess, fearing her harsh dark side and preferring instead to cast your allegiance with her nurturing Mother and playful Virgin aspects.

Sometime before the end of that first year and a day of study, you began to understand that the left-hand path didn't always refer to negative magick. It could also mean simple chaos that, in spite of what it sounded like, could be every bit as spiritually illuminating as light and order. These were lessons that boggled your mind; ones that had to wait until the dissonance inside the student was ready before the teacher of discord could appear.

As an intermediate student of Witchcraft, the dark Crone is as familiar to you as the Virgin and Mother aspects of the Goddess. You cherished what she could teach you and you learned not to fear her but to embrace her wisdom.

You learned that the terms "black magick" and "white magick" are frowned upon in many Craft practices, and you began to understand the power to be found in shades of gray.

You learned that casting a circle by walking in a widdershins direction did not make a spell or ritual negative any more than performing these acts deosil made them assuredly positive. That only the intent of the person or group doing the working determined which energies were put into play was a major turning point in your understanding of how magickal energy worked.

You no longer shunned the dark but recognized it as a component of the spiritual world that was no lesser and no greater than the light. It was just different. Chaos occasionally reared its harlequin head, and you learned in time to laugh with it, not at it, and to go where the forces of chaos took you. To your eternal surprise, you learned as much from chaos as you did from order.

The Darkness Inside Us All

While light or the sun represents our outer selves, the dark and the moon correlate to our inner selves or those parts we either keep hidden or which are hidden even from us. This can include any incident or idea we don't want to face or any idea with which we cannot come to terms. Knowing our dark side may not solve those problems, and there may always be aspects of ourselves—both light and dark—that we wish we could change, but understanding that they're there is the first step in making any change.

Twentieth-century psychologist Carl Gustav Jung wrote "Enlightenment is not found in the light, but in illuminating the darkness." An old Irish triad tells us "Three candles illuminate every darkness: truth, nature, knowledge."

It's that illumination we must have to peer into the dark corners of ourselves if we are to continue to grow toward our deities. Always remember that dark is not necessarily bad, but can be as enlightening as the light. It's all in the way we look at the two seemingly diverse concepts and how we internalize them.

Chaos Magick

It has often been said that chaos, not order, is the natural state of the universe. In many cases, this is true. Just as the light has a darkness that is of equal importance, so does order have chaos.

An entire tradition has developed around its chaotic nature. Appropriately, it's called the Discordian Tradition, named for the goddess of chaos, Discordia. She has a habit of shaking things up when we get too complaisant, and shows us new ways of performing old tasks that can open our eyes and souls to new experiences. She is also a deity of our own creation. Though commonly thought to be Greek in origin, no myths have been recorded of a deity named Discordia, though many other deities of chaos abound. Perhaps Discordianism is the Witches' way of personifying them all.

The gnosis, or spiritual alchemy, created by chaos tends to fill in the areas of our spiritual selves that we have not already filled with other clutter. It remains there as an integral part of us. In some ways it becomes our personal trickster spirit guide that stops us when we start to take ourselves too seriously. It allows us to work magick without sweetness and light, and illumines the darkest corners of our desires to show us what is right and wrong with our desires. Face it, nothing is ever perfect, and how many times has someone said to you, "The reality didn't measure up to the fantasy"?

In chaos magick the process is of supreme importance, not the resulting goal. This means that the constant state of flux, which we have been acculturated by the mundane world to abhor, is what we should embrace instead.

A *curandera*, or wise woman, I knew when I lived in Texas once told me that the best defense against negative magick—or any chaos—is laughter. She was right on so many levels. Not only does laughter knock the power base right out from under negative magick, it brings us in alignment with the joy of "things that go wrong," which is Discordia's delight. How we handle her tweaking of our spiritual noses can tell us a lot about our progress toward the creator. Learning to laugh at ourselves, and not take ourselves too seriously, is of supreme importance.

Newcomers to the Craft are often shocked when something goes wrong during a ritual and everyone starts to giggle until they are engulfed in hysterical laughter that won't go away. The newcomer is too serious and will need his daimon and some lessons from Discordia to make himself into a powerful Witch. To fill this gap in ourselves we must embrace the chaos and recognize it as part of the creative principle of our magick and of our deities.

The word *chaos* has a telling etymology. The *Oxford English Dictionary* defines it as "an abyss or large void." It is also linked to the primordial void from which life on Earth came to be. In other words, it is from chaos that order is born.

Chaos is the dark side of ritual and our spiritual sides, but like most things in the magickal world it rides that wheel of existence all over the universe. In other words, it also has an order all its own. We must learn to embrace both order and chaos, just as we learn to embrace both lightness and darkness. We must know how to change one into the other, and back again, to make our magick work its best and to know ourselves fully, and to keep that self in balance and harmony with all creation. As Carl Jung wrote, we must illuminate the darkness in order to find true enlightenment. From chaos comes order.

Integrate them within your spiritual self to learn many unusual lessons, and to move closer to unity with the creator who is made up of darkness and light, and chaos and order.

The Principia Discordia: The Book and the Philosophy

The primary discussion of the Discordian Tradition is outlined in *The Principia Discordia*, a small book that comes in several variations, all penned by different men and women who, in the the spirit of what you'd expect from Discordian thought, argue over who owns the copyrights and which version of the book is the oldest or most accurate. Of course, it's only natural to discover infighting over authorship and whether the work belongs to Christian mystics or Pagans worshipping the goddess Eris, a Roman version of the goddess Discordia.

In some classical mythology Eris's toy of folly and disorganization was called the Apple of Discord, the root cause of the Trojan War. She is called the daughter of the night, and various myths mate her with a variety of gods who govern the realms of sorrow, pain, want, confusion, malicious mischief, wrong turns, and mistakes.

If you wish to obtain your own copy of *The Principia Discordia*, I recommend first searching out "Discordia" on the Internet and reading some of the pages. One of the basic tenets is that it is chaos, rather than order, that is the natural state of the universe. Order, or any illusions of order, is the work of "the devil," who lulls us into a false sense of security through our desire for an order that is always doomed to decay into its natural chaotic state. Examination of the ever-evolving and expanding universe gives evidence that chaos is always at work. Order implies something which is static, fixed. The universe is neither, therefore it is in a constant state of chaos.

One website, jubal.westnet.com/hyperdiscordia/, refers to Discordianism as a "psychohazard," and warns that you either "get it" or you don't. This is yet another example of the assertion we made in an earlier chapter, which said "Everything you know is wrong."

Kerry Thornley, a cofounder of the Discordian Society, contrasts his tradition as being disorganized religion, as opposed to the organized religions that have thus far preached order over chaos to us for centuries. On a Discordian website (www-2.cs. cmu. edu/tilt/principia/intro5.html), he argues that religious thought is no more than a desperate need for order, a superstructure on which we can hang our well-ordered version of reality, one doomed to eventually crumble before the mighty Eris.

The Dark Side of the Moon and Our Inner Being

Somewhere in your Craft studies you touched upon astrology, probably in some depth. The positioning of the moon in your chart can shed light on your dark side, even before you venture out at night or walk into the world of the goddess Discordia. Night, as we shall see, is a tangible, living thing, as is daylight. Each is of equal value. The light allows our outer selves to shine for all to see; our dark side, as personified by the moon, is where we hide our inner selves, our emotions, our instincts, and even our unconscious desires.

Most of you reading this book can probably recite the planets and their whereabouts on your natal chart like a kindergartner can recite "Mary Had a Little Lamb." If you don't know the position of the moon at the time of your birth, any ephemeris or good book on astrology will give you that position. These can be found at most bookstores and many libraries.

To understand your inner self, those conflicts that don't seem to match your sun sign (or what most people call their birth sign), you have to understand the position of the moon at your birth. All planets have their negative aspects. Depending upon which of the twelve houses they are in, or how they are positioned against other planets, their negative traits may show up more in you than their positive traits.

The sun is the planet of the outer self, the one the world sees. The moon is the inner self, the psychic self, that part of us we hide from the world. We often try to hide it from ourselves to our own detriment. Understanding our dark side is fundamental to understanding what is at the soul of dark Witchcraft.

MOON IN ARIES

The positive lunar traits are optimism, energy, and good organizational ability. The negative traits are acting on impulse, impatience, lack of energy, lack of organization, and temper tantrums.

MOON IN TAURUS

The positive traits are determination, supportiveness of others, refusal to give up on someone or something, and love of the arts. The negative traits are being set in your ways, stubborn, wanting to have your own way, possessiveness, and love of luxury at any price.

MOON IN GEMINI

The positive traits are being able to juggle more than one project at once, the ability to multitask, the ability to move seamlessly from one set of ideals to another, and tolerance. The negative aspects are a love of manipulating others, inability to focus, disorganization, capriciousness, and the ability to stab even your dearest friend in the back for some small gain to yourself.

MOON IN CANCER

Positive traits are powers of empathy, loyalty, attachment to loved ones, good imagination, and compassion. The negative traits are a tendency to mood swings, finding fault in others, being judgmental, irritability, and dwelling on your losses when you have many gains to rejoice over.

MOON IN LEO

The positive traits are creativity, open-mindedness, deep compassion for others, a need to give of the self, and an enjoyment of friendships. The negative traits are selfishness, arrogance, stubbornness, dictatorial manners, and bullying others.

MOON IN VIRGO

The positive aspects uphold all your positive sun sign attributes. This lunar position gives you an eye for detail, makes you meticulous in your efforts, provides a need to give to serve others, makes you a hard worker and loyal employee, and you are seen as someone who can be relied upon to see any task through to its end, even if that end fails. The negative traits make you critical and argumentative. You become upset when small details go awry, and are untrustworthy and controlling.

MOON IN LIBRA

The positive lunar traits are your sense of fairness, your diplomacy, your ability to see what everyone needs and wants, and a tendency to be even-tempered. Your negative traits are being too judgmental, arbitrary, unreliable, or as changeable as the winds, and throwing otherwise strong aspects of yourself or your personal relationships into chaos.

MOON IN SCORPIO

The positive traits inside a vivid imagination, ambition in the workplace, and always having a contingency plan in case something goes awry. The negative traits include secrecy, lying, jealousy, suspiciousness, unforgivingness, holding grudges, and harboring a deep hatred of anyone who gets ahead of you in your academic or career pursuits. You also tend to project your qualities onto others and to judge them by that standard.

MOON IN SAGITTARIUS

The positive lunar traits are your natural love of life, your open-mindedness, and your ability to change as situations warrant. The negative traits are lack of loyalty and commitment, emotional withdrawal from those whom you care about, a preference for play rather than work, shifting blame to others, a disregard for the feelings or well-being of others, and general irresponsibility.

MOON IN CAPRICORN

The positive traits are self-discipline, willingness to accept and see through your responsibilities, loyalty to friends, and determination to complete any project at hand. The negative traits are pessimism, anxiety, a sense of failure, rigidity, and a general aura of "pity poor me" that drives others away.

MOON IN AQUARIUS

The positive traits support your sun sign. They are idealism, creativity in thought, love for all humanity, and a general sense of idealism. The negative traits are disorganized thinking, selfishness, being opinionated, capriciousness, and not being able to see projects or ideas through to completion.

MOON IN PISCES

The positive lunar traits are compassion, loyalty, open and balanced emotions, willingness to help others, the ability to think for yourself, and having an intuitive and psychic nature. The negative traits are chronic discontent, emotional imbalance, secrecy, snappishness, depression, inability to concentrate, and a tendency to believe the last thing you heard about an issue.

All these lunar traits are further exacerbated by whichever of the twelve houses of the zodiac your moon resides in. This may take more than an ephemeris to figure out. You may need a professional natal chart drawn up for you. There are many computer programs that can do this for you, as well as Internet sources.

Think about what the houses mean and where your moon falls. You might be surprised how much the negative qualities of your lunar self get in the way of your daily living. Why those instead of the positive ones? I have no answer other than perhaps we've let ourselves become negative thinkers in the mundane world, a trait that rubs off easily from those with whom we come into daily contact.

When we take ourselves too seriously, much of the joy of life leaves us. We get so determined to get that A on our history test or bring in that three-million-dollar account that we can't enjoy the process of learning or doing the work. The end goal becomes our sole purpose for being, and that takes away from our enjoyment of simply being. Chaos teaches us to slow down and learn to laugh at ourselves.

I once knew an executive, an accountant, who used to wear ties that had subtle patterns in them that looked like mere decorations unless you looked closely. This man was a meticulous, detail-oriented Virgo with a fiery Leo rising. When you looked at the pattern of his tie you might have seen Mickey Mouse, Winnie the Pooh, the Tasmanian Devil, or some other cartoon character or silliness. When asked why he wore those subtle cartoon characters on his work clothes, his answer was honest and insightful: "I do it to remind myself not to take myself too seriously."

That's one executive who will never have ulcers or other stress-related illnesses, for he's already learned the valuable art of integrating chaos into order and finding his balance within their dynamic.

If your moon is sitting in a house that exacerbates its negative side even more, then you have harsh lessons to learn. Every successful lesson begins with the simple concept of "Know Thyself."

HOUSE	DEFINITION
First House	The House of Self
Second House	The House of Physicality
Third House	The House of Communication
Fourth House	The House of Home and Family
Fifth House	The House of Creativity

Sixth House	The House of Health and Giving
Seventh House	The House of Partnerships
Eighth House	The House of Death and Rebirth
Ninth House	The House of Spirituality
Tenth House	The House of Career
Eleventh House	The House of Hopes and Wishes
Twelfth House	The House of Self-Undoing

Turning a Negative Into a Positive

Negative lunar traits are not insurmountable. Our lunar-inspired negatives are our dark aspects, parts of our nature we must work to overcome. This is the point of knowing our horoscopes, so that we can see our weaknesses and work to enhance our positive aspects while downplaying the negative. The negative aspects of our lunar selves can show us where our weaknesses are, but only we can figure out how to turn them into positive traits.

Keep in mind that none of us can maintain a constant stream of positive energy. If the natural order of the universe is disorder, our moments of tranquility will eventually cycle back to us—as all things do—changed by the other energies that joined it on its journey.

We cannot afford to ignore our dark side, for it is part of us, and some of our negative or dark traits protect us. For example, it's smart to be distrustful around certain people or in certain situations. Blind trust can get us in a lot of trouble. It can even get us killed. Suspicion can serve the same purpose, but when it's projected onto trusted loved ones, it's a dark aspect that needs correcting. This allows you to balance your light and dark sides and, because our deities also have light and dark aspects, it can bring us closer to them.

The New or Dark Moon

Witches get so used to gathering and working under the light of the full moon that even the most experienced among us sometimes forgets the power in the darkness. The changing tide of the new moon, when darkness rules the night skies, can be a metaphor for creating new selves from our old.

Covens who meet at the new moon, or what I prefer to call the dark moon, are likely to find their rituals take on a distinct character that separates it from rituals held under a full moon. The individuals involved may may even find that the dark moon brings out their dark tendencies. It may take longer to learn to work in harmony with one another on the new moon. However, the chaos this can create does not have to be a negative experience—it can be a healing one.

Even solitaries who work on the dark moon notice this distinct difference. Many choose to work at this time to take advantage of seeing their dark sides come out so they can see what they like least about themselves and work to change it.

Spells designed for the new or dark moon often involve the start of something new or the banishing of something old. It's a moment in time when one cycle ends and a new one begins. It's one of those times-in-between-times where magick can be its most potent.

The dark moon often enables us to discover the true name of something in our dark side, and we all know from Witchcraft 101 that knowing something's true name, and using that name out loud, gives us a large measure of power over it. In my tradition, this is why we adopt two Craft names: one by which we are known to others, and another known only to the deities.

The next dark moon you may want to try surrendering yourself to its capricious and chaotic power to find out what it can teach you. If it's warm enough, lay on the ground or on a blanket in a place where you know you will be safe from harm (from the two-legged, four-legged, and two-fanged), and go into a light meditative trance. Allow your inner self to be given over to the power of the moon. Know that she floats above you even though her face is hidden in shadow.

Then lie still and deepen your meditative state. Focus on the energy of the dark moon and what it can tell you about yourself, your spirituality, and your chosen path. As with any inner world work, the answers may come to you as symbols, words, pictures, or as just a feeling. When you are finished you should take the time to record any impressions or other experiences you had. Do this ritual again on the next dark moon and compare experiences to see where the darkness is leading you.

You will be surprised how accurately it reaches into your darkest secrets and desires and pulls them out for you to examine in the light. It's only by knowing all our many selves, including our dark side, that we can grow into the spiritual being we wish to become.

Daimonic Dynamics

Now that you have a general idea about the nature of your own dark side, you can use it for magick. In the dark realms our will does more than set manifestation in motion, it creates challenges we must meet and overcome. Often we must learn the lessons of the dark before we can have what we want in the light.

Most of us have heard the term "spirit guides," those beings who may or may not once have had human form whose job it is to help guide us through this current life-time. Many of us have met these beings in meditations and astral projections and rely on them like the old and cherished friends they are.

There are other beings who can be our inner guides through life, ones that under-stand and work with our dark aspects, in particular those we wish to overcome. These beings are known as daimons or daemons. They are never to be confused with demons, or the servants of the anti-God of Christian theology.

Daimons can be found at our side when an inner journey takes us into a realm in which our dark side will manifest, such as when we meet with our shadow self. Greek folklore says at least one of these beings is attached to each of us at birth. The daimon is the voice in your head that asks, "Are you *sure* you know what you're doing?" and "Are you *sure* you want what you say you want?"

Daimons concern themselves almost solely with our spiritual lives and help us in our quest to reunite with the deities. They could care less about our spell to get a new car or the talisman we crafted to help us win the lottery. However, if the wish remains strong enough to project itself onto the astral plane as a thoughtform that the daimon can see and understand, it will try to assist you in attaining what you want. This is where we must be careful in our expressions of desire: be careful what you wish for, or you just might get it.

In some ways our daimon becomes our alter ego, that part of us that stays the course when the rest of us goes off on a crazy run up the wrong tree. In other ways, they are our selfish children who grab what they want whether it's theirs or not.

Early in life our daimon internalizes itself with our subconsciousness and our con-sciousness, and it may or may not be visible in our astral plane work. Many Witches go through an entire lifetime unaware of this creature's existence. Other know it's there and they fear it, which is silly. Make friends with it. The only thing we have to truly fear is the unknown.

Daimons are powerful spirit guides and helpers, ones which have the power to create situations and conditions in which we must make choices that the daimon hopes will force us back onto the proper spiritual path. Sometimes they can be hard lessons, but they will always be of value in the end.

Also, never try and run from a lesson from your daimon, for that is like trying to out-run yourself. The daimon is part of you and no matter how far or fast you travel, there it is, hitching a ride wherever you go. Like your shadow, you can hide from it for a while, but you can never escape it.

Contrary to popular myth, daimons are not negative beings. That reputation no doubt originated because of their hideous appearance and their harsh lessons. In truth, your daimon has your best interests at heart, but it teaches harsh lessons when the person to whom it is attached repeatedly refuses to learn.

You can ask your daimon for assistance while in meditation. Ask it to help you find your way through the spiritual maze to the godhead. Your daimon will be a trustworthy guardian in times of crisis and learning to heed its warnings can save your from danger or allow you to slip into the arms of someone who can help or comfort you.

Next time you find yourself in deep meditation, ask your daimon to show itself. Don't be surprised if it slips right out of your body or steps our from behind you. It is part of you and has been from your birth. Also, be prepared for a being who looks more like a monster than a benevolent spirit guide. Daimons have a ferocious and, well, demonic look about them.

It's rare that a trickster spirit can mimic your daimon while you're working on the astral plane, because few spirits want to take the blistering punishment your daimon can give it for such effrontery.

Tough Love

What's the best reason to know your daimon? It is one of the few beings who will actively try to block you from acting against your own best interests in any situation. Though their power is strongest on a dark moon, or during the dark half of the year, or when you're in meditation or on the astral plane, the daimon will do whatever it can to keep your self-interest at heart.

Thus the help of the daimon can be a blade that cuts both ways. You must remind the daimon of the rede of "harm none," for so programmed is he to look after your best interest that sometimes he will allow someone else's interests to be harmed, or at least dented, until you get what your daimon thinks you need. It's this focus on self-interest that has caused it to be associated with the negative path of the Craft.

This is not love in any sense that we know it. Even those who want the best for us know that it's not ethical to take from someone else so that you can have it. The daimon is not programmed to understand this. Maybe its weakness is selfishness, but this is how determined it is to serve your will. Use the daimon wisely, but curb its overzealousness.

Remember, the bottom line when dealing with your daimon is that the best rule is the old adage "Be careful what you wish for, or you just might get it."

The Labyrinth and the Maze

In the beginning you may not have been exposed to labyrinth and maze archetypes or their spiritual uses. Unless you belonged to a teaching coven that was fond of using them, meaning they had a large area of land to work on and a fair assurance of privacy, you may not have been taught about these powerful configurations, even after your year-and-a-day initiation.

As an intermediate your own reading and study would expose you to the spiritual concepts of the labyrinth and the maze. Whether or not they were part of your actual Craft practice was determined by availability of land and if you were or were not part of a coven or study group used to using these devices for seasonal ritual and spiritual growth.

Again, it must be kept in mind that it is in the mind that spiritual change—all change—ultimately takes place. The world we think we see is merely a reflection of what our minds accept.

No student of Witchcraft need ever be limited by time or space in any magickal or ritual endeavor. Through meditative states of consciousness, guided meditation, or astral projection, the whole universe is ours to explore.

Vive la Différence

There's a common misconception that the labyrinth and the maze are two names for the same configuration. This is not true. A labyrinth has one path that spirals to the center and out again. A maze is more like a game where you have to find the one correct path to the center and back again. A labyrinth can be walked while your thoughts remain on the purpose of your ritual. A maze will have many dead ends and false trails that won't get you where you want to go, and will require your concentration and magickal instincts to be completed by you.

In Craft practices these two configurations also have different uses and meanings. The labyrinth is the one most often used by covens and study groups. Symbolically it is the spiral journey in and out of the other world. It represents creation, death and rebirth, the cycles of the seasons, the path to the divine, and the attainment of wisdom. Its one path leads you on what at first seems an aimless wandering, but eventually your faith takes you to its center, where its power can be found, used, and projected.

A maze has many paths, but only one leads to the center. There are many false starts, dead ends, and backtracking that represent a wrong turn toward your spiritual goal. It can be compared to climbing the tree of life and finding yourself out on a branch that you thought led to the top but, once you got out onto it, you realized it was nothing but an attractive branch with a few useful limbs, but it was mostly for show.

Where the labyrinth can be seen as the spiral journey of life's many cycles, the maze can be compared to the classic hero's journey, a mythic adventure with its tests, enemies, and challenges that allows only the most determined to reach their goal.

Making and Using a Spiritual Labyrinth

Of the two configurations, the labyrinth is by far the older. The Greek historian Herodotus refers to labyrinths inside temples and sacred structures as early as 2000 BCE. Even at the time of his writing, it is estimated that the labyrinth had been there for close to three hundred years.

The most famous of the ancient labyrinths was at Knossos in Crete. In Cretan mythology the goddess Ariadne, a deity of the underworld and of germination, gave her lover Theseus a roll of thread so he could find his way out of King Minos' famous labyrinth that imprisoned the dreaded monster known as the Minotaur. Ariadne was widely worshiped by women in both her native Crete and in Greece where she was paired and polarized with the god of wine and hedonism, Dionysus. Ariadne was a creator deity, associated with spinning into being the threads of which existence was woven.

The labyrinth's image as a spiritual symbol spread throughout Europe. Cave draw-ings, chalk markings, stone embankments and other evidence exists of the labyrinth's ancient history. Depictions of them, or their remains, have been found in Egypt, Greece, France, England, and Ireland.

Most interesting are those found in churches and cathedrals. It's common knowledge that Christianity spread throughout Europe by adopting and adapting Pagan festivals and sacred sites. As early as 400 CE a church in Algeria sported a labyrinth in its vesti-bule, and the Christian pilgrimage site in Ireland, Glendalough, had a drawing of a large labyrinth on one of the rock formations. Though taken over by the priests of the new religion, Glendalough and its holy well were once sacred to the Mother Goddess Brighid.

The most famous church-based labyrinth is probably the Great Labyrinth inside the Chartres Cathedral in France. Visitors to the church will often walk its circuitous route to the center. Many have no idea what compels them to do this, or what the labyrinth's spiritual powers are. Nonetheless, the genetic imprinting is there, and we are drawn to the spiral's center as our souls are drawn to the deities.

The center of the labyrinth is a physical representation of the otherworld, the realm where knowledge is shared and given freely as a reward for the challenge of walking the long and winding road.

The winding itself mimics the spiral of creation. The spiral has stood for creative and regenerative energy since ancient times, and modern DNA, the building threads of all life, has proven this ancient instinct to idealize the spiral as the most infinitesimal par-ticle of life. It's no accident feminist traditions, such as Dianic, adopted the labrys as their emblem. A comparison between the double-headed axe and the most common labyrinth patterns show two circular halves with two straight paths leading toward the center, similar to the construction of the labrys.

If you or your coven wish to make a labyrinth, you can use one of the classic designs, one of which is depicted here (see next page), or sit down with a piece of paper and an open mind to create your own. Some labyrinths have a path that leads almost straight to the center before winding outward, circling around, then taking the journeyer back up another straight path into the center. Others wind in slowly to the center, and others have you travel circles in both halves, or even in four quarters, before finding the road that leads to the middle.

The center of the labyrinth represents the otherworld. It can be an underworld, upperworld, faery world, etc., depending on the time of year or on the desire of the person or persons using it. Everyone using it at the same time must agree on the place they are heading and the purpose to keep the group mind's energy from scrambling the native energy of the labyrinth, rendering its magick useless for all.

There existed in Europe and Africa a belief that even if a labyrinth was not constructed at a natural power spot on the land, the careful construction of one would cause a power vortex to slowly build on that site. Consistent use of the labyrinth will enhance these natural powers of the land.

Your labyrinth may be constructed with a trench dug into the earth or outlined with stones. The ones using stones are the most popular. Landscaping and home improvement centers have a large variety of attractive blocks, or you can scour your community for large rocks lying about unused.

Make sure you line up the stones far enough apart that the pathway is clear for the walker. This is especially important if the ritual will be done after sundown.

The labyrinth (left) and Chartres labyrinth (right)

Some groups and individuals like to add candles every few inches throughout the labyrinth, or at least at the entrance and in the middle. Extreme caution is needed whenever candles are employed in a labyrinth. Outdoor candles should be globed or placed in votive jars, or anchored with sand or some other stable substance. This will prevent the burning of clothing as your group passes through. However, dry grass can ignite from the heat alone, spreading flames rapidly in all directions. Keep safety in mind at all times and, if you find candles are not practical, you can use small penlights or other battery- operated items.

Another reason to be cautious with candles has to do with ritual dress. Most of us are attracted to flowing robes that drag the ground, or that have long, flowing sleeves. The experienced Witch already knows the drawbacks of these types of robes, but they still draw us. I have one that I've owned for many years, but I find I wear it less often because the sleeves knock things off altars, drag through candle flames and other ritual accouterments, and the long hemline makes it impractical for dancing. Walking a candle-lined labyrinth in such ritual dress would be a disaster.

If land space is an issue, or you need a portable labyrinth to move to different working sites, you can draw your pattern out on a large sheet. If you have no space you can use a drawing to enter into astrally or through visualization.

Be sure to keep in mind the spiritual significance of the labyrinth as you create it, just as you would when creating or empowering any other magickal catalyst.

The labyrinth can then be used for a variety of reasons, such as:

- During an initiation, have the new Witch tread the path either alone or with her teacher to the center, where the coven waits. Her entry represents her willingness to seek and serve the deities, and her exit represents her rebirth into a new life as a Witch.

- Use it at the spring or fall equinoxes to mimic the going to and returning from the underworld of the goddess of regeneration.

- Use the center for performing healing magick and rituals. The vortex-like energy in the center of a labyrinth is reputed to aid in healing of all kinds.

- Use it for handfasting or Pagan marriage ceremonies. The couple should enter the labyrinth separately, or with various members of the coven and their guests.

The ceremony should be held in the center, where the deities dwell, to mimic the sacred marriage of the divine.

- Use at the summer and winter solstices as a battleground for the Oak King and Holly King. Both may enter, but only the victor of the season should exit until the ritual is complete. The Oak King rules the waxing year, from December through June. The Holly King rules the waning year, from June through December.

- Use it as a place for a passing-over or memorial ritual. Envision yourself leading the newly passed-over spirit into the otherworld, saying your goodbyes, and then leaving without the spirit, who now knows his way to the otherworld but is left free to go where he wishes.

If you are a solitary, or simply want a more dramatic labyrinth experience, all you need is a drawing of labyrinth that you have memorized in perfect detail. Take yourself into a deep meditative state and enter the labyrinth.

Within the universe of your mind there is no limit to where your labyrinth can be. You can enter through a cave and allow yourself to spiral downward with each concentric circle. You can place it on a mountaintop and set the center at its summit. You can use a dense forest, or a meadow with hedgerows. You can see your labyrinth as an ancient sacred site made of standing stones.

Each location of your labyrinth will provide a ritual character all its own to enrich your current spirituality.

Making and Using a Maze

The maze became a popular playground during the later half of the Elizabethan period (late sixteenth century), but its concept is one of deeper spiritual meaning. Where the labyrinth represents the spiritual journey into and out of life, and into and out of our many cycles of regeneration, the maze represents the impediments that block our spiritual progression.

In many ways the maze mimics the classic hero's journey with its tests, allies, enemies, confrontations, trials, and rewards. These can be enhanced by undergoing the experience with a large group, or by treading the maze as an inner-world journey.

My only experience in a physical world maze was when I was seven and living in southern Indiana. Nearby was the small town of New Harmony, the remnants of a nineteenth-century utopian community experiment led by Robert Owen and his followers. Not only is there a replica of the Chartres Cathedral labyrinth within the town, but there is also a famous maze crafted in the Elizabethan style by using hedgerows that have to be threaded through to find the one path to the center.

My four-year-old brother held tight to my mother's hand, and the two of them ventured only a few steps into the maze. My father and I were determined to find our way to the center. Though I was just tall enough to see over the hedgerows and try to plan my path, I was stymied at many places that had appeared earlier to be the correct path to the center.

I refused to give up, even after I saw my father waving in triumph from the center. I was so frustrated by that point that I wanted to just break through the tightly packed hedgerows and plow my way to the center.

My father guided me the rest of the way from his position of height, where he could see the clear path and any false turns. I finally made it to the center where we both stopped to give a victory wave to my exhausted mother, who was having trouble occupying a four-year-old while Dad and I played.

I stayed by his side as we exited the maze, which for reasons beyond my understanding seemed easier than entering, even though it was the same path in both directions.

A good maze cannot be made with stones. It's too confusing to be sure where one path dead-ends or where two do not join. A small fence, hedgerows, or anything else you can find that sticks out above the ground at least a foot high and makes a solid wall is best.

Like the labyrinth, the center of the maze is the realm of the divine. In the terms of Joseph Campbell and others who have studied world myths, they would call it the place of the supreme ordeal or the inmost cave.

One of the advantages of having a large group to help you or of performing this experience in a meditative state is having divine and semi-divine beings along the paths—the false ones and the true one. If you're in a group, some members can take on these roles while the others work through the maze.

In the meditative state these otherworld beings can be there just for you. They can offer you assistance, answer questions, or give you tokens or talismans you may need later. They can also give you false information and try to thwart your journey to the center.

There are numerous divine and semi-divine archetypes to be met as you trace your own hero's journey into the center:

Shaper/Bender	Shapeshifter
Trickster	Magician
Nurturer	Priest/ess
The Fey	Animal Spirit
Ancestor Spirit	Ally
Energizer	Measurer
Enemy	Polarity
Shadow	Teacher
Defender	Initiator
Warrior	Hunter
Challenger	Guardian
Deliverer	Gifter
Spinner	Oracle
Weaver	Preserver
Empowerer	Catalyst
The Silent	The Misruler
Queen/King	The Great Fear
Pathfinder	Hermit
Destroyer	Parent
Child	Earth Spirit

Each of these, or several of them, can block or aid your journey. Your goal is to sort out which is which, reach the inmost cave, gain the knowledge to be attained there, and return to your own world, where that knowledge is put to work for you so that it can become wisdom.

Advanced Tree Spirituality

In the beginning of your Witchcraft studies you learned a lot about the power of trees. The study went side by side with your learning about herbalism and the elementals who inhabited and protected herbs and trees. You learned that willowbark contains the salicyclic acid that makes up aspirin, and that the poisonous foxglove plant contains the life-saving digitalis given to heart patients.

You also learned the magickal properties of trees: which woods made the best wands for which kind of magick, and which leaves, barks, and berries, etc., made the best catalysts for a specific type of spell.

Tree knowledge seemed at that point to be endless, but you optimistically presumed that by the time your year and a day was up you'd have exhausted the topic and be ready to wander into the woodlands and forests with an intimate familiarity.

As an intermediate you found there was still much more tree lore to learn. You kept learning and you developed a deeper appreciation for the subtleties and nuances of the vast tree kingdom. You read all about their archetypes and other references to them in mythology and various folklores.

You had it hammered into your head that the world tree was the center point of the universe, from where you could travel anywhere. In Norse mythology this great tree was central to the ability to traverse the many realms. In Celtic mythology you read of the Battle of the Trees, and of the five magickal trees of Ireland's five provinces. There was wisdom in the west, warfare in the north, abundance in the east, music in the south, and rulership or sovereignty in the center.

As you explored the world beyond Witchcraft you found that there was no culture that did not cherish its trees and whose people did not, at one time or another, hold them sacred. Though "civilized" cultures today can seem callous about their trees, our ancestors felt different.

In modern Judaism the post-biblical festival of Tu B'Shavat, usually occurring in January or February on the fifteenth day of the lunar month of Shavat, celebrates the "new year" of trees. The original purpose was for calculating the age of fruit-bearing trees for tithing purposes. Planting trees and eating their fruit have become traditions of this festival. Around the world Jewish children collect money to send to Israel to plant new trees for this holiday.

As an intermediate student you learned more about the guardian spirits of the trees: the capricious, the good, and the wicked. You learned how to talk to these beings and how to placate them so that the tree could yield its knowledge. Most of all, you learned never to harm a tree or to take anything from it without its permission.

Why Trees?

Trees make our lives more enjoyable. Without them life might not even be possible. The oxygen they produce is vital to sustaining our lives. We might even call our relationship symbiotic. Trees inhale carbon dioxide and exhale oxygen. We inhale oxygen and exhale carbon dioxide. We need each other to exist.

The long lives of trees, and of the spirits and wildlife that are attached to them, and their root systems that mirror their upper branches all combine to make trees appear immortal. They are thriving when we are born, and they are still thriving when we leave the earth plane at death. Their thick summer branches hang over us like the roof of a great cathedral, providing shade, shelter, and helping to cleanse our air. In spring many trees provide a rich display of flowers, and in autumn their vibrant colors are unequaled in nature.

In all cultures worldwide trees have been looked to as symbols of traveling to other worlds, as healing objects, and as sources of knowledge—if we can only humble ourselves to listen to their teachings.

The Celts believed trees had long memories of things which took place near them, and had a special connection to heroic events. Thirteen of their trees were made sacred and developed into the Celtic tree calendar we know today of one tree for each lunar cycle in the solar year. Claims to its antiquity may be exaggerated but the cycle of the moons and trees works to bring us in closer harmony with nature, so its wisdom is well used no matter how old it is.

Higher Learning from Trees

By the time you're ready for advanced Witchcraft practices, you probably thought you knew all there was to know about trees and their magickal or medicinal properties. This information is something we can find from many books and through experienced teachers. We don't have to get it from the tree itself. Yet we need that connection with nature to work at our best, and trees can communicate with us directly, telling about themselves and ourselves and what they can do to help us.

Some trees have been abused to make way for new housing communities or stripped away for factory farming. They've been chopped down, pruned back until many of their branches are dead, cut off above the roots to be sold as seasonal ornaments, and been used as posting boards for those selling products of dubious value or for those hunting for lost pets.

When you find a tree you wish to approach for its knowledge, do so slowly, showing reverence for the tree and any wildlife and spirits who make it their home. Respect it as a sentient being with a free will that is just as precious and meaningful as your own. If you're sensitive enough you might feel the tree tremble in fright as you come near.

It's sad but true that some have been so abused by humans that they actively fear us. The mere presence of a human in their vicinity makes them nervous as they wonder what new atrocity you will heap on them. It may take time to get these trees to trust you, but the effort is worthwhile, especially if the tree is on your land and you can assure its continued protection.

If you feel the tree's fear, mentally connect with the tree to let it know you mean it no harm. In fact, if you notice nails or other items embedded in its trunk, let the tree know you can remove these and help heal the scars. It may take several weeks of approaching the tree day by day to gain its trust and put it at ease. If the tree is willing to let you, take out each nail or staple slowly so as not to create more damage, then visualize the scar being sealed with bright green light you draw up from Mother Earth. This will help heal the pain and make for a faster healing of the damaged bark.

The same is true for trees that have been ruthlessly pruned back by utility company employees whose job it is to remove excess growth around power lines. You may not be able to stop this from occurring, as your city or county has the right of eminent domain over all property within its boundaries. You might be able to forestall the damage by doing gentle pruning yourself, but as the tree grows taller it threatens to push power lines to the breaking point.

All you can do in this case is ask the utility crew to do as little damage as possible, and to send loving messages to the tree and heal it with green light.

You may offer gifts to the trees you want to work with. Common gifts are bright ribbons, bells, seasonal decorations (hung on branches and not hammered in), a coin buried at its base for the faeries, or food for the creatures who call the tree home.

As I approach any tree that attracts my attention, whether I intend to work with it magickally or not, I give it my standard greeting: "Blessed be, ancient tree."

If the tree is still a sapling, or very young, I find it hard to establish communication. It may be that, like humans, it takes a long life and much experience to attain knowledge worth passing along. Even so, I greet it with: "Blessed be, fine young tree."

There was a beautiful old tree near the edge of a farm field I used to pass when I was out running. At one time the whole of the Midwest was forest land, most of it gone now to make way for farms, housing developments, and businesses. Why this one large tree was left at the edge of the field near a rural road is a mystery, but it was a beautiful old thing. I sensed its loneliness and its fear that it would be destroyed as its neighbors once were. Sometimes I look back and think it recognized me as a Witch and spoke to me first.

Since I used the tree as my west point marker before turning around and going down the road the other way, I would arrive at its side several times a day. Each time I gave it my greeting, then turned around and continued my exercise.

It took several weeks before I could sense the tree no longer feared me, and was even glad to see me. Sometimes I could sense it hailing me in greeting before I could hail it. It was definitely lonely. Sometimes I would mentally encase it in a rich green light to promote its health and growth. Other times I left items at its base for the small animals who lived in the area: rabbits, raccoons, and opossums. A tree that houses wildlife will not be lonely.

Though I never used the tree for any other purpose, I feel good that I taught that old tree that not all humans are bad.

At that same time I had three younger trees in my front yard that I liked to adorn with seasonal decorations—colorful eggs at Ostara, ghosts at Samhain, and bells at Midsummer. I made sure the trees knew in advance what my plans were and that no harm would come to them through my actions. I just wanted to adorn them and make them look festive for the season. One tree seemed to not care for decoration until it saw the other two trees in their seasonal finery. I then sensed it wished to be a part of the holiday and it allowed me to decorate it as I did the other two.

When working with trees for the purpose of attaining knowledge you should be aware of information that comes to you within the next twenty-four hours that might relate to a question you asked of a tree. In one instance I was concerned with the toxicity of a particular tree's leaves. I have intense allergies and wasn't sure if I'd made a mistake with the leaves or whether I was just the victim of my hyperactive immune system. I got no answer that day from the tree itself, but while reading later that night I came across a quote from seventeenth-century magician and physician Paracelsus, who reminded me of the old magickal adage that tells us the same substance that kills can cure:

> All things are poisons, for there is nothing without poisonous qualities. It is only the dose which makes a thing poison.

I had to admit the truth of Paracelsus' observation. His commentary segued right into modern homeopathy, in which a small part of the item that made you sick is used to make you well. This was also lesson in moderation. As you would with all herbal potions, please work with a doctor or reliable homeopathist before trying to use these cures on yourself or your family.

Obtaining Knowledge from Trees That Can Become Wisdom

This is not a book on mythology. Those of you interested in exploring trees in mythology can find them in virtually all books on myth from all known cultures. There is not space or time to go over all of these or comment upon them here. The myths are useful to know, and they can help you better understand a specific species' magickal properties. In this book we are seeking advanced learning, finding ways to gather deeper knowledge from the trees.

The trees don't speak to all of us the same way, though there are many points of commonality. Most of what's imparted to you will apply only to you at the time you ask, and will be of little value to anyone else. This is why you should keep detailed records of your tree exchanges.

Most of us already know the magickal properties of common trees and the lore surrounding them. This information usually comes to us hand in hand with our herbal studies as beginning Witches. Some of us are gifted in knowing how to use parts of trees for healing rituals. What most of us lack is the secrets of the trees.

All trees possess a knowledge of their own which is separate from, though often correlated with, their magickal properties. They have a great wisdom and can reach into many worlds to seek out what they want to know. Deities to whom they are sacred, the totem animals and birds who dwell within them, and the elementals and faeries who protect and live within their branches or root systems all can give the tree information they think you should have.

To gain higher learning from trees in your area you will need a notebook and pen, and probably a pictorial guidebook to the trees in your region. Once you identify a tree you can go to it and ask it to share its knowledge with you.

Approach the tree with a simple greeting and let it know you are a follower of the faith of the earth, and that you will do it no harm. Let it know you have brought it a gift of some kind. If you feel the tree is nervous in your presence, leave the gift and come back again the next day or in several days.

Greet the tree again, making sure it knows you are not planning harm. If you can see damage from human misuse of the tree, you can offer to help heal it. A badly abused tree will probably still not be comfortable with you. It will take more time. But leave it your gift anyway and try again in another day or two.

Most trees are receptive to you without all the day after day efforts. Only those traumatized by past events will send off vibrations of fear and will be too paralyzed with terror to work with you.

Approach the tree you wish to work with and tell it you wish it to impart knowledge to you. Take a quick look at the trunk and base and make sure no creatures are there who could harm you or surprise you. An army of ants crawling over you will not be conducive to learning.

If everything looks safe, and you sense the tree agrees to work with you, step up to it and press your forehead, the psychic chakra center known as the third eye, to its trunk. Wrap your arms around the tree and place your palms flat against it.

Take a few moments to get the feel of the tree and allow it to get the feel of you. Trees are as individual as we are, and one oak tree may tell you things another oak tree is unable to or won't tell you. Like humans, they can carry grudges, and they can feel entitled to proprietary information that they don't want you to have. You'll learn soon enough which trees are most helpful and trustworthy. Just don't decide which is which based solely on the species.

Another thing to keep in mind is what you had to remember about birds when you learned augury: there are many subspecies of trees, and each will have a character all its own. Keeping your tree records in a looseleaf binder where you can move the pages around is best. This will ensure that you don't confuse something one maple tree told you with another.

You will make special bonds with some trees, just as you would people you work with, and there will be others who never warm up to you as you'd like. As I said, they all have their own personalities, just as humans do. Not all Irish Americans are the same. Not all African Americans are the same. Don't expect all elms or maples to be the same either. They share characteristics and a sense of who is one of their own and who is not, but they all have different attitudes toward other species.

Record your experience each time you go to a tree, whether it's the same one or different ones. Add whatever notes you need to make so you will remember the details of the event. In your tree knowledge notebook you should also have the following entries about each tree encounter:

Type

Subspecies

Location

Damage assessment

Fear assessment

Approximate age

Day and date

Time of day

Moon phase

Weather

Gift offered

First approach scenario

Second approach scenario

How many approaches occurred before trust was established

What or who made the tree its home

What you were seeking

What the tree told you

Did your energy feel compatible?

Does it want you to come back?

Did it share its name?

The power inherent in words is drummed into a Witch from day one of his studies. We know that discovering or being given the true name of someone or something gives us a measure of power over it. Being given a tree's name is a great gift, an act of trust on the part of the tree. It may give you a special name that is not its true name. Call it by what it asks to be called. When and if it does give you its true name, treat that knowledge with respect and do not share it with anyone else. Remember, the tree trusts you. Don't ruin your relationship with it by abusing the information it shares with you.

The following is a list of knowledge I've gained from various trees, or information given to me by others who enjoy the companionship of trees. Use it as a starting point for gaining knowledge, remembering that until you put that knowledge to work for you and actually experience it for yourself, it will never become wisdom. Knowledge is surface fluff, static and still. Wisdom is dynamic, ever-changing magick in action.

TREE	KNOWLEDGE
Alder	One of the Celtic sacred trees. Its wood is strong and slow to decompose. Alder can teach you about strength and how to know when to fight or when to let something roll off you. The alder helps you overcome resistance to those things you cannot change. Celtic smiths used alder to stock their fires.
Apple	Apple trees are said to line the boundary of the otherworld in Celtic mythology. This is a tree that knows many secrets about nature and about connecting with the divine. It can advise you on spell preparation, and will offer both its flowers and fruit if you need them. Though it is beautiful and helpful, never forget that the seeds inside its fruit are a deadly poison.
Apricot	Ask this tree about romance, love, and humanity. Its expansive energies can teach us to love ourselves and others.
Ash	The world tree of Norse mythology is said to be an ash. The Celts also held it in reverence as one of their sacred trees. Ash helps you separate what something appears to be from what it actually is. It can also offer its branches for potent wands, but let it make the offer. Do not ask.
Aspen	The aspen is one of the most fearless trees and it can teach you about overcoming fears. If you're not sure what your own strengths are, ask an aspen to help.
Beech	The beech is a tree of patience and can help you learn to wait. It may even help you to discover what it is you really seek. The beech can also help you unmask your creative instincts.
Birch	A birch can help clear your mind so you can better think through a problem. It also calms and centers you so you can stay emotionally balanced through any ritual. Ask the birch how to overcome and correct past mistakes.
Cherry	The cherry tree bubbles with the energy of new life. It can help you change what you do not like about yourself. It can also impart lessons of the life cycles we must all endure.

TREE	KNOWLEDGE
Crab Apple	Though named for ugliness and age, this tree is always on a quest for beauty, inside and out. Ask it how you can learn to attain a nonjudgmental attitude with people and things.
Cypress	Cypress understands sacrifice and the many ways it has been handled and mishandled in human societies. Allow it to counsel you on when, where, and how any sacrifice should be made in order for you to attain your desire. It will never condone harming any living thing. The sacrifice asked will be something of yourself.
Dogwood	Though it blooms in spring with gentle pink blossoms, this is a tree associated with Mars, the Roman god of war. The dogwood can teach about deception and disguise. It can also help you with your astral projection if this is not one of your areas of strength.
Elm	There are several species of elm; all can help you learn the healing arts. Be cautious, for some elms have poisonous parts. In Norse mythology the elm is a symbol of the first woman, and the ash the first man. Allow the elm to teach you about the importance of polarities.
Elder	In western Europe babies were put to sleep in elder cradles to protect them from the faeries. Its blossoms and berries it will readily offer, but be cautious in taking them. The elder will expect you to be committed to the magick for which you asked its help. In Germanic mythology, the elder is a tree of the underworld and it can help you better understand this realm.
Hazel	Hazel is the traditional wood used for crafting divining rods. Ask the hazel to help you find what is lost, even if what you've lost is yourself. It also uncovers hidden wisdom.
Horse Chestnut	This tree assists us in clear thinking. The pods on it, known as buckeyes, are toxic if eaten, but feel free to gather them from the ground to use as protective talismans.

TREE	KNOWLEDGE
Linden	Once sacred to the rulers of Germany, this is a wishing tree, one which can teach us where to find our true happiness. It also helps us find ways to ease chronic ailments and where to seek our prosperity.
Magnolia	This tree shows us where beauty lies. Its fragrant blossoms are said to promote fidelity. Let this tree teach you about faithfulness and loyalty, or to help you uncover those who deceive you behind your back.
Maple	The maple is a tree of balance and harmony. Let it help you center and balance yourself.
Mimosa	This is a tree that helps you bring out your psychic self.
Mulberry	Teaches us how to communicate.
Oak	Oak is one of the sacred trees of the Celts. It's knowledgeable about discord, strength, and courage. Ask it to help you when tests of endurance arise.
Orange	Teaches us about the sweetness and sorrow of life, and how they intertwine.
Palm, Date	Gives advice on fertility, planting, reaping, and the weather.
Palm, Coconut	Teaches you lessons about inner beauty and gives advice on warding and psychic self-defense.
Pecan	Gives lessons on abundance.
Pine	Be aware there are a wide variety of pine trees. They can counsel you on the meaning of true abundance. They do not tolerate self-pity and will help you find your inner strength.
Peach	Teaches us about protection and how to turn knowledge to wisdom.
Poplar	There are several varieties of poplar. They can teach us about beauty and good use of the land.
Rowan	Another of the sacred trees of the Celts, the rowan helps us get over self-doubt and raises our self-esteem. They also teach us about self-protection.

TREE	KNOWLEDGE
Sycamore	Teaches us about the value of work.
Tamarisk	This tree is often used in banishment spells. Let it teach you how to decide what or who needs to be banished from your life so you can be set free to continue your spiritual growth.
Walnut	The walnut teaches us lessons about things that are hidden and when they should be revealed.
Willow	Sacred to the moon, the willow opens our psychic channels.
Yew	Sacred to Uller, the Norse god of archery, this tree is poisonous. Its lessons are those of sorrow and missed opportunities.

Augury and Advanced Divination

In the beginning you became acquainted with tarot cards, stones, lots, runes, scrying, sortilege, the I Ching, and possibly several other forms of divination. Whether you knew how they operated or whether you'd ever worked with them before was another matter. Not long into your Craft studies you were asked to select one you felt a strong draw toward and to make this your primary divination tool for the time being. Your teachers wanted you to get reliable readings before adding more learning to your already considerable tasks.

There are no statistics—or at least none of which I'm aware—to document which divination methods are most often chosen for a first study. My own experience tells me the tarot is the form most often chosen by the new student of Witchcraft. We are naturally drawn to the rich symbolism of the cards and they provide stimulation of the mind and the imagination, tweaking our intuitive natures. With hundreds of decks in print from which to choose, you can have—or even create—a deck that is perfectly in tune with your psyche, culture, needs, or one you just think is attractive.

As an intermediate Craft student you branched out, dug deeper, perhaps even wrote your own book of interpretations for various methods of divinations you studied. Still, you had your favorites, the reliable sources you could turn to for accurate readings. You even made notes on interpretations you found to be more accurate than the ones others found. This made sense to you. You are a unique individual, and you have affinities and talents all your own, so you will naturally find some unique interpretations of age-old divination devices.

Now as you stand at the threshold of advanced Craft practice, you're being asked to branch out even further, looking more deeply into both the natural world around you and into your tarot cards for greater guidance, clearer answers, and connection with the divine.

The Art of Augury

Augury is often misdefined as being any type of divination using objects or beings who inhabit the natural world. This is not true. Each type of divination with natural phenomenon has a name all its own. For example:

Apantomancy: Divination based on the sudden appearance of a creature in the wild

Aeromancy: Divination based on wind patterns

Austromancy: Divination based on sounds in nature

Botanomancy: Divination based on the manipulation of specific plants and trees

Capnomancy: Divination done by reading smoke patterns

Chiromancy: A fancy name for palmistry, or reading the lines and rises on one's hand

Critomancy: A sortilege type of divination done by tossing and reading grain patterns

Estrellomancy: Divination by reading shooting stars or comet patterns

Geomancy: Complex divination process using holes poked into fresh earth or sand

Herbomancy: Divination using herbs and other plants

Hippomancy: Divination done by examining the movements of wild horses

Hydromancy: Any divination process using water

Ichthyomancy: Divination using the movements or appearance of fish or of fish entrails

Lithomancy: Divination using gemstones or pieces of glass

Margaritomancy: Divination done by tossing stones

Meteoromancy: Divination using weather patterns

Nephelomancy: Divination by watching cloud shape and movements

Myomancy: Divination from the movement and appearance of rodents

Ololygmancy: Divination derived from the barking or howling patterns of wolves or dogs

Ophiomancy: Divination by examining the trails left by passing serpents

Ovomancy: Divination using eggs

Pegomancy: Reading the patterns of bubbles in natural springs

Pessomancy: Divination using the naturally occurring patterns on creek beds or river banks

Pyromancy: Divination using fire

Selenomancy: Divination using the appearance of the moon, named for Grecian lunar goddess Selena

Spodomancy: Reading pattern of embers and falling logs in dying fires

Zoomancy: General name for any divination using animals, principally mammals

Birds, Shapeshifters, and Otherworldly Guides

Augury as it is practiced in Witchcraft focuses on birds, a divination properly called orinthomancy, and their activities and immediate appearance and relationship to their environment. This involves other "mancies," including alueromancy, which examines the packing patterns of birds, and meteoromancy, the reading of weather patterns. A knowledge of the magickal and divinatory meaning of trees and plants is also useful.

Augury is documented back to Roman times and was used in Anglo-Celtic traditions both old and new. From Britain and Ireland, bird lore—particularly omens and portents—

came to the New World, where it is still in common use in the Appalachian and Ozark Mountain regions of the United States.

In many mythologies we see characters shapeshifting or being transformed into birds after a magickal experience or battle. This usually indicates a shifting of body or consciousness from this world to the otherworld. This does not necessarily mean a physical death has taken place, but may be interpreted as a shift to a higher level of consciousness.

Some auguries are dependent upon which trees a bird chooses to settle in, and a thorough study of augury requires at least a basic understanding of the magickal power of trees. For example, the bluebird has long been touted as a symbol of happiness, but what if you find one sitting in a yew tree? The yew is poisonous and associated with negative magick and the otherworld. Does this mean your happiness is not firmly settled yet, or that its foundation needs strengthening? Yet the yew is the world tree in some societies. What about if the bird is in an ash tree, another world tree? Does this mean your joy is assured in all worlds? Or how about a hawthorn bush, the quintessential faery tree? Is this omen telling you you may need to seek out the elemental kingdom to find the key to your happiness?

Many books have been written on the topic of magickal tree lore, and it is covered in some detail in chapter 12. It is a huge study in and of itself and is almost a requirement for advanced divination and for many advanced magickal rites. If you had good teachers, or access to a good bookstore or library, no doubt you started on this study as a beginner in the Craft.

The list that follows attempts to identify common birds and various meanings or omens they may represent. Keep in mind that many of these birds have hundreds of subspecies around the world. The duck alone has over 200 noted subspecies, each with its own swimming, migration, behavior, and flight patterns.

If you wish to embark on a serious venture into augury you will need to make notes each and every day of birds you see both in your environment and in your dreams or visions. You will need to do this for a full year so that you gain a sense of which birds appear at which times of the year, which migrate elsewhere, and which stay close to home.

Remember, too, that your particular area or region will have birds native only to your area. This is especially true of subspecies of common birds, such as the aforementioned duck. These local birds can tell you much when you look to them for help, but you first have to establish what they mean by keeping that year-long augury diary.

When making your augury notes it's good to include as much information as possible so that you have a complete picture of what was being shown to you. Consider including the following as a minimum:

Species

Subspecies

Gender, if possible

Unusual mannerism

Unusual coloring

Date and day

Time of day

Moon phase

Weather

Where seen

Associated deities

Type of roost (tree, phone wire, etc.)

Meaning of roosting place

Flight pattern

Flight partners

Behavior

Activity

Does species prey on other birds?

Does species mate for life?

Is species prolific?

Others of species nearby

Other birds nearby

World news of the day

Personal news of the day

Your health on the day

Your emotions on the day

Special events

Unexpected events

Plans or magick that succeeded

Plans or magick that failed

Rituals done and result

Remember that my list and yours may be very different. My notations of the birds I observe are dependent on the climate in which I live, which culture's legends I believe in, and the personal meaning the bird may have for me because of its status as a state or national emblem, through the experience of owning a pet bird, or from making nesting areas near my home to attract specific birds.

BIRD	MEANING
Blue Jay	Aggression, unnecessary fighting, beware of unexpected attack
Bluebird	Contentment, follow your dreams
Cardinal	Hardiness, adaptability, work rewarded
Crane, in flight	Transportation to otherworld

BIRD	MEANING
Crane, roosting	Imminent change, stormy times ahead
Crow	Sacred to Crone Goddess, magick of night, getting what you want; ill omen in southern Appalachia
Curlew	Danger on the horizon, caution to take cover and make sure you cannot be found at fault
Dove, in flight	Peace, solace, prayers taken to their source, creation, purity
Doves, in flight	More of good dove omens
Dove, roosting	Stagnation, challenges unmet
Doves, roosting	More of ill dove omens
Duck, in flight	Change, moving as environment changes, need to get on with work toward goal
Duck, swimming	Caution to beware of enemies, preparing for next onslaught
Ducks, swimming	Safety in numbers
Eagle, in flight	Travel into higher consciousness, movement between worlds
Eagle, roosting	Waiting to see which way the deities want you to go; longevity, protection
Falcon	Sacred to Odin in Norse mythology, used to travel to the otherworld; caution to look at the larger picture
Finch	Abundance, cordiality, regeneration
Geese, in flight	Sacred to Sun God, travel between worlds, harbingers of sacred change
Geese, on ground	Loss of connection to divine, change stagnating, possible loss
Goose, alone	Caution to wake up and realize what's taking place around you; sacred to war goddess Athena
Hawk	Many subspecies, generally a sign of change; observe behavior and surroundings to divine precise meaning
Heron	Sacred to moon; caution to find that which is hidden, night magick

BIRD	MEANING
Hen	Fertility, protection
Hummingbird	Abundance, prosperity, contentment; bigger is not always better; Basques believe if you see a hummingbird while someone is speaking you can be sure he is telling the truth
Kingfisher	Success in endeavors, good weather ahead
Lark	Seen in the morning is a positive omen, seen at night is a negative omen
Loon	Partnership, asking for assistance, going after the love you seek
Magpie	An old English Mother Goose verse tells us one magpie means sorrow, two are for happiness, three partnership or weddings, four foretells a birth, five or six herald wealth to come, and seven is for that which is hidden, or the thing "which cannot be told" (movement to higher consciousness?)
Martin	Community, partnership, teamwork; allowances for those who are not "up to speed"
Mourning Dove	Need for others, warning of change, consolation
Oriole	Chinese symbol of joy; harmony, balance, polarity, sexuality
Ostrich	Caution not to hide from or ignore what you do not wish to see or know
Owl	Many subspecies; generally associated with the night, moon, Goddess, wisdom, successful hunting, good divination skills
Parrot	Lack of creativity; caution of going for appearance over substance, longevity
Peacock	Sun magick, pride, going for what you want, showing off, leonine energy
Peahen	Camouflage, shyness, demurring or hiding one's talents, lunar energy waning
Pelican	Shapeshifting, hidden hostilities, making do with what you have

BIRD	MEANING
Penguin	Survivors, slow but steady, finding joy in what you are lacking, a turn away from materialism
Pheasant	Chinese omen of ill; generally a harbinger of bad news or poor weather
Quail	Good luck, renewal, sacred to Greek major deities
Raven	Sacred to Celtic battle deities, ill omen in Appalachia, change, death, shifting worlds coming together, the thinning of the veil
Rooster	Sacred to solar deities, harbinger of change, virility, aggression
Robin	Harbinger of change, abundance, rebirth
Sandpiper	Tenacity, water magick, look to other realms for assistance but be willing to do the work for yourself
Sparrow	Romance goes sour, look to higher consciousness for happiness
Starling	Weather omens associated with this bird, if low flying it will rain, generally an omen of contentment
Stork	Fertility, youth, childbirth
Swallow	Harbinger of change, general happiness
Swan	Otherworld in disguise, ability to move between worlds, the faery kingdom, faery royalty
Vulture	Caution to be aware of predators, or caution to know what is going on around you
Woodpecker	Harbinger of good news and positive change, note tree in which bird is seen to get some idea of the type of news on the horizon
Wren	Knowledge ready to turn to wisdom, an omen of good things to come because they've been earned

Power Animals and Animal Omens

Though other animal archetypes remain consistent throughout most of the world's cultures, there are some subtle differences. The best place to look for these is in the mythology of the Pagan tradition you follow or wish to follow.

For example, Celtic researchers and writers Caitlín and John Matthews have tallied up more than 150 different animals that appear in Celtic myths and legends alone, including mythical ones—and these are the myths of only one culture. There are five times that many creatures, and even more subspecies of creatures, that may appear in myths or come to you in a meditative trance or while astral projecting.

Another way to gauge any single animal's meaning to you is by your personal experience and feelings about that animal. For example, if you were bitten by a dog as a child, you may fear dogs and have a mental concept of them as aggressors rather than as protectors. A lot of people suffer chronic phobias toward specific creatures, such as spiders. Instead of seeing the spider as a symbol of the goddess of creation, who spun all things into being, they see only an eight-legged monster whose sole purpose is to torment or poison.

Be sure to take all these things into consideration when looking at an animal's archetypical profile to divine its full meaning for you or for whomever you are performing your divination.

ANIMAL	POSSIBLE MEANING
Alligator	Caution of hidden enemies, or caution to hide and create a battle plan of your own
Anteater	Thrift and resourcefulness
Antelope	Grace under pressure, or caution to move swiftly and silently away
Armadillo	Caution to put on your armor or to draw in your energies until danger passes
Badger	If you can't hide, turn and take a stand; take care of yourself
Bat	Rely on your sixth sense, look inward
Bee	Look outside yourself for answers

ANIMAL	POSSIBLE MEANING
Beetle	Sacred in Egypt; hidden magickal powers
Bear	Protective energy, awakening to new consciousness, battle animal in Celtic lore
Beaver	Industriousness pays off, teamwork, power of times in between
Butterfly	Need for self-change to find what you're seeking
Cat	Guardians at work, things hidden, looking inside yourself, nocturnal magick, working in partnership with others may not pan out, sacred to rulers of Egypt
Cricket	Communication is subtle, translate with caution, a turn to home and hearth
Coyote	Classic trickster in Native American lore, caution for the trick, or advise using your wiles to achieve your goals
Deer	Symbolic of wintertime abundance, swift, know when to fight and when to flee
Dog	Caution to stay on your path, friendship, protection, loyalty
Dolphin	Look to higher consciousness, beings from other realms offer assistance
Donkey	Stubborn attention to task at hand, caution to put all your will into effort if you want it to manifest
Eel	Hidden danger, treasure in places unexpected
Elephant	Symbol of royalty in Asia, strength, power in gentle presence, sacred beings offer aid
Fox	Look for ways to get around an enemy, or look for the enemy fooling you; astral projection, the shapeshifter
Frog	Power in the night, look to moon and water element for assistance
Giraffe	Gift of prophecy, use reliable divination to assist with problem
Goat	Surefooted animal who stands its ground

ANIMAL	POSSIBLE MEANING
Grasshopper	Go after your goal methodically in planned leaps and bounds
Groundhog	Industry, prophecy, harbinger of needed change
Hare	The shapeshifter, power of the Witch, consider changes that must be made to reach goal—are they worth the effort?
Hedgehog	Go inward for protection, seek answers within
Horse	Classic bridge between the worlds, battle, fearlessness, speed, independence
Jaguar	Main power animal of Native Central America, power in independence and the night, lunar magick can be potent
Lady Bug	Gentleness, help from Goddess, use feminine powers to win goal
Lightning Bug	The world of the fey, transportation to other realms, need for clearer sight into what is now murky
Lion	Male and female power in tandem, you can find what you seek and have it, power is in the clan's teamwork
Lizard	Power in camouflage, astral projection, the water, move swiftly and be ready to abandon material goal for better one or for personal growth
Lynx	Powers of second sight; look to past to understand present and plan future
Moose	Harbinger of winter and crone energy, end of a cycle, time for rest between efforts
Monkey	Agility, ability to surprise others with hidden talents, look below the surface
Mouse	Industriousness, attention to detail, knowing when to be still and when to move, beware of traps set by enemies
Opossum	Acting abilities needed for success, or caution to beware of lies and tricks

ANIMAL	POSSIBLE MEANING
Otter	Ability to move swiftly between realms, independence; sometimes fun is its own reward, share the bounty
Panther	Power in the self, reconsider partnerships
Porcupine	"Speak softly and carry a big stick"
Rabbit	Move in unexpected ways to avoid traps, know when to run and when to stand still, do the surprising, hidden aggression, fertility
Raccoon	Agility, theft, resourcefulness, consider using disguise to achieve goals, caution to look out for those appearing to you in false guise, the unfaithful friend
Salmon	Fish of knowledge and wisdom in Celtic mythology
Seals	Disguise of the water faeries in Europe, look to otherworld and its inhabitants for answers, be imaginative, try dream incubation
Skunk	Quiet respect, fearlessness, accuracy, take no chances when enemy approaches
Snake	Goddess power, regeneration, cycles of time, phallic symbol in some cultures
Spider	Sacred to the creator, industriousness, creativity, building networks, allow nothing of value to slip past you, lunar power
Squirrel	"Be prepared," reward for hard work, need for action
Stag	Message from the otherworld, sacred marriage
Tiger	Devotion to loved ones, knowing how to wait for the perfect time to strike, lunar and water powers are helpful, be ferocious when you must be
Weasel	Now is not the time to face problem head on, find a way around it and plan new approach
Whale	Creative power, power in the arts and their magickal energies, higher consciousness

ANIMAL	POSSIBLE MEANING
Wildebeest	Caution not to be the weak link, protection to be found within the circle of those who love you
Wolf	Loyalty, fidelity, family, teamwork, power of the group mind, the guardian spirit, power in times in between
Zebra	Adaptability, dependence on group for achieving goals, caution in travel

Advanced Tarot Divination

Astral projecting or pathworking into and through a tarot card is a time-honored practice, one considered advanced because of the many symbols and images the magician has to keep in mind in order to enter the card's world.

Late in your intermediate studies you may have been introduced to the tattwa symbols, old Aryan representations for the elements:

Earth	Yellow Square, sitting firm
Water	Silver Crescent, on its back
Fire	Red Equilateral Triangle
Air	Blue Perfect Circle
Spirit	Black Egg, upright on wide end

The most common technique for entering these elemental worlds is to make a set of the cards for yourself, select one, then gaze at it for several minutes while allowing yourself to sink into an eyes-open meditative state of consciousness. (I give complete instructions for making and using all twenty-five tattwas in my book *Making Magick* [Llewellyn, 1997]). When ready, look away from the symbol at some clear white area such as a blank wall, a hung sheet, or a movie screen. You will notice that the symbol is now in its complementary color, the one opposite it on a standard color wheel (for tattwa symbols and color wheel, see illustrations on page 38). In other words, red appears green, yellow appears purple, etc. Firmly set this image in your mind, close your eyes, and step into the elemental world.

For advanced divination with the tarot cards, you must first feel comfortable reading them for yourself and for others. If you still need a guidebook to look up a symbol or concept occasionally, this is fine. Better to be accurate than to make a mistake when you've gone to all the effort of doing a divination. You also need a good understanding of how the cards read as a flow—in other words, what certain cards mean in their relation to others that turn up in the spread. And, lastly, you need to have a good idea of what the card means when it is reversed. Don't make the mistake of thinking "reversed" always means "opposite." The meaning of a reversed card depends on where in a reading it falls, and what other cards surround it.

There are dozens of good books on tarot, and studying any of them can help you develop your own intuitive sense of any particular deck.

To perform this advanced divination, separate out the cards of the major arcana. These are the easiest to work with at first. Place them all facedown while you remain focused on the question or issue you want answered or clarified, then select one card and turn it over in an upright position.

Study the card's details to make sure you know it intimately, then close your eyes.

We will enter the tarot card just like we entered the tattwas, but we will not attempt to visualize each color as its opposite, though they may well appear to you as such. What you want is enough familiarity with a particular deck that you feel you can walk into the scenes depicted and interact with the characters.

This is best done by closing your eyes and visualizing every detail of the card. As you continue to observe with your mind's eye, allow the card to grow life-sized before you. Then see it thinning as if it were a curtain you could part and walk through. You might rather visualize it as becoming liquid so you can press your way through it, as you might walk through a waterfall.

The scene should come to life as soon as you enter. You should hear, feel, and see all that was on the face of the card, and the areas not shown on the card as well.

If you find your cards remain static and do not come to life for you, you might want to start with some guided meditations of the cards to help get you started. Yasmine Galenorn wrote a wonderful book, rich with Pagan symbolism, called *Tarot Journeys: Adventures in Self-Transformation* (Llewellyn, 1999). This is an excellent book to start with if you want to do advanced tarot work by entering the astral world in which the archetype you wish to examine resides.

You may remain in the card for as long as it takes to gather the information you want; however, be aware that the card itself may dictate to you when it has told you all it intends to tell. The dynamics of the card will slow down, beings will stop speaking or gesturing, or you may be led by someone back to where you entered the card. In some cases the card will freeze-frame itself and you will sense the veil separating its world from yours thinning so that you may step back through.

When the card has given up all the information it intends to for the time being, it is pointless to continue to stay. It's like watching a blank movie screen after the show is over and the credits have rolled. It's over.

What happens when you feel the need to leave the card before it has imparted all you ask of it?

First of all, make sure you're not wanting to leave because of an irrational fear or because the information you're receiving is not what you want it to be. There are some unpleasant scenes to be viewed in the cards, but these are symbols meant to give you information you have asked to have. They cannot harm you, though they can be disturbing at times.

This is when you have to remember Witchcraft 101 again: you are always in control. The cards tell us only of the future based on potentials currently set in motion. When we change that potential, we change the outcome.

If a reading is not clear, you may draw two more cards and try the divination again, but please be sure you're doing this to gain clarity and not because you don't like the answers. If this is your goal you may find the cards not communicating with you. They may stay in freeze frame rather than becoming dynamic, or no one may speak to you.

If you try three times and the answer is still not clear, put your cards away and try again in another twenty-four hours. It is traditional to ask the same question no more than three times in one sitting. To do more is considered impolite to the spirits of the cards. It also clouds your thoughts with too much information. The overload is hard to sort out and can confuse what started out as a clear reading.

the earth chapters

Where our powers live

fourteen

Advanced-Intermediate Magick

In the beginning of your magickal studies you were so thrilled to find that your simple candle or herbal spells worked that your bedazzled brain wouldn't dare peer around the next corner to look ahead. You felt at the top of your game, as if you were the most powerful being in the universe. Admit it, at that moment of first success all you wanted to do was toss a red cape over your shoulder and leap off a tall building while your rich tenor voice echoed across the sky with a rousing "Here I come to save the day."

Don't deny it. I was the same. We all were. Such is the emotional high that accompanies our first magickal success.

As an intermediate student of magick you found that bigger spells required bigger efforts, ones that sometimes seemed far beyond your skills. You began to be less enamored of your personal power, and even began to see magickal achievements come to manifestation more often and with less work, even when their setup and execution took more implements and more time.

You forced yourself to remember that the power at your disposal was intended to make you humble, not egotistical, and that those who use their magick without arrogance gain more from their efforts and are more likely to have their work blessed by the deities. You had to be reminded that magick and religion are not the same thing, though keeping the purpose of each straight sometimes muddled your mind.

In Witchcraft we use magick because we want to work with the flow of energy in the universe, to get closer to nature, and to bring about positive change in our lives, in the lives of those we love, and for our communities and country. While other religions' methods of effecting change may be prayer or chanting, ours is the positive manipulation of these natural energies.

In Witchcraft magick is never mandatory, it is simply part of what we are. At this point we had to stop thinking of the word "spell" as a noun. "Spell" is a verb, a process, an action intended to created an equal and opposite reaction. Basic physics—the stuff you learned in high school.

Magick is also not supernatural. We might on occasion think of it as paranormal because it operates on principles science cannot yet define, but those principles exist all the same. They have to exist or magick would not work. Magick must comply with the natural laws of the universe, just like everything else must comply, whether we understand those natural laws or not. Nothing supernatural can or does exist. Nothing.

As an intermediate you also learned to better distinguish between magick and mysticism. That which sought to bring desires into your world, the will you projected into other realms to obtain them, was magick, or what some magicians call thaumaturgy. That which sought to raise you up to the level of the deities, to connect with your creator, was a spiritual experience known as theurgy, or mysticism. Both in their own ways are forms of magick, but one seeks earthly goals and the other seeks spiritual goals. This does not imply that anyone is placing a value judgment on either magick or mysticism; it's just a factual statement of what is.

Is Magick Part of Advanced Witchcraft?

I debated for several months whether this chapter had any place in a book on advanced Witchcraft. If we go back to the definitions of an advanced Witch discussed by various Witches in chapter 1, virtually no one who has committed to this religion long-term mentions magick as a hallmark of advancement. We know there are such things as advanced spells, but they seem to coincide rather than cohabitate with our faith.

Anyone can do magick if they wish. The mechanisms are in place because that's the way the energy of the universe flows, and it cannot be tricked, fooled, or bypassed. Neither can the consequences of your magickal actions be avoided. Because this is a text for the advanced practitioner we will not dwell on magickal ethics, nor will we debate the often misunderstood aphorism, "The Witch who cannot kill cannot cure." Power is power and ever more shall be so. We draw from it and can do as we will, hopefully with a mind and heart set on harming none.

The best news I can give those of you already into, or ready to step into, advanced Witchcraft is that we will not use this chapter to digress by launching onto another long and tedious discussion of the magickal prerequisites that you've known and practiced for years.

The more you learn about your Craft, the more success you will have. Spells done with emotional input and with a desire to harm none rarely fail. If you think one of your spells has failed, go back and take a good look at all aspects of the spell and what you reaped from it. You may be surprised to find you got just what you asked for, whether or not it came in the form you intended.

When a spell fails, it fails for only one of two reasons:

1) Enough effort was not put into the original spell.

2) A greater will was opposing your will.

Enough with the preamble, and on to the advanced methods of making magick.

Five Basic Methods of Advanced-Intermediate Magick

True advanced magick uses the self as its only catalyst. Advanced-intermediate magick, such as the techniques we are discussing in this chapter, allows us to use multiple catalysts to assist us and to carry our energy born of desire over the long term. This is something beginners do not have the mental discipline to do until they have practiced for several years.

There are five basic methods of advanced-intermediate spellwork. They may be used individually or in combination as you choose. These are:

1) Using multiple catalysts

2) Sex magick techniques

3) Time bending

4) Ritualized spells

5) Long-term spellcrafting

USING MULTIPLE CATALYSTS

By the time of your first initiation you have already learned that true magick is inside you and not in anything you use to help you craft that magick. With the visualization skills you have developed as an intermediate Witch you can enhance your magickal workings by adding more catalysts to a spell. By catalysts we mean items that are used to help you focus and direct your magickal energy. These can be ritual tools, candles, stones, herbs, photographs, or a myriad of other items to help you get a clearer mental picture of your desired outcome. These have no power on their own, and cannot make magick happen for you until you charge them toward your goal.

When you are an advanced intermediate, you are ready to handle more complex visualizations and to keep in mind what the many items you have chosen to use as catalysts symbolize. Much of this is instinctive, a skill that grew from your years of Craft training.

Let's say, for example, you wish to do a spell to draw love into your life. You would want at the center of your altar a candle in a color that represents love to you. Common color choices are red, pink, and green. You might carve that candle with symbols of love and commitment using hearts and other mundane symbols, rune markings, oghams, or any other decorations that seem appropriate. You might wish to surround that center candle with magnetic sands or bits of rose quartz. If your goal is marriage you might add candles shaped like a male and a female, tying them together so as they melt they blend together as one. Plain white candles bound together with white thread work well as a substitute for these figure candles.

Around the outside of your center goal candle, you might add others to represent your other hopes for your relationship. You might add blue or white candles for fidelity, an apple for eternity, a geode stone for fertility (if you want children), a cup of wine for unity, a wedding ring doused with jasmine oil to draw love to you, lavender incense to put the essence of romance into the air, a pen to symbolize good communication, and an open book to represent trust.

You may add anything else you like, but since this is a spell of something you wish to draw to you, the more important symbols should be at the center of your altar, and the lesser elements toward the outside.

The opposite is true of a spell for something you wish to have taken away, such as a bad habit or an illness. Let's say you want to enact a spell to eliminate your debts. Start by placing green candles anointed with pine oil around the outside of your altar. These are the primary symbols of what you seek. You want debt removed from you, not drawn to you, so you place the most important parts of the spell nearer to the outside of the altar to push the debt away. Inside the ring of candles you might add photographs of successful people, old paystubs on which you've written yourself in a generous raise, and some coins for wealth. At the center you would place of symbol of you being debt free, such as a checkbook that shows lots of money and all your bills zeroed out.

The trick is to be able to keep all these catalysts and their symbolic meanings in your mind at the same time.

You should empower each catalyst individually prior to working your spell. This not only is easier on you, but allows you to put more time and focus into your spell. However, as you do the spell—always starting with the most important elements first—you will need to spend time visualizing and using words of power that incorporate all your catalysts. This takes practice, usually from past use of these items so that their representative meanings are impressed on your deep mind.

Any spell can be turned into an advanced spell by taking the basic blueprint, which as you should know by now is not meant to be slavishly adhered to but serves as an outline for a spell's enactment. Spells you get from someone else, or from a book on magick, should always be viewed as blueprints and not as rules. Use your knowledge, or find a book to help you, and you can add as many catalysts to a single spell as your mind can keep track of. If you have trouble coming up with more than one or two items, it may be time to step down a branch or two on that tree of life and do some more study in this area before pressing onward.

USING SEX MAGICK

Sex magick is often classed in the intermediate-advanced category because of its association with the Eastern arts of sexual magick known as tantra and kundalini, both of which allow for a mystical experience while magick is being made. The details of both of these arts have been written about by people who've devoted their lives to this study, and we can only skim them here.

Basic sex magick involves the creation of a symbol that the two partners agree represents their shared goal. The symbol can be as elaborate or as simple as the participants want it to be. What's important is that it symbolizes for them the desired outcome of their shared goal.

These symbols are studied and meditated over by the couple for several days until a mere glance at it evokes all the mental imagery and emotional desire of the end goal.

The symbol is then reproduced and placed in many strategic locations around the room where the sexual act will take place. You want it to be seen from any position in which you may find yourself. At the moment of orgasm you shouldn't be thinking about your spell, but about the joy and intimacy of having sex with your partner. This produces the strongest orgasms and therefore the strongest magick. As you climax, keep your eyes focused on the symbol you created. Your subconscious can handle the rest.

You can even try some basic kundalini techniques if you're familiar with the body's seven primary chakras and with the concept behind body posture magick. Various body postures in myths and folklore often represent some type of deity or elemental energy. In the art of kundalini, these two concepts unite.

No symbols are needed for this unless you wish to combine magick with your mysticism. The two partners should face one another, sitting cross-legged with their legs and arms wrapped around one another. Begin your sexual encounters with gentle touching and kissing, all the while maintaining this body posture. When you feel the first stirrings of sexual desire, envision it as a huge spiral of energy, or even as a sacred serpent, rising from the root chakra at the base of your tailbone and slowly rising through your belly.

As you continue teasing your partner with loving acts, visualize the kundalini energy moving snakelike into the navel chakra, lighting it, opening it, and charging it as a pathway to the divine.

As the energy rises through each of your chakras you will become more and more sexually aroused. At this point you should be seeing your partner not as just a man or a woman but as a representation of the God or Goddess.

When the kundalini energy reaches your crown chakra, allow it to intertwine with your partner's. This is symbolic of the union of God and Goddess in sacred marriage.

You may complete your sexual encounter at this time, then sit together while the kundalini energy unwinds and travels back down to the base of your tailbone, where you can ground it.

THE ART OF BENDING TIME

Today it is an accepted fact of physics that time does not exist outside of our known universe. In fact, time as we perceive it doesn't exist at all. We see it taking place in a linear fashion, or sometimes a cyclical manner, when in truth time is omnipresent with all past, present, and future occurring at once.

Because all time exists right now, a smart Witch can change the past to affect her present, just as she can affect the present to affect her future.

In a deep meditative state, go back to an event you wish to change or erase and visualize it happening differently. You will need to do this over and over to see true change taking place. For example, you may want to go back to a traffic accident and try to remove it from your space-time continuum. As your magick takes shape you may find your car was not damaged as badly as was first estimated, and you'll see injuries healing more rapidly or vanishing altogether.

Remember that you have all the time in world when it comes to making magick. You simply have to have the mind of an advanced Witch to see the power in simultaneous events. It's not easy, but it can be done.

RITUALIZED SPELLS

Basic ritual concepts and practices were probably the first thing you learned after your teachers were sure you had an understanding of the basic tenets and beliefs of the Craft. Whether you're enacting magick on your own or with a group, any form of ritualization can make the spell stronger.

The calling of the quarters, and perhaps even the cross quarters, and all the formality that accompanies such ritual allows you more time to infuse your spell with your personal energy and draws in the elements, deities, and any other helpful spirits to assist you.

The circular shape of your work area is a symbol of eternity and completion, and the ritual act tells your mind where you want it to go. Someone practiced in ritual can make any spell ten times as potent by adding ritual elements.

THE WAXING AND WANING OF LONG-TERM SPELLCRAFT

The closest thing to true advanced magick at the intermediate-advanced level is enacting a long-term spell. This is to be done for something you want that you know will not come to you quickly or easily. You will have to take this spell and work with it daily over several weeks, perhaps even several months.

Examples of this are when you are looking for a new home, seeking a life partner, or doing healing for someone with a chronic illness.

Of all types of natural magick, this is the one in which magical timing is the most important. Where you can do other spells anytime, knowing they are enhanced by using astrology but never harmed, the long-term spells work with the rise and fall of the lunar tides, and takes into consideration other astrological events.

Let's say you want to do a spell to seek a new love. You may wish to start on a full or waxing moon, gearing all your visualization, words of power, and other imagery to the idea of gaining love. When the lunar cycle turns to waning, you reverse your visualization to that of losing your loneliness.

You will be doing long-term spells daily if possible, even using everyday objects to assist with the rhythms in chants. The hum of a sewing machine, the rhythmic wobble of a photocopier, the drone of a computer—all can be tapped anytime without anyone else knowing what you're up to.

The only time you will not want to fully enact your spell will be when the moon is what is termed "void of course." This is when the moon has passed its last major aspect with another planet before moving into another zodiac sign. This is considered a poor time to begin any new venture and, unless you desperately feel the need to do the spell once more, these magickally neutral periods should be avoided.

MAGICKAL TIMING FOR LONG-TERM SPELLS

For long-term spells you will also want to pay attention to the energy of the days of the week and the sign in which the moon is traversing. Tuning into these by making subtle changes in your words of power or visualization can boost your spell's effectiveness.

Each planet has its own magickal affinities and arenas it governs:

Moon (Monday)	Goddess mysteries, the home, children, childbirth, fertility, divination, motherhood, psychicism, women, life cycles, dream magick, inner growth, astral projection, the subconscious, water magick, sleep, reincarnation, private matters, the night, the home, nocturnal creatures, peace, tranquility, nurturing, dancing, painting, general divination
Sun (Sunday)	God mysteries, employment, the law, leadership, prosperity, money, protection, strength, men, royalty, theater, entertain-

ment, the performing arts, heat, charity, volunteering, government, law, self-confidence, fire magick, personal power, physical
self-defense, warding, purification, public matters, banishing,
exorcism

Mercury (Wedn.)   Communication, the intellect, fickleness, healing, herbalism,
                  writing, wisdom, mental prowess, books, computers, reading,
                  gossip, vocal music, travel, correspondence, diplomacy, travel,
                  mathematics, the sciences, history, education, study, mass
                  media, visiting others, libraries, teachers, students, air magick

Venus (Friday)   Love, romance, beauty, family matters, interpersonal relation-
                  ships, peace, fashion, architecture, light amusements, intimate
                  social gatherings, shopping, friendships, gardening, fidelity,
                  emotions, music, pets, acts of kindness and generosity, art,
                  sculpture, poetry

Mars (Tuesday)   Anger, power, lust, construction, war, combat, sex, lust, cour-
                  age, banishing, medicine, passion, the military, conflict, fear,
                  police, soldiers, disagreement, physical exertion, competi-
                  tion, group power, group strength, machinery, carpentry,
                  bargaining power, needle crafts, endurance

Jupiter (Thurs.) Prosperity, money, employment, good luck, fair judgments,
                  friendship, investments, ambition, wealth, the law, prestige,
                  success, courtrooms, gambling, foreign interests, attraction,
                  astronomy, social events, psychology, the clergy, self-
                  improvement

Saturn (Sat.)   The hidden, past lives, transits, rebirth, self-undoing, lies,
                  mental and emotional distress, losses, the elderly, comple-
                  tion, spirit communication, excavations, archaeology, death,
                  morality, meditation, accepting or changing bad situations,
                  psychic self-defense, understanding karma

Using the Planetary Hours for Greater Precision

You can harness even more planetary energy by calculating the planetary hours of the day and night. This system of planetary hours dates back at least to the medieval period.

The concept is simple once you catch on. The planetary hours aren't whole hours except on the vernal and autumnal equinoxes. This system divides the hours of daylight and the hours of darkness each into twelve equal divisions so that "day" and "night" planetary hours may be calculated.

To calculate the moments when each of the hours begin and end, you will need a chart of the exact sunrise and sunset times for your location. These can be obtained from local television stations, local fish and game departments, or synagogues who all report these times to their immediate area. These times vary by latitude, so a chart reckoned for a city more than an hour to the south or north of you will be useless unless you plan to drive all that way simply to work your spell.

To figure an "hour," take the total number of hours and minutes of daylight and divide by twelve. This will tell you exactly how long each planetary hour will be from sunrise to sunset. Take the total number of hours and minutes of darkness and divide by twelve and you will get the length of each planetary hour from sunset to sunrise. In other words, there are twelve hours in every day (from sunrise to sunset) and twelve more every night (from sunset to sunrise). At the spring or autumn equinox every planet has exactly one hour of uninterrupted influence. At the winter solstice the night is longer, and every planet has about an hour and twenty minutes during the night, and about forty-seven minutes during the day.

The planetary hours chart you'll find here shows you the sequence of planets governing each planetary hour.

DAYLIGHT HOURS

	SUNDAY	MONDAY	TUESDAY	WEDNESDAY	THURSDAY	FRIDAY	SATURDAY
1	Sun	Moon	Mars	Mercury	Jupiter	Venus	Saturn
2	Venus	Saturn	Sun	Moon	Mars	Mercury	Jupiter
3	Mercury	Jupiter	Venus	Saturn	Sun	Moon	Mars
4	Moon	Mars	Mercury	Jupiter	Venus	Saturn	Sun
5	Saturn	Sun	Moon	Mars	Mercury	Jupiter	Venus
6	Jupiter	Venus	Saturn	Sun	Moon	Mars	Mercury
7	Mars	Mercury	Jupiter	Venus	Saturn	Sun	Moon
8	Sun	Moon	Mars	Mercury	Jupiter	Venus	Saturn
9	Venus	Saturn	Sun	Moon	Mars	Mercury	Jupiter
10	Mercury	Jupiter	Venus	Saturn	Sun	Moon	Mars
11	Moon	Mars	Mercury	Jupiter	Venus	Saturn	Sun
12	Saturn	Sun	Moon	Mars	Mercury	Jupiter	Venus

NIGHTTIME HOURS

	SUNDAY	MONDAY	TUESDAY	WEDNESDAY	THURSDAY	FRIDAY	SATURDAY
1	Jupiter	Venus	Saturn	Sun	Moon	Mars	Mercury
2	Mars	Mercury	Jupiter	Venus	Saturn	Sun	Moon
3	Sun	Moon	Mars	Mercury	Jupiter	Venus	Saturn
4	Venus	Saturn	Sun	Moon	Mars	Mercury	Jupiter
5	Mercury	Jupiter	Venus	Saturn	Sun	Moon	Mars
6	Moon	Mars	Mercury	Jupiter	Venus	Saturn	Sun
7	Saturn	Sun	Moon	Mars	Mercury	Jupiter	Venus
8	Jupiter	Venus	Saturn	Sun	Moon	Mars	Mercury
9	Mars	Mercury	Jupiter	Venus	Saturn	Sun	Moon
10	Sun	Moon	Mars	Mercury	Jupiter	Venus	Saturn
11	Venus	Saturn	Sun	Moon	Mars	Mercury	Jupiter
12	Mercury	Jupiter	Venus	Saturn	Sun	Moon	Mars

Magick and Ritual Using the Fine Arts

As a beginning student of natural magick you found it hard to think past the next spell. It was still hard for you to focus for longer than fifteen minutes, and group magick still worked better for you than solitary spells. By the time your year and a day of initial study was complete, you were a competent folk magician, a Witch who could make magick happen.

As an intermediate you finally realized what you'd been told from the start: the power is not in the tools and accouterments of a spell, but in the Witch who enacts them to life. The ritual implements are merely catalysts to share affinities with and help you focus upon your goal.

Suddenly your magick is like a supercharged ball. You give it a casual toss, and it rockets off in strange, new directions that you find both to easy to be real and too hard to bother with. This consternation is felt most by those who have an affinity or talent in one of the fine arts, or who are dedicated scholars in most any field. Something about using the fine arts as a bridge from advanced-intermediate magick to advanced magick seems as if you've just taken a wrong turn as you climb up those tree branches heading for the top.

Spiritual Advancement and Expression Using the Fine Arts

In many ways this chapter is Witchcraft 101 material; in others it ranks among the great mysteries of the Craft. I decided to place it in between the chapter on advanced-intermediate magick, which uses lots of accouterments and advanced visual-ization, and the chapter on advanced magick in which the Witch alone is the catalyst for change.

Music began with the earliest of protohumans, with percussion instrumentation as sticks and stones were struck together, producing rhythm. These crude instruments developed into drums and prompted people to dance, raising energy for magick and worship. These led to the construction of the first musical instruments in ancient Assyria, the lyre and the flute.

Egyptian and Etruscan sculptures and cave paintings in Europe that date to at least 4500 BCE attest to the interest our ancestors had in preserving their tribal legends, tell-ing heroic stories, transmitting their values to their young, making magick, and praising the deities, such as when a hunt was successful. Dancers mimicked these animals, and the arts kept intertwining.

In Greece, the Eleusinian mysteries indulged in ritual dramas that told the stories of the gods. Later, when markings on stone, wood, or papyrus were used, characters were created that made the spoken language visible to the human eye so that a story could be retold again and again without change.

When enacted with a sacred purpose, choreography, writing, poetry, music composi-tion, drawing, painting, sculpting, acting, puppeteering, singing, and recording actions are all forms of inner alchemy. Like meditation, they allow your mind to transcend earthbound reality and soar into the realms where true changes can occur.

That such simple acts can bring about such profound change strikes many as unusual, especially when you've worked so hard thus far to get to this point. This is one of those things "which can never be told." It has to be experienced, and as we travel through this and the next chapter, experience it you will.

Once Upon a Time . . .

According to classical mythology, a race of deities known as the Titans ruled ancient Greece. In a massive battle the Titans were defeated by the Hellenic deities who replaced them, with Zeus being the supreme god who made his home at the top of Mount Olympus, where the divine pantheon of the Greeks found their inspirations.

The deities were so thrilled with their victory that they asked Zeus if there wasn't something he could do to create some method of preserving the full glory of the story of their victory.

The result of this request was the birth of the nine Muses.

Zeus lay with Mnemosyne, the goddess of memory, for nine consecutive nights. When the Muses were born they were divine beings who ranked somewhere beneath the rest of Greece's gods and were charged with assisting humanity to learn their arts so that the whole world could recount its stories in song, story, and art. They were each given their dominions and symbolic totems, and were collectively symbolized by the nightingale, a bird known to make sweet song.

It's also interesting to note that the symbol of two of the most powerful Muses live on in modern theater. The twin harlequin masks of comedy (Thaleia) and tragedy (Melpomene) that symbolize the dramatic arts first belonged to the Muses. Their symbols were appropriated by the theater to inspire performance magick.

The names and transliterations of the Muses vary by translation, but there are almost always nine of them, headed by Calliope, the firstborn and most powerful of the nine.

THE NINE MUSES

Muse: Calliope. *Meaning:* Fair-voiced. *Arena:* Poetry, epics. *Symbols and Affinities:* Writing implements, wind. *Tarot:* the Hermit; the firstborn of the Muses. *Anathemas:* Discordant sounds.

Muse: Cleio. *Meaning:* The proclaimer. *Arena:* History. *Symbols and Affinities:* Scrolls, pens, memory, bards. *Tarot:* Justice; some myths call her the mother of the Sirens. *Anathemas:* Lies, blemishes, injustice.

Muse: Euterpe. *Meaning:* Giver of pleasure. *Arena:* Music. *Symbols and Affinities:* The flute. *Tarot:* the Magician, the Fool. *Anathemas:* Refusal to enjoy the gifts of life.

Muse: Melpomene. *Meaning:* Singer. *Arena:* Tragedy. *Symbols and Affinities:* The sad mask of the twin harlequins representing tragedy and comedy in theater. *Tarot:* the Chariot, the Moon, Temperance. *Anathemas:* Frivolity—she prefers those in deep contemplation.

Muse: Polyhymnia. *Meaning:* She of many hymns. *Arena:* Drama, art, mime. *Symbols and Affinities:* Halos, all sacred books, reborn deities, sacred music. *Tarot:* the High Priestess. *Anathemas:* Those who use her gifts without honoring their sacred source.

Muse: Terpsichore. *Meaning:* The whirler. *Arena:* Dance, lyric. *Symbols and Affinities:* The lyre. *Tarot:* the Tower, Death or Change. *Anathemas:* Those who do not help themselves but want others to do for them.

Muse: Thaleia. *Meaning:* The flourisher. *Arena:* Comedy. *Symbols and Affinities:* The laughing mask of the twin harlequins representing comedy in the theater. *Tarot:* the Chariot, the Sun, the World. *Anathemas:* Sadness—she cannot abide those who refuse to enjoy.

Muse: Urania. *Meaning:* Heavenly one. *Arena:* Astronomy. *Symbols and Affinities:* The globe and maps of the heavens. *Tarot:* the Wheel of Fortune. *Anathemas:* Those who do not seek the answers that lie before them.

Muse: Erato. *Meaning:* Romantic love. *Arena:* Love songs. *Symbols and Affinities:* Bow and arrow. *Tarot:* the Lovers. *Anathemas:* Magick used to destroy love.

In a few stories there are three additional minor Muses:

Aoide, the Muse of Singing

Melete, the Muse of Rehearsal

Mnene, the Muse of Remembering

Finding Your Muse

Because the Muses are charged with assisting humankind to excel in the arts, they can be easier to evoke and invoke than many other deities. Fine artists of all types have claimed to be blessed by their Muse. This usually happens when the inner spirit or collective unconscious seems to take over the creative process and, though the artist still labors, it seems as if a partner is at work within, guiding their way. It was fashionable until the late Middle Ages for poets to end their works by thanking their Muses for their gifts of inspiration.

As the Muse legends spread throughout Europe just ahead of the rise of Christianity, many of the Muses were reduced to demigods, evil faeries, or demons to whom your soul would belong should you seek inspiration from any other than the Christian God or one of his appointed archangels.

One example of such a distortion is the Leanansidhe of Ireland. It is a certainty that she was once a goddess of poetic inspiration similar to Brighid, or St. Bridget, but while Brighid's sainthood and forced connection to the Virgin Mary made her a "safe" source of artistic inspiration, Leanansidhe became a vampire who sucked the lifeblood from those who came to her for their inspiration.

Today those in the arts still seek their Muse. Most of them use the term while remaining unaware of the importance of the Muse to the arts, yet the term continues to be used, especially by ballet dancers, poets, and Pagan artists of all kinds.

Writing and Using Story Spells

The process by which writing took over from oral storytelling tradition was slow. Part of this was because paper was expensive to make and hard to get. Another problem was that markings we think of as letters were at first treated as sacred objects, something that should not be out of the hands of the clergy. This also allowed Europe's myths to be written down by the conquering religion, making subtle changes that the advanced Pagan eye can still see. It was through the oral repetitions of the peasantry's faery tales where Craft lore was preserved.

With the exception of Catholic clergy and a few of the nobility and royalty, the population of Europe was illiterate until the nineteenth century when reformers—mostly women—worldwide sought to change the worlds of children, taking them from the workhouses and farm fields and placing them into classrooms where they could learn.

Learning alone does not make writing easy. When American novelist and screenwriter F. Scott Fitzgerald (1896–1940) was asked how he wrote, he said he sat down at his typewriter, rolled up his sleeves, and opened up a vein.

Story spells don't have to be difficult; you need only to be infused with your will. In fact, the less detail you put into them the better. Keep in mind that magick, like all forms of energy, follows the path of least resistance. You don't want to be so detailed in your story that you hinder your progress.

When I was thirteen I got into a loud argument with another girl right in the middle of the classroom. I fumed for the next two hours, barely able to contain my anger and needing to take it out on someone or something. Fortunately, I had a wonderful social studies teacher who was wise enough to understand I had to find an outlet for my anger or it was only going to grow until it erupted again.

She took me into a corner of the teacher's lounge and sat me down in front of a pad of paper and a pen. "Write it out," she said. Then she left to go back to her classroom.

At the end of that period I had amassed seven pages of vitriolic prose. My teacher returned and folded up the papers. She said she wouldn't look at them and that I should go back to class. As much as I wanted to still be outraged at the girl who made me mad, I found I could no longer summon up the righteous anger I had earlier. It had been poured into those seven sheets of paper, which were destroyed a week later. It was an effective spell—though I didn't know it at the time—that channeled dangerous energies from me into an inanimate object.

The simple act of making lists is an easy variation on the story spell. I keep a personal journal as well as a Book of Shadows. In my journal I keep a running list of things I want to achieve in different areas of my life. I tweak and change it almost weekly as the items on the list come to fruition or take me in a new direction that is even better than I first envisioned.

It took me a long time to realize the ongoing list in my journal, which I have headed THE PLAN, was a form of story spell. Listed in chronological order, I take broad ideas of where I want to be and what I want to be doing as far into the future as five years from now and make my notes. Many times I have been surprised when steps are skipped over and I land in a spot further down on the list than I intended. This is usually a good thing, as I am that much closer to my ultimate goals. I've also found that sometimes writing out my desires puts them into perspective and I'm not getting what I want confused with what I need. That makes the magick work all the faster.

Writer and speaker Marion Weinstein, author of the popular book *Positive Magic* (Phoenix, 1980), writes of a system of "List Moons." Every third full moon, usually the one closest to the nearest sabbat, she sits down and makes a list of things she wants, needs, or would like to accomplish. This is part of her esbat ritual. She keeps the list until the next List Moon, crosses off the completed items, and makes a new one.

As with all magick, simply writing down ideas won't do the work for you, but because words are symbols they speak to the subconscious mind and tell it what it is you want. The subconscious then tries to make it happen, whether it is in your best interest or not. You help it by working toward your goals in the physical world.

Music and Song Spells

Since music was first written down by composers in early Assyria, people have felt its magick move them to tears, cheers, or laughter. Music's ability to evoke emotion, stir memory, soothe anger, bring out tenderness, arouse warriors for battle, rally partisans for a campaign, prepare congregations for worship, and tell a story have all been noted and used everywhere for many, many centuries. If you have any doubts, just look to the various popular songs of World Wars I and II that sought to inspire and console.

One of my closest friends, and fellow Witch, did her master's thesis in musicology at the University of Texas on the spiritual dimensions of music, focusing on the area that is now modern India and Pakistan. The research required looking into how the ancient Aryans believed individual notes, chords, or intervals affected the human psyche. She also discovered many mathematical correlations to individual notes. Most interesting was noting how a standard key of C major scale correlated with the seven chakras, or energy centers, of the human body. Middle C (the center white key on a standard piano) represented the root chakra, and the next highest key the next chakra, etc.

NOTE	CHAKRA	ACTION
C	Root Chakra	Beginning
D	Navel Chakra	Discord and Will
E	Solar Plexus	Creation and Energy
F	Heart Center	Growth and Emotion
G	Throat Chakra	Accord and Unity
A	Third Eye Chakra	Separation
B	Crown Chakra	Resolution

The Aryans also noted that when a chord or selection of harmonies was diminished, augmented, or otherwise manipulated, it produced other new emotions or physical reactions. These were noted in great detail and matched to deities, emotions, desires, animals, and other creatures and ideas, much like Aleister Crowley's compilation *Liber 777* has for the Western magickal traditions.

Her research showed that certain harmonies were supposed to evoke specific emotions, including sexual arousal. Though neither she nor anyone in class during her presentation admitted to experiencing randy feelings when she played some of this music, it's an interesting area to ponder, one almost as powerful as verbal or visual subliminal programming.

Of course the debate rages on about how music used to sound, and this is not an argument likely to ever be solved. Some researchers claim that even when we reproduce the instruments of the past, align them with tuning forks so they are what we now call "perfect pitch," and play from the original scores, the music has to sound different today.

Others argue that there is little or no difference in the sounds, but that cultural differences affect how music stirs us. Perhaps only in India would the music my friend played be arousing because those who were acculturated there were taught to be stirred.

This is certainly true in the case of military music. Strike up the band with the official songs of the various branches of the armed forces, or play a nation's anthem, and watch the divisions that normally separate these people melt away as the music unites the partisans in a common emotion.

To use music for magick you don't have to be a composer. Take a tune you like, preferably one to which no lyric has ever existed, and use it as a symbol of your magickal goal. Hum it, play it, or put your own words to it to create your own magick.

If you are interested in delving deeper into this subject without becoming mired in too much techno-jargon and mathematics, I recommend R. J. Stewart's *The Spiritual Dimension of Music* (Destiny Books, 1987, 1990) and Joanne Crandall's *Self-Transformation Through Music* (Theosophical Publishing House, 1986) as excellent resources. Both contain more practical information than can be contained in this single chapter.

Dance Spells

Dancing was such an integral part of ancient worship that the early Christian Church dubbed it an evil act, one which induced lust and caused people to come under influences other than that of the church.

They were right.

The Sufis of old Arabia, known as the whirling dervishes, were an early sect in the Middle East who used ecstatic dance in their worship. Modern Judaism still celebrates the annual festival of Simkhat Torah (Celebration of the Torah) where the sacred scrolls are taken from their arks, paraded around the synagogue, and honored with song and dance.

We all have an emotional response to dance, just as we do to the music that accompanies it. In the past, dance was not only used in early worship but in early social gatherings. Interest in social dance is on the rise again today with modern ballroom dancing, now being called DanceSport, on the verge of its debut as an Olympic sport. Dance has also been used to express antisocial ideas by many countercultures, most recently that of the youth peace movement of the 1960s.

In Iris J. Stewart's well-researched and beautifully photographed book *Sacred Woman, Sacred Dance* (Inner Traditions, 2000), she constructs a thesis that dance was once the realm of females who used body movement to invoke the goddesses. As humanity's first language, movement was sacred, and to her credit Ms. Stewart carries her strong argument into modern times to the circles of our modern Witches and other New Age groups who seek to awaken their inner spirit through specially choreographed movements.

Those who cannot dance can view these pictures or create dances in their minds and work through them, as in a pathworking. Eric Franklin, author of *Dance Imagery for Technique and Performance* (Human Kinetics, 1996), shows how professional dancers can use mental imagery to improve their performance. The concept intrigued me and I bought the book for myself. The entire tome is creative visualization at its finest and would work for anyone wanting to work with the Muse of dance, whether or not they possess any talent or ability.

Art and Sculpture Spells

The Great Sphinx of Egypt.

Rodin's *Thinker*.

The *Mona Lisa*.

Michelangelo's *David*.

The Sistine Chapel ceiling.

Whistler's mother.

Great works of art and sculpture are known around the world. There seems to be a magick in the work itself, the ability to take a palette of wet colors or a lump of clay or stone and turn it into a thing of beauty recognizable to others.

Sand paintings and drawings designed to be destroyed in ritual are used frequently in modern magick. Blessed by the Muses, these temporary works of art can be sent onto the wheel of existence to be returned as magickal fulfillments.

There's something almost therapeutic about creating something, even when you have no talent. Show an adult a coloring book and big box of crayons or a piece of modeling clay and watch them play like children. Those of us who know how to infuse these works with magick can create potent spells with very few accouterments and catalysts.

Modern medicine uses art to help discover what lurks in the subconsciousness of troubled patients, or to help those with physical disabilities regain their lost dexterity.

Ritual Drama

Ritual drama is believed to have originated in ancient Greece in the temples of the Eleusinian mysteries to commemorate the return of Kore from the underworld as spring approached. This is a difficult one to do alone unless you do it on the spirit planes.

Most covens who do ritual drama do it to honor the life cycles of the deities and not to provide a magickal vehicle for one of their members. Alone, or with a single loved one, you should have no trouble making this work. Call on your Muse and let her guide your words and actions to avoid cluttering the path of least resistance.

From the Fine Arts to Advanced Magick

It's time to shed the masks, the tragedy and comedy, put away the wands and athames, the paint jars, the books, and move into the world of true advanced magick.

Some surprises lie in store for those of you not already working at this level, but if your mind set is where it should be and you can make the work in the next chapter successful, no one would deny you the title of Honored Venerable Elder Witch.

Advanced Magick: The Art of Wishcraft

If you are a beginning Craft student reading this book you may be surprised, confused, or even outraged that this is one of its smallest chapters. In your first year and a day of study you probably couldn't get enough of the implements of the Craft. You loved their witchy feel and the atmosphere of gentle power they gave you. You couldn't wait to find your first wand or buy the perfect athame, and imagined that once you'd mastered the magickal arts your altar would look something like a fictional wizard's medieval tower temple.

If you're an intermediate student you're likely not so surprised by the relative shortness of this chapter. Perhaps you're already advanced enough to have experienced the magick that is you.

That's right—magick doesn't just flow through you, it *is* you. You are the ultimate catalyst for your spells.

Many Witches who have been diligently practicing their faith find that they get what they really want and need just by continuing to live their lives within the ethical boundaries they set for themselves. They meditate daily, observe the esbats and sabbats, and honor and serve their deities. They become a great conduit of positive energy flow that attracts what they want, and they send on more positive energy for others to draw from. The wheel turns and things just get better for everyone.

At this point you may even find out you don't need or want all the ritual tools you took so much time and effort to acquire.

Kerr Cuhulain, author of *The Wiccan Warrior*, sent me an e-mail saying he likes to look back at the early entries in his Book of Shadows and is amazed to note that all the accouterments, gestures, and ritualized effort he put into his early spells mean little now in comparison to the life he lives. He has become a conduit of a positive energy flow that benefits not only himself, but all those whom his life touches.

You don't have to give up using your traditional tools if you don't want to. I have a special zodiac-style wand I made from a three-foot dowel rod in my intermediate days that I enjoy using. It feels good in my hands. It's familiar and warm and makes me feel good to have it nearby, but I don't rely on it for crafting spells.

What Is the Secret of Advanced Magick?

Once again, the secret is that there is no secret. Talk with some long-time practitioners via one of the Internet chat rooms or use groups. Advanced magick comes to you through living as a Witch, and begins with what Sybil Leek called "seeing to your own house first."

Though she meant this as a metaphor for putting the major aspects of your life in order before you embark on your initial year-and-a-day study of basic Witchcraft, you can also take her advice literally. Having your gingerbread cottage, your office, or any-where you spend lots of time in some semblance of order and beauty helps provide what I call *soul peace*, the deep-down, satisfying sense of comfort that makes your chakras shine and opens you as a conduit for that positive magick flow.

This is where you discover that all the things you thought were the right way to do something have new rules. For example, the times in between that we are taught hold the power of magick because their place in the universe is mutable or hard to define can be tossed out. We are always at some time in between, just as we are always at some place in between.

You also realize now the truth of the all the talk about the process being just as important, if not more so, than the end result. Psychologist Carl Jung called this realiza-tion the "process of becoming"—a necessary step, he believed, to achieving the higher level of physical and spiritual existence known as "individualization."

Spells are now processes, even long after the goal has been won. You no longer have just the knowledge that the word *spell* is a verb and not a noun, but you have that wis-dom. Now your processes work better for you because you've lost the anxiety newcom-ers often feel toward their first spells.

The breath control, mind control, and body postures that seemed so hard to master at first are second nature to you. You may have a bad day every now and then, but for the most part your efforts at entering a meditative state of consciousness begin to happen as soon as you think about it. You breathe on an object and immediately infuse it with your energy. You think about something and it starts to take shape. You make plans and find them taking on a life of their own. Channeling your magickal energy just seems to happen in accordance with your will, your true will. As you think about things and live your life in harmony with the deities you serve, you find you ask for less but you gain so much more.

This point in the Craft career is also where you start to discover other disciplines that you merge with your magickal and mystical practices. For instance, many Pagans have discovered the Asian art of Feng Shui and are using its principles to help clean up the disordered areas of their lives. Feng Shui teaches that each section of a room or place you occupy shares an energy attachment to a specific area of your life. In this way it is not too much different than laying a map of the twelve houses of the zodiac over your home and looking to see which region of your home is lying within each specific house, and which ones most closely relate to which part of your life.

In fact, if Feng Shui is not your thing, try using a drawing of the twelve houses in Western astrology as your template instead. There are some variations in locales, but I've found this method works better for me than Feng Shui, and maybe it would for you, too.

A profusion of books on Feng Shui are available right now, from the technically complex to the Keep It Simple Stupid schools of thought. I have three that I use and recommend. The first is Richard Webster's *Feng Shui for Beginners* (Llewellyn, 2000), which outlines the two major methods of Feng Shui. Then there is Terah Kathryn Collins' *The Western Guide to Feng Shui: Room by Room* (Hay House, 1999), which takes some of the Asian mystique from the process. I also love *Sacred Space: Clearing and Enhancing the Energy of Your Home* by Denise Linn (Ballantine, 1995), which is not a book on Feng Shui or Witchcraft but still teaches the importance and methods of arranging your living space to give yourself the soul peace in which you can live, work, and make magick with success.

In Feng Shui you mentally take a basic layout (see illustrations, next page) and place it over the area in which you're working. Each region in the layout corresponds to an

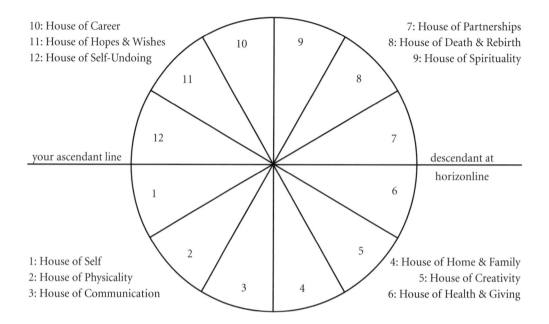

10: House of Career
11: House of Hopes & Wishes
12: House of Self-Undoing

7: House of Partnerships
8: House of Death & Rebirth
9: House of Spirituality

your ascendant line

descendant at
horizonline

1: House of Self
2: House of Physicality
3: House of Communication

4: House of Home & Family
5: House of Creativity
6: House of Health & Giving

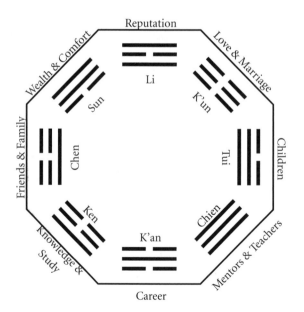

The standard natal chart with corresponding houses (top) and the Feng Shui layout (bottom)

area of your life and also to a specific set of lines that make up a glyph in the I Ching, or the Chinese Book of Changes. Going into the details of the I Ching is beyond the scope of this book, but reading what each glyph has to say about the area in which you're working, and the divinatory work that can be done with the book, can be successful.

The basic idea is to look for clutter or items that block the flow of positive energy, called chi. Mirrors, fish bowls, and lights (among other things) all help the flow. Items with hard edges, dark areas, disorganized space, or no windows or mirrors can all impede chi and keep that corresponding area of your life in turmoil.

Other ways to see to your own house are just to keep it neat and clean. Love it because it's your space whether it's large or small. Use the power of color energy—another Wicca 101 lesson—to increase your comfort.

Decorate to your taste and no one else's. This not only includes color but items you wish to use as accent pieces and overall style. You can be as rigid or eclectic as you like. This is *your* order and beauty and, the power of chaos not withstanding, it shouldn't be the concern of anyone else. I recently saw a wall hanging in a craft store that said, "If you're coming to see me, you're welcome anytime. If you're coming to see my house, make a damn appointment."

Incense is another way to help clear your home of negative energy. Popular incenses for clearing are:

Frankincense

Cinnamon

Cedar or Pine

Sandalwood

Myrrh

Spiritual habits are also important to advanced practice, and many advanced Witches are in the habit of setting aside some portion of their day for devotions. I can't imagine a single day going by when I don't at least think about my patron goddess and speak with her, even it's only a brief "thank you for helping see me through another day." My connection to her is that vital to my life, and I probably speak with her and spend more time with her than I do interacting with any human individual. And, yes, I *do* have a life—a busy one. That's why taking that time to commune with the deity you serve is so vital. And, by the way, try charting the amount of time you actually spend interacting with others during an average day. Then mark out the amount of that time where communications of true importance or intimacy are exchanged. You'll likely discover the sad but true fact that your time spent meaningfully with others is much less than you think.

Your devotions or time spent with your deities doesn't have to be long, formal, or ritualized if you don't want it to be. It can be as simple as saying a brief prayer upon awakening or going to sleep. This is not the time to ask your deities for what you want, but to honor and praise them. After all, it's you who serves them, not the other way around.

Not making direct requests has the side benefit of helping you learn to know yourself as each day passes. When you know yourself, it's easier to know what you really want so you don't get that "be careful what you wish for or you just might get it" rebound.

Wishcraft Forever!

Advanced magick doesn't mean more complexity. In fact, it means just the opposite. Advanced magick is:

Simpler

Connected to the web of being

Living in harmony with all beings, and

Being what and who you are.

By knowing yourself you gain a sense of soul peace. This doesn't mean your life is perfect or that you're always clear about your personal goals, but that you take time each day to contemplate your life and to thank your deities for what you have been given in life this far. We can all find those worse off than ourselves, and it's easy to forget that we have lots to be thankful for already.

Janet Farrar and Maggie Shayne, both well-known writers and Witches, have noted that they no longer enact spells as we normally think of them, at least not often. They find, as I have found, that things come to them through wishing and spending time thinking about that wish. They tend to focus more on what they really need, not just what they want. In contrast to many wants, needs are those things which make us truly happy, give us soul peace, and allow us to live satisfying lives.

Other advanced Witches also confess to no longer performing elaborate spells, but that what they desire seems to weave itself into their lives as if—as if by magick! As advanced Witches we find our energies in such harmony with all that is that we can't help but draw our desires to us. The channels are clear, and the path of least resistance runs right from our thoughtforms to our physical lives.

It's only been in the last two years—maybe less—that I've noticed how this has worked for me. Two recent examples from my own Wishcraft concerned my job. I am a licensed stockbroker, and almost believe the word "stress" didn't exist until the New York Stock Exchange opened for business in 1792. Unless you've been living under a rock, you're aware the market took a huge dive in April 1999 and has been on a wild rollercoaster ride ever since. Concerns for preserving capital caused a lot of investors to pull back into more conservative investments such as government bonds. This caused an even greater drop in the open market as money shifted from equity investments to fixed income and the money flow began to slow, prompting the drop in interest rates.

Stockbrokers, registered support staff, general principals, operations managers, and other licensed investment professionals began to notice the money flow slowing, but not the influx of calls from investors asking for opinions and assistance. I was nervous. I knew the industry was talking about inevitable layoffs, and at the time, though I was doing work requiring a securities license, I was not working in an area of the brokerage where I was bringing in appreciable assets. After several weeks of fretting and sensing trouble approaching, I made a simple "job security" talisman and placed it deep inside my desk at work.

Mostly I thought about my job. I didn't think of this as being magick, but it was feeding my spell all the same. I was weighing the pros and cons. I was considering options. I was worn out. I spent lots of time thinking about the ten years I'd put in of falling markets, trading deadlines, other time-critical issues, and handling millions of theoretical dollars each day. I thought about the terror of thinking you made an error on a billion-dollar institutional trade.

I also thought I was crazy to be doing what I was doing. There is a reason most successful brokers are either young or started young, and why heart attacks and burnout plague the industry. A telling example is, for instance, if I were to commit assault, the incident would be reported to the Exchange and I could lose my license. However, if a psychiatrist decided to commit me to a mental institution, this was not a reportable incident and I would not lose my license. The whole industry was nuts.

A month later I was the first of many to be laid off from a major international investment firm.

But my spell worked.

How can I say that when I was not only laid off, but was the first person to go?

Because I was one of the first to be laid off, I had more opportunity to take a look around town at other niches of the investment world requiring a licensed professional but which didn't depend on daily trading to make ends meet. Because of this I was one of the first to apply at an investment advisory firm that needed another licensed employee. The job was less stressful, paid more, and because advisory services tend to be more buy-and-hold oriented and fee-based rather than depending on commissions, the job was much more secure.

I had been wanting to write full time for many years, but it just never seemed the right time to make the leap. Moreover, I'd become used to a double income and, no matter how much hard work I put in, it seemed worth it—for a while. Then I became ill. Chronically ill, and the energy to do one job was hard to muster. There was no way I could do two. The more I tried, the sicker I became.

I knew I wasn't giving my best to either my writing or my other employer. I kept thinking about what I should do and when; my mind seemed to constantly be wrestling with the problem.

Then, bang! Another downsizing. I decided that rather than allow someone to lose their job who really needed it, I would volunteer to bow out and take my chances on my own.

I'm still not as healthy as I want to be, but I know with my magickal will backing me that wholeness and well-being are coming my way at this very moment.

The spell worked. The non-spell worked. The trick now is to have faith in the powers that created this chance for me, the process, and the success.

"That's All, Folks"

If this chapter is too short for your taste, I apologize, but that's about all there is to say about real advanced magick. You don't achieve it through complexity, but through simplicity and by living in harmony with the flow of energy surrounding you. It takes time to learn the Wishcraft art. It's one skill that cannot be rushed by reading lots of books or doing lots of spells. It comes with true elderhood, with growing in your Craft, with amassing learning and gaining power but still finding it humbling.

This definition of elderhood does not refer to a degree given for some tasks or accomplishments, but as a reward from the web for spending positive time within it learning and growing. Elder power flows to you naturally as you live your daily life as a Witch, year in and year out, until you not only believe yourself to be a positive conduit on the wheel of all that is, you know it.

Experience.

Knowledge.

Wisdom.

That which can never be told.

Keeping silent.

The words are spoken only by the soul.

There's no need now for spoken words.

You are the magick.

The Healing Arts

In the beginning you probably heard the term "Witches heal," and learned the rich history of Witches as healers. They were the wise women and cunning men of the countryside long before the rise of the organized professionalization of physicians. However, the church saw the link between natural healing and the worship of the earth as a manifestation of the divine. It sought to put an end to this by accusing the natural healers of Witchcraft. It charged that these healers interfered with God's plans for life and death, therefore they must derive their power from anti-God forces. The church got rid of this problem and its challenge to their authority with the cry of "Witch," predictably followed by the usual flames, hangings, and drownings.

If you belonged to a teaching coven when you first began to study Witchcraft, or if you worked with a teacher skilled in the healing arts, you probably were taught some basic healing techniques such as placing someone at the center of a circle or spiral, and having the rest of the group send energy to them. You also learned about breathing on someone to effect healing.

The hardest part of all was being told you needed permission to help someone heal. Some people like being sick, and some need it to work out a karmic issue. Some people may not even be able to tell you why they don't want your help, but you should respect their wishes. The only time you should do whatever you can for someone, by both traditional and modern means, is in the case of a medical emergency. The important thing in that case is to save the life of a fellow human being—or a beloved pet—and deal with any repercussions later.

As an intermediate Craft student your knowledge of healing grew to include color magick, where color was used with breath or visualization to heal. Cool colors brought down fevers, warm colors stopped chills. When the right color couldn't be picked, then plain, pure, true white always came to the rescue.

Healing with color was considered an intermediate skill because the wrong color can be harmful in some cases. For example, feeding a warm orange color to someone with a fever may cure a pain in the side, but it also may ramp up the fever a few notches. A healer with color has to be absolutely sure what he is doing, which is why the neutral white is used often by those who do not have the innate gift of sensing which color is best.

There is a small, inexpensive book called *How to Heal with Color* by Ted Andrews (Llewellyn, 1992) that goes into color healing, color breathing, and color painting in great detail. Those who feel skilled in this area may wish to start with this book before branching out.

As an intermediate Witch you learned about the placebo effect, one of the negative consequences associated with metaphysical healing. Many of your "patients" will suddenly feel better after you treat them simply because something is being done. It makes them feel that they have some control and are not just waiting around for medicines and doctors to do the work. The danger is that many of these people are ready to shun modern medicine and leave themselves in your hands. You must insist to them that this placebo effect is only a short-term fix and that you could do more harm than good by taking them out of the hands of a skilled physician. Metaphysical and medical healing work best in tandem, with both Witch and doctor having full knowledge about what treatments are being used and how often.

The other problem is that dispensing medical advice without a license is a crime, one which is punished with all the severity the law allows. Never pretend to dispense medical, legal, or financial advice to anyone unless you are licensed to do so. But don't hesitate to use your magickal intuition to assist any professional who is trying to help you.

The first step in healing is to put your "patient" at ease by telling him that you are only adding to the doctor's work and that not following the doctor's instructions not only hurts him, but makes your job all the harder.

As an advanced practitioner of the Craft, your healing skills have grown and, if you have a talent in this area, it is now apparent. There are basically three categories of advanced metaphysical healing:

1) Remote Healing

2) Chakra Healing

3) Hands-On Healing

You've probably already noticed that this is a very short chapter. In part, this is because healing is an art all to itself, and you can find many books on metaphysical and alternative healing. If you find you have a talent for these, then they are well worth exploring in greater depth. The other reason is that healing practices are common events among covens and other groups of occultists, so there are few truly advanced practices that are not in common use and easy for us to be exposed to and learned.

REMOTE HEALING

Remote healing is an advanced art because it requires expert skill in both astral projection and in second sight. Many Witches find they have a problem doing one or the other, and only those gifted with this talent, or who practice long and hard, usually master this art.

When you know your patient is sleeping, astral project to his bedside. Take a look at his entire body from a few feet away. Note any dark spots or any negative beings hovering around. These should all be banished with a shot of white light from you. Look also for symbols or unusual colors in the aura that might indicate a problem area.

Now step closer to your patient. Look at his chakras. Note any that are not clear, open, and vibrant in color. You may use your mind or your hands to remove dark spots or colors in the aura that don't appear healthy. Ground them away from the patient.

Also look at areas where there are no chakra points. You want to make sure there is no darkness or any spots that appear "angry." If there are, use your mind or hands to heal them.

Before you leave the patient's bedside to return to your own normal consciousness, check your astral body to make sure you've grounded everything you've collected from the patient. You don't want to carry it back into your own world.

When the patient is awake you may give him a call and give a full report of what you found and what you did.

CHAKRA HEALING

You can do chakra healing either as a remote exercise or by standing at the bedside of your patient. All it takes is the ability to see the chakras and sense if they're open, how far they're open, and how clear and clean they are or are not.

If you're not skilled at seeing the chakras of another person, their aura might be able to tell you just as much about the state of their chakras. Dark spots or unpleasant patterns on certain parts of the body should clue you in to the fact that there is something wrong in that area, or in the area governed by that specific chakra. You may use your hands or your mind to clear and cleanse these areas.

Some practitioners use a crystal pendulum to discern the condition of the chakras. They hold it over each one. If it moves clockwise, that chakra is open and healthy; if it moves counterclockwise or back and forth, it means there is damage here and that the chakra needs some attention.

Each chakra governs a specific part of the body, mind, and spirit. In general, these are as follows:

> *Chakra:* Root. *Location:* Base of the tail bone. *Color:* Red. *Associated with:* Health, the intestines, sexuality, element of earth, centering, individuality, stability, personal security, sense of smell, lead poisoning, Saturn, the earth itself, trees, the square.

> *Chakra:* Navel. *Location:* Just below the navel. *Color:* Orange. *Associated with:* Desire, willpower, feminine power, blood, emotions, the element of water, sea herbs and stones, sea animals, grief and joy, the reproductive organs, the circle, Neptune.

> *Chakra:* Solar plexus. *Location:* Center of the solar plexus. *Color:* Yellow. *Associated with:* Digestion, masculine power, the element of fire, heat, deep emotions, anger, need for revenge.

> *Chakra:* Heart center. *Location:* Center of the breast bone. *Color:* Green. *Associated with:* Love, good emotions, memory birds, the element of air, compassion, the heart and lungs, the moon.

> *Chakra:* Throat. *Location:* Center hollow of throat. *Color:* Blue. *Associated with:* Speech, communication, music, hearing, writing, creativity, the triangle, Mercury, the thyroid, the mouth, elephants and lions.

Chakra: Third eye. *Location:* Above and between the eyes. *Color:* Indigo. *Associated with:* Psychism, the oval, sight, light, perception, winged deities, quartz, the mental body.

Chakra: Crown. *Location:* Just above the head. *Color:* Violet, silver or gold. *Associated with:* Higher self, the element of spirit, the brain, thought, all time, diamond, the full moon, the nervous system, spirituality, the astral body, connection to the divine.

HANDS-ON HEALING

The concept of healing touch is becoming more and more accepted in the mainstream medical community. Part of this is common sense. Without physical contact with other human beings we sicken and die. Infants who are not cuddled do not thrive, and elderly patients who have no one to touch them with caring hands are sicker and die younger than those who have the benefit of the frequent loving caress.

Start this healing by having your patient lie down and relax. Soothing music, a light incense, semidarkness, and a light head massage can help. Allow the person to tell you where they hurt or what they believe their problem to be. They may have seen several doctors already and know what their problems are, but it may seem overwhelming to have so many doctors doing so many different things to them. You are one person trying to tie all this together, and this gives many people a sense of comfort.

You need to know precisely what your patient knows about his condition because you will use your hands as magnets to draw the pain or illness out of your patient without causing harm to yourself.

For example, if your patient is suffering from a migraine, place your right or dominant hand at the base of the neck and your left or nondominant hand on the forehead. Draw in energy from the deities or from Mother Earth and allow it to flow through your hands into that person's head. Visualize this as a clear white light filling the head with soothing, healing energy.

After a minute or two you will sense your patient begin to relax as the white light begins to work.

As soon as this happens, visualize the energy you placed in your patient's head polarizing and being pulled into your hands.

One of the reasons this is an advanced skill is that newcomers tend to not be able to stop the spread of the energy at the wrists or elbow where they can be easily grounded. They tend to let the energy of the pain or illness continue on into their bodies, and they can also become ill.

Keep your hands where they are until you sense that the pain is gone, or until you feel you've done all you can for one session.

Be sure to ground well and run your hands under some cool water to make sure you're carrying no residual energies of the pain or illness.

If the patient still is in pain, you may try this again until the pain is gone, or at least is bearable. You will usually be able to get a sense of it because your hands will cease to feel as if they're gathering any more painful energy.

the spirit chapters

Where our web is woven

The Faeries and the Power in a Name

In the beginning, esoteric concepts like nature spirits, faeries, alien beings from other planets, and the nature of the elemental world were subjects that seemed relegated to other disciplines of study, not to Witchcraft. Of course, as you grew in your knowledge you began to suspect that there weren't many topics that Witchcraft did not touch upon in some way or another. Certainly anything in the world of nature was firmly in the realm of the Craft. But what about other magickal elements?

You soon discovered that magick was all around you, and—more importantly—within you as well. Nowhere was this more true than when you entered the elemental world. Four simple elements: earth, water, fire, and air. By the time you were first initiated, you probably felt you knew them all and that you couldn't possibly learn more.

As an intermediate Craft student you realized you'd never master all there was to learn about the complex world of the elements and their essential spirits, beings you might have referred to as faeries or the fey.

With the tenacity that has marked our people for centuries, you embarked upon the mind-boggling study of these beings and the many concepts, theories, and ideas about who they are, where they came from, where they live, and what they can and cannot do.

Witches and Faeries

Witches have always been believed to have a special awareness, sometimes even a working relationship with the fey. Since my book *A Witch's Guide to Faery Folk* came out in 1993, the e-mails and letters I've received from readers tell me this is true today, as it probably was in the past.

Enough Witches have related their experiences—both the fleeting and the ongoing—to me that I've had cause to wonder if those early experiences made us more aware of the natural world and predisposed us to Witchcraft, or if there was an inborn awareness already in us which caused the fey to appear to us or made us able to simply see what others could not. Faeries were seen in foliage, in the wood grain of an antique dresser, under crawlspaces, in the dark corners of closets, and in gardens and grass.

The first time I saw faeries was the spring of my sixth year. I was never a good sleeper, much to my parents' distress, so I learned to entertain myself without waking them up. One spring night I wasn't able to sleep, so I was sitting in the upstairs dormer window looking out on our neighbor's English garden. I liked to sit there and make up my own little songs and stories. I recall a gentle spring breeze coming in the window. The memory of that sensual feeling is written on the book of my life.

As I looked down to the garden I saw several translucent beings dancing around a circular flower display. At first I thought I was seeing ghosts, and opened my mouth for a blood-chilling scream for my mother.

Then I looked again.

These beings were not tall enough to be human discarnates. They were about three feet tall, almost child-sized, but were clearly adults in their facial features. They were winged, but the wings were hard to see and didn't seem to have anything to do with their ability to move or fly. They all appeared to be female, all robed in diaphanous gowns of pastel colors. The gowns became almost nonexistent as they swept the spring grass, as if the beings had no feet, or their feet were on another plane of existence.

I don't know how long I watched them or how I came to the decision that these were faeries. The real kicker to this story is that, several weeks later, my paternal grandmother gave me a book of Easter stories and poems. I turned through the book, admiring the artwork, and then I came upon a page that showed the exact beings I saw that night from my window. They were called faeries. There were other pictures of faeries in the book, but only the one page with the unique figures I had seen. I've been a believer in them since.

In some ways these early faery sightings that many Witches experience is another model of the heroic journey of mythology. It's comparable to the otherworld or underworld initiation concept wherein the hero-Witch is taken into another realm, changed by the experiences there, then rereleased into his own world again, only to find that everything he believes, sees, and touches is no longer the same as it was before. This initiation can be profound, a complete life-changing event, or a subtle shifting in beliefs. It also may bring a new power or talent with it, especially the power to communicate with faeries in the future.

Not all faeries like humans; some never have, and others have learned to dislike us for our callous treatment of them and our natural environment. Still, many can lend their elemental energy to your magick. As you travel in the astral worlds, they can assist you, guide you, and protect you.

Sometimes the fey know the answers to questions you have, but they often give you their answers in the form of a riddle which you must decode to use. You may or may not figure out what they're telling you until it happens. I recommend recording any such riddles in your Book of Shadows just like you would any other divination. The message may come in a dream that you know was more than a dream, or while you're astral projecting or working in your astral temple, or even in the physical world setting.

There are many trickster spirits among the faeries, and many will tell you what you want to hear. Finding special allies is important. When astral projecting, will yourself to go to that otherworld known as the land of Faery and try meeting different beings. Or bring them to your astral temple by leaving them libations and "verbally" calling for their presence.

You'll know when you've made a faery ally, for it will tell you what to call him. This may not be his true name, for they guard these closely, but it will be similar to our Craft names, something we know is the essence of us for the time we are in the circle of magick, and to which we will respond.

Who Are the Faeries?

Ask any Witch to define the term *faery* and you'll likely get as many answers as there are Witches. We tend to use the term to describe a wide variety of beings, including deities, simply because we don't know where else to class them in our mental hierarchy of otherworld inhabitants.

Just because you haven't seen a particular type of faery, or had any personal interaction with it, doesn't mean it doesn't exist. This is especially true of the small winged variety of faery that many claim was only an invention of the Victorians. I believe that the Victorians enjoyed this type of faery because it felt safe, and the staid Victorians were desperate for entertainment. Remember that this is the same age that gave birth to the religion of Spiritualism, where otherworld spirits are part of their worship and are consulted for assistance.

Some scholars who've studied the Celtic faery world believe the faeries to be memories of the old deities, the Tuatha de Danann. These are tall, shining, blonde beings, and bear no resemblance to the Celtic dwarf faeries such as the leprechauns of Ireland or the knockers of Cornwall.

In most cultures there exists a rich body of faery lore that has been passed down as faery tales. They portray a wide variety of otherworldly beings who are clearly not of divine origin, but have characteristics and powers that exclude them from the human race.

The origins of these beliefs have been examined by historians and mythologists, and those who do not believe in otherworldly beings hypothesize that faeries are distant memories of dwarfish protohuman races that were small and dwelled in underground sod shelters or within stone hives and cairns. England's King James I (1566–1625), a notorious Witch slayer, believed faeries to be demons, servants of Satan in a pleasant guise. Clerics of that same period believed faeries to be fallen angels who were not evil enough for Hell but ineligible to remain in Heaven, so they were doomed to walk the earth in a world not wholly astral and not wholly physical.

There have even been some interesting theories linking faeries to alien beings from other planets. Famous magician and Witch Dion Fortune believed elemental beings, or faeries, to be the projection of mass thoughtforms.

Folklorist David MacRitchie hypothesizes that our belief in faeries stems from memories of an earlier race of cave dwellers whose existence barely overlapped our own. These people would have been a compact, pre-Neolithic, protohuman race who lived underground, supporting themselves by hunting with the flint arrowheads we now refer to as "elf shot." This corresponds to the faery lore of many lands who believe their faeries to have been among the first inhabitants and who still dwell in their earth, and would explain the elf shot arrows often unearthed in Europe.

So what do Witches believe about the faery kingdom? There is no one answer, but there are several explanations for our having the belief in the first place. The mind-boggling part is that none, some, or all of these ideas could be true. All of the following have been called "faery" at one time or another:

PLANT SPIRITS

Some Witches see faeries as the spirits of the things that grow in nature. Poisonous plants yield capricious spirits, and helpful plants yield positive spirits. The positive ones are often referred to as plant totems, or the sentient part of the plant.

The most well-known of these are tree spirits or faeries who live in trees and protect them. They can be capricious, helpful, or unpleasant, depending upon the tree and the land in which it grows.

NATURE SPIRITS

Similar to plant spirits are nature spirits. Some Witches see these elemental beings as the astral bodies of nature's living things, able to appear to us the same way we can see other astral beings. These spirits guard and protect plants, trees, and animals. Their favor can be culled by being kind toward animals, respectful of nature, and leaving them libations of milk, bread, and butter.

Many of these are dwarf faeries, especially those who look after animals and homes. The winged creatures seem to be found in flowering plants and gardens, or among fields of wildflowers.

GUARDIAN SPIRITS

Some Witches have had nothing but positive experiences with the fey. Often these are Witches gifted in the natural healing arts who are assisted by the faery spirits. Scottish folklore and legends from other parts of western Europe are littered with tales of Witches who were taken into the world of Faery and taught the healing arts.

ELEMENTAL BEINGS

Many Witches believe that faeries are the representative spirits of the four elements:

Gnomes for Earth

Sylphs for Air

Salamanders for Fire

Undines for Water

EARTH-BOUND DISCARNATES

Some believe that faeries are spirits of deceased loved ones who can't, won't, or don't move on to become a part of the elemental environment. These earth-bound spirits might appear as ghosts or as part of the natural environment.

THE OLDEST DEITIES

A large number of Witches believe the fey to be the deities of the lands that were conquered by humans. This is a prominent belief especially among Anglo-Celtic traditions.

Separating Our Worlds

Do we stop believing as we get older? Are we blind to the spirits of nature as we age? Why is it that it takes second sight to see, meet, and work with the faery races? Why have so many of them become hostile to humans? There are no clear answers, though our collective disrespect for nature may be partly to blame.

In order to protect the faeries from human exploitation, legends exist that tell us how a deity decreed that we separate our worlds. As they did, they gave the surface of the earth to us, and the underworld and world of the astral to the fey.

One Welsh legend says a kindly Druid created a *ceo-druidechta* or Druid's Fog in which the faeries can move about unseen by us. Irish and Manx legends tell us that the sea god Manannan MacLir swept his magickal cloak between human warrior Cuchulain and his faery wife Fand, separating us by a veil of forgetfulness through which few can pass.

However, Witches seem to be passing through that barrier every day. What's more amazing is that large numbers of faeries seem to be reaching out to us as well. I don't know whether these faeries want to be part of our spiritual lives again, or whether the proliferation of earth religions has just made us more aware of what has been there all along. Over the past several years faeries seem to be seen more often in the physical world, and their appearance and assistance are strong on the astral plane.

Since they live not wholly in either world, they can be seen and can interact with us the way many spirits cannot.

True Naming

The term *words of power* is known to the beginning Witch, but it takes time to understand the power of words, in particular in knowing the true name of someone or some thing.

Sixteenth-century occultist and physician Henry Cornelius Agrippa wrote in one of his books of occult philosophy:

> An internal word is a conception of the mind, a motion of the soul, which is made without voice. . . . But an uttered word hath a certain act in the voice, and the properties of location, and is brought forth from the breath of man . . . [Words] often times they change not only the hearers, but also other bodies and things that have no life. (From Agrippa's *Three Books of Occult Philosophy* [Llewellyn, 1995], which first appeared in Latin in 1531. The Llewellyn edition was translated by James Freake and was edited and annotated by ceremonial magician and author Donald Tyson.)

The popular faery tale of Rumpelstiltskin tells the story of a young queen who was helped out of a hopeless task by a dwarf faery. He agreed to do this only if she would give him her first child. Desperate, she agreed. When the faery came to claim her new-born son, she didn't want to give him up, so she was given three days to guess his name. If she couldn't then the child was his. If she could, she kept the child. When she was able to tell him his name on the third day, the little creature literally stomped himself to pieces. Her knowing his name gave her enormous power over him.

This knowing of a true name is one explanation for why the elementals come to our circle when called upon in ritual. We do them the courtesy of asking rather than demanding their presence, but they come just the same. This may be because we know the name of their species even if we don't know their individual names. Gnomes, salamanders, undines, and sylphs come and lend their energy. We thank them and, when our ritual is complete, we tell them they may go. Sometimes they leave right away, other times they linger.

Because we do know these names we could get power happy and start making demands of these faeries. This is never a good idea in any magickal situation. That being you insult today may be the one you need help from tomorrow. You must also know that these creatures would love to find out your true name as well so that they have power over you. This is one reason you pick a magickal name to be used within the circle. In my tradition it is common practice to take a public Craft name and another known only to the deities. In this way we have a "true name" that is known only to the creator, and it cannot be used to gain any measure of power over us. Give only your "known by," or public Craft name, to any astral being.

Knowing someone's true name is another way of gaining power over them through magick. When I lived in Texas and was learning their native folk magick, I was told that to make any spell work I had to first know the birth name of the person I was working magick for, against, or with. In my case, I was at that time working for a boss that put no time or energy into the business. I was doing the work with the help of some motivated employees, but the boss was getting the credit. A curandera, or wise woman, was helping me to find ways to allow upper management to see who was doing the work. She said I didn't need the boss's middle name, but I had to find out her birth or maiden name. With knowledge of her first name and maiden name I was able to make the spell work. The boss moved on to a job in another industry that she liked and was better suited to her. Reports from friends said she was like a new person—earning more, doing more, and living happier.

Creating An Elemental

Using the power of your mind, you can create thoughtforms that result in the manifestation of an elemental being you have created. These beings can guard your home, watch out for natural disasters, or undertake most any task you ask of them.

Along with the ability to create comes a serious responsibility. We are creating an astral being who will be as real as any other spirit, and we must maintain control over our creations, keep watch over them, nurture them to keep them alive and working for us, and, when their job is done, to know what the best course of action is to un-create them.

Your creation will made by using the elements as building blocks, your mind as a potter's wheel, and your will as your programming. You will need to put energy into your elemental five times to make it strong.

Five is the legendary sacred number of the faeries. It makes sense when you think about it. Five is halfway to ten, the midpoint in a tarot suit. Like the faeries, the number five hovers between the beginning and the end. The word *quintessential*, meaning "to personify or accurately represent something," contains the root *quint*, meaning "five," and *essential*, meaning "elemental."

Creating your own elemental being who serves you as you ask it to until you dismantle its energy or banish it to the astral world has been a common practice among Witches, wizards, and other magicians for centuries. Why might you want to make one?

- To guard your home when you cannot be there.

- To protect you when you're in a dangerous place.

- To watch out for natural disasters which are, in essence,
  the energy of the elements gone out of control.

- To look after your children or pets like a guardian angel.

- To make those in your presence always tell the truth.

- To gather information and relay it back to you.

- To tap you on your psychic shoulder when your attention is needed elsewhere.

- To assist in a spell that you wish to manifest in the astral world
  but not the physical, such as when you create an astral temple.

- To help protect your children when they're away from home.

- To impart a specific atmosphere to a place, such as peace at home,
  calm in the office, or tranquil sleep.

- To accompany you on a trip or to a meeting where you feel you need
  an extra measure of safety and confidence.

Many Witches are uncomfortable with the idea of creating elemental beings. If you're one of them, then don't create one until the day comes—if it comes—when you feel the need and are comfortable with the process. Being unsure at first is actually a good thing. Magick should never be shot from the hip like a gunslinger in an old Western movie. Initial uncertainty makes you think critically about what you're doing, which makes it easier for you to act responsibly. It's usually the newer Witches who are the most hesitant, yet their skill level is still so weak that they probably cannot make a being of much strength. This requires detailed concentration and an iron will, skills that come with time and practice. An experienced Witch can create a powerful being whose presence can be felt, and sometimes seen, by others.

To put your mind at ease, I have known no one whose elemental has run amok, though I've heard claims ad nauseum of someone who knew someone who worked with someone else whose elemental did. This creature you create will be only as strong as you make it and, like any astral being unwanted in your physical life, it can be banished faster than it was created.

For many years I had a set of seven "dragon-dog" elementals who watched over my home. I had intended to make them look like huge guard dogs, but their faces took on the classic look of a Chinese roaring dragon. The parts seemed to fit, so I made no changes. Four of them were large and stationed at the four cardinal points of my home. Sometimes you could feel yourself passing through the primary guardian's astral body as you entered the front door. The other three protected special areas from harm and destruction: the roof, crawlspace, and attic. I kept all seven of them for years, renewing their energy on each full moon to keep them strong. I would talk to the main one who guarded my front door. It was a comfort to go out knowing I had my own security system in place.

Follow the steps below to create your elemental:

1) Decide on what you want your elemental to do for you.

2) Decide where your elemental will be. Will it stand at your front door? Follow you all the time?

3) Decide what you want your elemental to look like. Is it to be a fierce protector? A guardian? A comfort when you're alone? You'll find the elemental will have some ideas of its own about its physical appearance, but its look will be fashioned mostly by you impressing the thoughtform of what you want onto the astral plane. If it seems to fight you, or if it seems to want to work its own agenda and not yours, ground it and begin again in about a week. This gives the negative astral energy a chance to be banished.

4) Go into as deep a meditative state as you are able. Be sure to focus on your goal the whole time.

5) Hold your palms a few inches apart and envision a mass of unformed energy growing there. Draw it up from Mother Earth until it's strong. Watch it take shape as you create it in your hands. It can be an animal, a mix of animals, or look like whatever else you expect something assigned to its task should be. Feel its power growing, pushing your hands further and further apart.

6) Mentally move this energy to where you want the elemental to be. Let it know that this is where its place is. If you will need it to be mobile, show it where you want it to go or whom you wish it follow and for what purpose.

7) Bless and infuse energy into your being by each element. Call upon each as you would in a circle and ask that elemental power to be available to your elemental. You will also have the elements subject to your elemental being so it can protect you from the elements themselves, such as fire and flood. Do this five times, the last time sealing the process with the unifying power of spirit or akasha.

8) When it is complete and in place, mentally command it to do what you ask in the name of your patron deity.

9) Repeat steps seven and eight four more times. You can do this all at once, or space this out over several hours or days. I always did mine all at once because once my energy is engaged I felt stopping would be more detrimental than resting and then coming back to the task.

10) Know that the elemental is doing its job. Every now and then tell it so. Keep it happy and it will joyfully work for you.

11) Feed energy to the being each lunar month to keep it strong, working, viable, and doing what you ask of it—no more and no less.

12) If you want to change or add to your element's appearance or duties you can, but you will need to do this five times in succession. Do not do this often or the elemental's energies will be confused. If you want a whole new game, ground the first elemental and create another.

Don't expect your elementals to be your personal servants and spies. They will work tirelessly for you, but once created they are sentient lifeforms subject to the "harm none" rule, and they deserve respect. They want to be told they are doing their job well and they want to be rewarded. They know they are your creation—yours and Mother Earth's—and they have no fear of returning to their mother once you are finished with them. But they also do not want to be asked to cross that murky gray line onto the left-handed path.

You should never haphazardly create an elemental, intending to dispose of it the next day. If you undertake this task, then know that these are long-term creations meant to be working partners who will grow in power as you work with them, and they expect to remain around for a while. If you want something done fast, you're better off to try another form of magick. If you abuse this one on your first try, you may find that the other elementals you create will tend to be rebellious or less then helpful.

When the elemental's task is finished you may dismantle it, or send it into the astral world to live happy and safe. Make sure it is a positive entity and that allowing it to remain intact will harm none.

In most cases, simply grounding the elemental's energy to Mother Earth is best. It was energy you drew from her to make your creation, and this way you give it back to her to use as she sees fit.

If You Think Your House Is Haunted . . . and Even if You Don't

In the beginning you were taught about the multifaceted spirit world. You participated in rituals to honor ancestor spirits at Samhain or Hallows Eve. You learned how to conduct crossing-over rituals, or memorial rites to commemorate the life of one recently reborn into the Summerland, the Witches' land of the dead. If you were adept at this ritual, you found you could sense spirit presences and assist them along on their journey to the otherworld.

Still, in your mind, the world of the dead and that of the living remained separate and, with the exceptions of specific rituals, you believed a clear line of demarcation separated them. Unless you were a sensitive psychic, you had no cause to question this line of demarcation your mind had concocted.

As an intermediate your awareness of the subtle energy vibrations surrounding you heightened, and you could better sense when you were not alone. You may have studied parapsychology in more depth and drawn your own conclusions of what constituted a haunting, and that may have started you wondering just who and what shared your living space.

Your sixth sense for spirit presences strengthened to include faeries, astral beings and astral junk, ghosts, and a variety of other discarnate beings who occasionally wander through our lives or follow us back from our astral journeys.

There Is No Such Thing As "Haunted"

Got your attention, didn't I?

Haunting is another of those words we use because we don't know what else to call it when we seem to be sharing space with other beings from other times and places, especially if we can't see them. It's a word we'll continue to use because it helps us to have a common frame of reference. Haunting is an omnipresent phenomena, an illusion we find in our perception of time as linear; therefore, the word is redundant. We always share our space with someone or something else that is just as real as we are, even if they can't be seen.

All houses are haunted.

All places are haunted.

Many inanimate objects are haunted.

You haunt a few places and objects yourself, and you always will.

What we term haunted, especially when dealing with specific places or inanimate objects, is no more than awareness of the collection of residual energies that remains long after the events that caused them are over as we view it in linear time.

In most circumstances these residual energies would dissipate over time when there was no fresh energy being fed to them on a regular basis. Other times the spirit being chooses to move into other realms, but some like to hang around the edges of the earth plane, and some appear stuck here, confused and unable to go anywhere else.

You may be sharing living space with elemental beings, house faeries, thoughtforms, astral beings, ancestor spirits, guardian spirits, and perhaps a classic ghost or two. In other words, you have a very full house.

Determining Which Ghost Is Which

When we focus on the world of human discarnates, or "ghosts" as we like to call them, we all have our theories as to why they are here, and how and why they make themselves known to us. It won't take an in-depth discussion to determine that there are many kinds of ghosts, all of whom are as unique as their living selves had been.

You must first determine the type of spirit you have in your home, or in someone else's home, before you can decide to banish or to communicate with it. The steps you take will be determined not just by you, but by the willingness of the spirit to cooperate.

TRANSIENT SPIRITS

Does your ghost only want your attention once in a while? Did it suddenly just appear—seen or heard—one day? Did it stay only a short time, then disappear? Could there be some—any—plausible explanation for its presence other than that it is a human discarnate?

Sometimes a spirit is on the move and will pass through your world for only a brief time, perhaps for a few days or a few months. A few stay longer, but usually they don't. They don't seem to want to communicate, but are aware of your presence and seem to know they are dead. Why they don't or can't move on to a better plane of existence is not known. These solitary spirits appear unannounced, are usually harmless, and no one can think of a reason they might have been attracted to the places they visit. They will drift off when they are moved to do so and you'll probably not hear from them again or be able to understand why they chose to leave.

I once knew a family who had a ghost in the attic of their 1960s-style ranch house. The spirit was with them for about two years and seemed to want nothing more than to be acknowledged. As soon as one of the three inhabitants of the home came in the front door, they were sure to hear their resident spirit friend running back and forth across the attic floor over their heads. At first they thought they had squirrels in the attic, but a professional exterminator could find no trace of animal infestation.

The noises were heard by neighbors and friends, all agreeing that this was no animal, but the sound of running feet—human feet wearing shoes, no less.

The family decided just to live with their curiosity and they humored the noisemaker. They named him Edward, a label he seemed to be happy to have and to respond to. When family members arrived home and the running feet were heard overhead, they would call out, "Hi, Edward, how's it going?" As soon as Edward was acknowledged, his running feet would fall silent until the next time someone came home.

OBJECT SPIRITS

Have you ever been in an antique store or vintage clothing shop? Did you notice how different items felt to you? Did you find an object you loved, but something just didn't feel right about it? Did you find a lovely vintage outfit that made you feel uncomfortable when you put it on?

This is a haunted object.

Haunted objects may not be influenced by an actual ghost but by past uses of it by its former owner. That person's energies and vibrations, emotions and sensations have been impressed onto the object the same way you impress them onto a magickal catalyst.

If you're skilled in psychometry, the art of reading an object and its owner's history through touch, you might discover what caused the object to give off negative vibrations. Try holding the object in your receptive hand, or placing your receptive hand on top of the object, and closing your eyes. Focus on the object as you try to sink into as much of an altered state of consciousness as you can. At this point some Witches will see and hear things as clearly as if they're watching a movie, others will get only vague impressions, and most of us fall in between.

There are four primary reasons an object would appear haunted:

1) Someone deliberately cursed the item, or used it as a receptacle to transfer unwanted pain, sickness, or other negativity.

2) Someone in the "past" was emotionally attached to the item in life, and this attachment leaves its residue after death.

3) The item could have been used in a spell for the transfer of pain, as in moving a headache from your own head and into a receptacle such as a vase or glass jar. If it's not grounded it can cause haunting vibrations.

4) Someone with a strong personality used the object a lot and residue from that personality is reflected in the object.

5) The object was associated by a former owner with a time of extreme emotion, such as a wedding, death, or birth.

One of the most famous haunted objects is the Hope Diamond. Now housed in the Smithsonian Institute in Washington, D.C., it remains one of the museum's most popular displays. We can document its history and know that every one of its former owners met with serious misfortune, or even unexpected death.

RIP-IN-TIME SPIRIT

Did you see something once that appeared odd or unusual? When you looked again was it gone? Did the people you observed seem oblivious to you, but looked as if their dress and manners were from the past?

These are not really spirits, but a peek at a living person in another time who becomes visible at certain moments because the veil of time grows thin at the place where you both are standing. In this case the spirit may not even be aware of you, or the "spirit" may be seeing you as well and think *he's* the one seeing a ghost.

The story I told earlier about my friend who saw people waiting for a trolley car at the end of her yard was viewing a rip in time.

TIME-SLIP SPIRIT

This is similar to the rip in time, only this time you are the spirit the other time frame perceives as a ghost. There have been several famous stories circulated about such occurrences. They are common on old battlefields and state houses. At one moment you're in your own time, perhaps touring an old building or historic site, and the next you are in the past. The people who are in that other time see you and may express fear or wonder about your unusual clothing. To them, *you're* the ghost, the intruder.

There is a story I recall about some women who were touring the Petite Trianon near Versailles, France, and stumbled back to the time of Marie Antoinette when she played games with her wealthy courtiers. The tourists thought they were viewing a docudrama, but when they asked about it, no such thing was being done on the ground, and when they returned to the site it appeared radically different than when they'd entered the time-slip.

If anyone has become stuck in the past, unable to return, no one seems to be aware of this. Leaving the area where the slip has occurred usually breaks the spell. When you return to where you saw the past, it will probably be gone.

THE CLASSIC GHOST

A ghost is usually defined as being different from an apparition because a classic ghost appears to know who it is and where it is, and appears to be exercising free will. It appears when it wants and to whom it wants. It can go anywhere in your home or the place it haunts. It is aware of you and anyone else living with you, and it may try to communicate with someone in your home.

Sometimes the ghost will be a mean spirit who wants to upset your lives and, perhaps, chase you away. It may feel you're intruding on its property. Or it may like your company and even act as a guardian. I recall reading a story once about a young family who bought an old house they later found to have several spirits. One seemed determined to look after the couple's children, pulling up blankets that were tossed off in sleep, opening and closing windows to regulate temperature, and doing other small tasks that showed the owners the spirit meant no harm.

This is also the classic ghost that most people want removed from their home because it is unpredictable and does display free will and the ability to communicate with the living. Most people can sense this particular ghost is more substantial than a magnetic recording in the etheric continuum. This makes many homeowners nervous, and they want the being gone.

Unfortunately, it is exactly this type of spirit—the one that is still a sentient being acting in free will—that is the most difficult to remove. In many cases this ghost is a former inhabitant of the building who sees you as the intruder. A classic ghost is like a living person in that it possesses a personality and temperament all its own. Some wish to show you the hospitality of their home, others may see you as a trespasser or an unwanted guest.

STOP-ACTION SPIRITS

Do you see a spirit repeating an action over and over in the same place or at the same time of day? Is it so caught up in its actions that it appears to have no or little consciousness of your presence? This is a spirit who died with an unfinished task on his mind or in his hands. It could be as simple as a woman who died while doing a massive load of laundry she felt she had to finish, or a man working the railroad knowing he had to make sure the train took the right track. They feel responsible to continue seeing to these tasks long after their deaths.

The attitude of these spirits could be positive or negative, depending upon how that person felt about the task in life. If it made the spirit happy, he may not be thrilled that you are trying to take away his pleasure. If the repeated action is a compulsion caused by a lack of realizing that, now dead, the task does not have to be continued, your interference may be seen as salvation. I recall seeing a television program where the ghost of a woman who ran a boarding house in a small New England town was frantic with all the work she had to do. Her attempts at approaching the family were to ask for their help. A psychic was called in to help her understand that these tasks were not needed anymore and she could rest and rejoin her family now.

In some cases these spirits may not know their bodies have died. Their spirits just keep working. This is when you need to communicate carefully with the spirit and, if it wants to be free from its endless task, you can help it reach the otherworld by directing it to call for its spirit guides and enter that proverbial light. But if the spirit likes what it's doing, and you can live with its presence, so be it.

A skilled and sympathetic psychic can usually remove this type of spirit through mental communication. A psychic may be the only "verbal" contact the ghost has had in centuries, and most are quick to tell their stories. Some died by violence or treachery, others peacefully in their bed, but they all have a need to communicate with someone who can help them. The discarnate may not realize he or she is dead, it may feel it needs to deliver an important message to a loved one, it may feel tense because it left unfinished business behind, or perhaps the ghost just wants to watch over a still-living loved one.

Other free-will spirits have embraced the families who move into their homes and will look after children or pets with loving concern. This type of ghost will produce the strongest physical sensations we associate with a ghostly presence. These include a drop in air temperature, electromagnetic disturbance, unusual movement of light or shadow, or allowing themselves to be seen by those still living.

ETHERIC RECORDING SPIRIT

Does your resident spirit seem to be seen during specific conditions, such as when the air temperature is in a specific range, when the moon is full, or when there's some fog in the air? Does it seem to have an awareness of you, other people, walls, or anything else around it? Can you hear it speak, walk, or interact with other spirits? If so, then all you're seeing is something recorded in the atmosphere.

There are electromagnetic vibrations around us all the time and, like a piece of magnetic tape, the atmosphere can record these and play them back over and over again. This is especially true of places where traumatic or highly emotional events occurred. The stronger the emotions, the stronger the recording the event seems to make.

This is one type of haunting that is hard to banish because you cannot control your environment 100 percent of the time.

LOST SOULS

These are the wandering spirits who do not know they've died. They can appear as classic ghosts or stop-action spirits. They don't understand who you are and why you're in their home. They don't understand why they speak to people who don't answer, but only continue to look past them as if they're not there.

These are the spirits Witches can assist to pass into the otherworld. They usually don't put up much resistance, especially when they know their loved ones—whom they miss very much—will be awaiting them. Again, ask them to call for their spirit guides or another passed-over loved one to guide them, or to enter that proverbial light.

ANCESTOR SPIRITS

Is your spirit one who merely wants to remain near places or people she loved in life? This may be an ancestor spirit who will stay around for generations and watch over members of her family. They protect and cherish the family and the home. They can be banished if you want them to be, but most families seem to like the attention.

In African, Asian, and some Polynesian cultures, ancestor spirits are worshiped as deities and their presence is cultivated. In other cultures, most notably the Native Americans, the name of a deceased relative is never spoken, but its spirit is believed to watch over the tribe.

WARNING SPIRITS

This is an unusual phenomena where a spirit will appear over and over to one person, trying to communicate something. It could be anything as monumental as a natural disaster to something as small as finding a lost earring. Whatever the cause, it is of great importance to the spirit.

These spirits can't be banished until their message gets through. You can try, but they will put up a fight because they believe passing along what they know is essential. Only then can they rest in peace.

REVENGE SPIRITS

As the name suggests, these are ghosts with a purpose. Somehow they feel they were cheated out of something in life and they are back to do as much damage as possible to the person or persons they blame for their misfortune. Unfortunately, the spirit can't always tell one human being from another. Ghost story anthologies are packed with stories such as these.

The only thing you can do is try to banish the spirit from your home, but be prepared for a struggle.

OWNER SPIRITS

These spirits feel that the place you inhabit is not *your* home, place of business, etc., but theirs. They will express their anger at your redecorating efforts by shaking the walls and frightening away your clientele. In most cases, these spirits died in anger, and that emotion governs their after-death behavior. They must be banished but they will fight with you, even try to hurt you. Getting help from someone who can communicate with the spirit and who has experience in banishings is essential.

MANUFACTURED SPIRITS

Did you know you can haunt yourself? Experiments have shown that when enough people are told a ghost story that their collective thoughtforms are strong enough to manufacture a spirit to fit their beliefs. This is similar to creating an elemental, only in this case you've created one who conforms to a ghostly pattern. It will be seen, heard, and felt by many. The more who know and believe the story of the ghost—even though it is pure fiction—the stronger its presence will be.

Ground this type of spirit as you would any other elemental you created and spread the story to everyone you know that the spirit has moved on. Only when everyone stops believing in its presence will it go away and stay gone.

PET SPIRITS

Have you ever loved an animal and had that animal love you in return? That's a powerful bond. Has that animal appeared to you after its death when you needed protection or comfort? This is a common experience, especially with house pets. Any book on ghosts or on the unusual abilities of animals will have a few stories about dogs who chased away intruders weeks or months after their deaths. The pet's owner and the intruder can hear the dog, sometimes even see it, but it vanishes soon after its task is done.

Some critics of this type of spirit claim that when we're awakened in the middle of the night we are not thinking clearly and, because we were accustomed to having that dog look out for us, our minds manufacture the dog's habits. However, this doesn't explain how burglars, muggers, and others who didn't know the dog can hear and see it as well.

As I write this, my own sweet Sheltie, my pet and familiar of fourteen years, has been dead for over a year. I've had several years of chronic illness and some emotional and physical upheavals, the kind that my dog used to comfort me through. Over the last year I've heard his tags jingling around the house, and I've felt him placing his head near me as he did in life when he wanted my attention. I also feel his little paws jump up on my bed right where he used to leap, then pause, and then stumble across my ankles to the other side of the bed where he would curl up behind my knees. I don't know how long it will be before he moves on to wherever it is beloved pet spirits go when they die, but until he decides to leave, he's a welcome and comforting presence.

POLTERGEISTS

Is your resident spirit loud or destructive? Does it throw things? Break things? These noisy ghosts are called *poltergeists*, German for "noisy ghost."

Most people could find a way to cope with the noise, though it can be very loud and maddening. It's the destructiveness that is hard to endure. These spirits can destroy a home in minutes, shaking the walls, tossing objects off shelves, breaking glass, etc.

No one knows why these spirits are moved to destructiveness or where they come from. No one is even sure the poltergeist is one spirit or a spirit at all. They seem to come and go within a few months in most cases. Sometimes they are associated with the presence of an emotionally disturbed adolescent who may not realize she has the kinetic power to cause her own home to be haunted.

It's hard to banish a poltergeist. Many families simply stop fighting it and move away.

Banishing Beings and Closing Portals

Once you have determined what type of spirit you have, you will have a better idea if it can be banished or if you even want to banish it. Some people are quite comfortable sharing their home with a pleasant spirit, such as me with my Sheltie.

Some spirits can't be banished no matter what you do. For example, you obviously cannot will a living person you view through a rip in time to go away. If it keeps happening, you can mentally try to thicken the wall between your time frames, but you cannot make a person living in the past go away.

You will also have to determine if it is right for you to try to banish a specific spirit. Human discarnates should be given the courtesy of respect for their free will, within limits. If the spirit seems happy with its circumstances and is not threatening you, the best and most compassionate course of action may be to learn to live with it.

If you have access to any historical records or the records of titles to your property, you may learn the name of your ghost. This will give you some measure of power over him and give you an indication of why he is hanging around. A spirit who has gone unacknowledged for a long time might be startled that you know his name, and it may help you gain the spirit's confidence and put it at ease if it wants to move on to the otherworld but does not know how.

Before banishing, you will want to find out if there is a portal in your home that is allowing spirits to pass through from the otherworld into yours. These must be closed off before you can do anything about your haunting problem. Otherwise it's like trying to fix a leaky pipe while the water's still running—you may fix the leak but you'll have more water to deal with later.

A portal is a thinning or opening between the world of spirit and our world of form that allows the free passage of beings from one world to the other. These can best be located while in an altered state of consciousness by "feeling" out each part of your home, or by actually seeing a spirit pass into your home through one specific location. For instance, if you see it walk through a wall, you know you've pinpointed its portal.

Oftentimes old blueprints of your house can help you locate possible portals. Look for places that used to have doors or windows that have been covered over during various remodeling projects. These are often portals for those who once lived there. If you work magick in a specific place or have a room set aside as a "temple" room, these can also become portals.

When you sense a moment when there are no spirit presences around, seal off all possible portals. Envision a flaming blue pentagram over the portal through which nothing can pass. You may want to place some ghost bane herbs there for a few months just to make sure that you've covered yourself. Herbs that work well are rosemary, basil, angelica, frankincense, lilac, juniper, rue, or sandalwood.

Next, go through your whole house room by room and find out if you still sense any presences. If you do, mentally communicate with them and try to get them to leave. Open the nearest portal if they agree, then close it after them.

The final step is going through your home with vanilla water and frankincense incense, blessing and warding. Frankincense is a wonderful purifier and will rid your home of any residue from the unwanted spirits. The vanilla water should be lightly tossed about from your fingertips. Be careful not to do damage to wood or fabrics.

Determining which spirit is which can be hard unless you do it often. This one of the few Craft arts that cannot be taught easily from a book. There is just too much involved, and to learn properly one really needs hands-on lessons with an experienced teacher who is actively involved in the banishing and can take you step by step through the process. I would probably never have learned or even thought about learning anything about ghosts. It just happened that my own teacher had the situation come up during my training and I was with her during her work. I am glad I learned something of this art, though I would not presume to think myself an expert, and I have to confess that it is a circumstance I would rather not find myself in again.

Don't take your exorcism rites from badly produced horror movies and attempt to send a spirit elsewhere if you are not skilled at spirit contact or you do not have some solid knowledge of parapsychology. Trying to coax a belligerent spirit, perhaps one who sees you as an intruder in his home, into the light may find you the recipient of an unpleasant outburst of ghostly rage.

Will the ghost stay gone? Who knows. Most of the time they do, but not always.

Traditional protections from ghosts are placing salt around the perimeter of your home, wearing silk clothing, spinning three times counterclockwise before entering your home, placing rosemary at each window, and keeping yourself well grounded after any magick or divinations.

Witches' Ways of Communicating with Ghosts

The study of parapsychology has gone high tech, just as every other industry. Professional ghost hunters use a wide range of equipment to measure temperature, air pressure, etc. This book cannot hope to cover the scope of communication techniques you can find in other, meatier works on parapsychology. One ghost hunter's website I visited listed three pages of expensive equipment he was using.

There are many ways to communicate with a spirit. Talking boards, automatic writing, and trance channeling are popular among Spiritualists, but are not common Craft practices. A Witch's connection with ghosts seems to be more spontaneous than planned, occurring only when something meaningful needs to be exchanged. It's not something most of us can turn on and off with ease. However, if the spirit is willing, and you really want one in your home, it can be done. Just please recall the adage "Be careful what you wish for or you just might get it."

A Witch's sensitivity to the presence of a spirit being seems to grow with our growth within the Craft. Communication with these beings also becomes easier. The three best communication methods are telepathic communication, hypnogogic communication, and slowing time by bending light with mirrors.

Use the power of your mind if you wish to speak with a ghost. If your skills are well-developed enough they will hear and respond. Do this near where you think there is a portal or where spirits have been seen before. Resist the urge to call a spirit to you just to see if it can be done. Trust me, it can, but you have no control over who or what you're drawing to yourself, and that's just as dumb as leaving your front door wide open with a "welcome" sign hung in neon lights. You just never know what trouble you'll bring yourself.

Hypnogogic communication is done during that netherworld between sleep and wakefulness where you're not clearly asleep or awake. I learned the power of this state after my maternal grandmother passed over. Many times I would hear her voice call my name as I entered this state. I admit, it jarred me awake the first half dozen times, but once you get used to hearing familiar, though disembodied, voices in your head, you can enjoy the communication.

The third method allows you to see any spirits present with greater ease, but it doesn't always enhance communication. Set up several mirrors—three is the minimum—so that you can look into one and have it reflect the image of the second, which reflects the image of a third mirror, etc., until the last one projects the image of a portal in your home, such as a door.

Einstein did numerous experiments with mirrors when he was doing his time experiments, and he discovered that blending light, as a mirror can do, actually causes the slowing of time. This slowing allows us to see more clearly into a world where the vibrational rate is higher than our own here on the dense earth plane. This otherworld is the realm where higher beings and positive spirits reside. They share our space but not our plane of existence, and vibrate so fast as to remain unseen to the naked eye, though those who are psychic sensitives are aware of these presences.

I discovered a place where I could peer at the spirits on this higher vibrational plane within my former home when, quite by accident, my bathroom mirror, bathroom door mirror, and dresser mirror all happened to be aligned so that I could see down the long hallway into the family room at the other end of the house. I could clearly see beings that could only be human discarnates going about their business.

I was so stunned at first that I stood statue-still just watching them. Then I began to wonder what would happen if I saw someone looking back. I was sure I wouldn't handle it well, and I could even have inadvertently opened a portal. I readjusted the mirrors until I could sort out in my mind just what it was that happened.

The best way to communicate with spirits in general is through mental telepathy from inside the safety of your sacred circle. If you are interested in other methods of communication, such as those previously mentioned, please look into the bibliography or at your library or local bookstore for titles on mediumship and parapsychology.

The Dark Night of the Soul

In the beginning the darkest thing you encountered was the new moon. Even in-depth exposure to the Crone aspect of the Goddess was withheld until your teachers were sure you could grasp the concept that there was no danger in the dark aspects of divinity any more than in the light ones. They both had value, though it may have taken you a few months to get past your acculturated fears of darkness.

As an intermediate Witch you'd been given opportunities to work with darker forces, such as the Crone and new moon (see chapter 10, Dark Witchery). Your Witchcraft vocabulary expanded rapidly and you soon became acquainted with a new term that surpassed all others in the realms of darkness. This is one you had a right to fear, for it alone could produce the gnosis or alchemy that moves us up from the astral and physical worlds into the sphere of the creator. The name of the boogieman stalking you?

The Dark Night of the Soul.

Of Inquisitions and Adepts

The term *Dark Night of the Soul* is credited to sixteenth-century Spanish monk and poet San Juan de la Cruz, or St. John of the Cross (1542–1591). The term was part of a subtitle of a 1583 treatise based on his poem "Songs of the Soul Which Rejoices at Having Reached Holy and Ecstatic Union with God by the Road of Spiritual Navigation." The treatise was part worship and part diary of San Juan's own spiritual progression to the godhead. He makes it clear to anyone with knowledge of spiritual metaphysics that what is described is another terror of the threshold that, in this case, takes the form of extreme spiritual doubts and desolation. He likens it to feeling lost on a lonely road, feeling as if no one cares where you end up and that the divine has deserted you. Only your faith in the divine being there around the next curve or the next will see you through. To give up would have been, to the mind of San Juan, giving up on God and casting one's self into eternal damnation.

If the term "Dark Night of the Soul," or "La Noche Oscura de la Alma," was in use before that time, it was probably used only by Christian mystics such as San Juan. Keep in mind that he was writing just a few decades after the end of the Spanish Inquisition, a vicious blot on history ordained by Queen Isabela in 1478 and petering out somewhere around 1512, when it is said that the last of the Moors had been expelled from the Iberian Peninsula.

The Spanish Inquisition sought to purify Spain by enforcing Christianity on all who lived within her borders. The Moors, who were Islamic, and Jews who had lived there peacefully for several centuries suddenly were faced with a "convert or die" ultimatum. This system worked, or appeared to work for a while. Eventually some overzealous priests, whose sadistic instincts were given free reign by Isabela's proclamation, made it clear that the existence of the Moors and Jews in Spain would no longer be tolerated, even if conversion had been made.

Some Moors tried to adopt the Eastern Orthodox faith as codified by the Emperor Constantine (274–337) who, though raised as a Roman Pagan who worshipped Sol, eventually converted to Christianity and, from his seat of power in what is now modern-day Turkey, split the church in two pieces: the Eastern Orthodox, of which Constantine was the supreme ruler, and Catholicism, which adhered to the edicts of the pope in Rome.

By 1512 all non-Catholics has been expelled from the country, or had been tortured and executed.

The purification frenzy was further fed by religious unrest in nearby Germany where, on All Hallows Eve of 1517, an unknown monk named Martin Luther published his infamous *Ninety-Five Theses* in which he condemned many routine church practices, such as the buying and selling of "indulgences" as a method of cleansing humanity of their sins. Luther eventually nailed a copy of his *Ninety-Five Theses* to the door of the All Saints Cathedral in Whittenberg, and the Protestant Reformation was born. Europe, religion, and the world would never be the same again.

Because of the many religious persecutions sweeping across Europe at this time, it's doubtful that Pagans, who remained hidden on penalty of death, ever heard the term "Dark Night of the Soul." The concept of a Dark Night of the Soul probably came into Witchcraft through ceremonial magick sometime in the late nineteenth century, in the same way and during the same period we adopted many of their ritual tools and directional correspondences. As far as modern Witchcraft goes, the term was probably not in common use until at least the middle of the twentieth century.

This doesn't mean that spiritual crises didn't exist in the Pagan world before that time. To the contrary, the priests and priestesses and, more notably, the Celtic Druids often experienced spiritual doubts and were reputed to endure their own rigorous rituals to help the seeker get past them.

San Juan believed, as did many clerics at that time, that suffering was a necessary component of spiritual progress, and the Dark Night of the Soul was the worst of all sufferings for one who sought God. He likened it to feeling as if one had been abandoned by God, leaving a void that would be filled with a deep fear that spiritual blessings and growth were at an end. Much of San Juan's most famous poetry was written during 1576 and 1577, when he spent two years in a Spanish prison for trying to reform some of the monastic rules Rome imposed on Spanish clerics. Little wonder he felt abandoned by the God he served.

The Pagan Experience of the Dark Night of the Soul

In Pagan mysticism, the Dark Night of the Soul also refers to that same sense of spiritual desolation, but one in which we must remember the lessons of all our past terrors of the threshold. We must recall that 90 percent of our fears are of our own making. We use them to gauge our spiritual progress, not just to attain union with God or to lose all hope of doing so. This is because of our concept of deity. They aren't all good or bad but many shades of gray, which blur the black and white thinking of mainstream beliefs. Pagan deities are not all perfect and infallible, but they are always nearby when we call for them. We also have no anti-God or Satanic equivalent to compare to the imaginative hellfires of fundamentalist Christianity.

Recall the mantra on the top sephira of the Tree of Life, the one often borrowed for our own Charge of the Goddess: "I am that which is attained at the end of desire."

Can we truly stop having mortal desires? Would we want to? Does the next logical step after the Dark Night of the Soul have to be death? I say "no" to all these questions. Asceticism has never been part of Pagan practice. We are human and expected to act like humans. To the contrary, we are taught as Witches that acts of love and pleasure are forms of sacraments so long as they harm none. Life is a gift and it is to be enjoyed. Unlike San Juan and his co-religionists, our purpose for this night of desolation is not seeking an ecstatic trance in which the seeker courts death in order to reach the god-head, but to show us where we may be going wrong in our search for reunion with the deities. The Dark Night of the Soul makes clear to us our spiritual shortcomings and allows us to reset our course toward the divine.

Paradoxes and conundrums are part of a universe we perceive as linear but is actually cyclical or omnipresent. The conundrum I find here is that if you stop desiring the material things, you are still desiring to unite with the creator, so there can truly be no end of desire in any spiritual life until it is over. At that point, many of us believe the quest continues with us in another form of being, be that human or spirit.

The Sorrow and Satisfaction of Spiritual Crisis

A Witch's spiritual crisis is not going to be same as that of a medieval monk. As with all our rites, we remain in charge of how it progresses and we are free to halt the process at any time if something doesn't feel right. We certainly don't see pain and suffering as being necessary prerequisites to gaining the love or assistance of our deities.

The pain factor seems to be disappearing in Paganism altogether. Many modern covens, including that of famous Witch author and teacher Janet Farrar, have even done away with the process of scourging. Scouring was a light whipping action with a cat-o'-nine-tails meant to purify the soul for entry into the ritual circle. It was never meant to inflict true pain, though often it did.

Assessing Your Spiritual Crisis

How do you know when you've reached a state of spiritual crisis? Perhaps you find yourself doubting the validity of your chosen path, or maybe you find you doubt the existence of the deities. Sometimes you feel all your rituals, prayers, and study have been for nothing, that what you seek does not exist outside of your imagination.

You may feel lost, depressed, and without purpose. Your spells may all be failing and you believe your patrons are rejecting you as their servant.

All these can be signs that it's time to reevaluate your progress and adjust your course. This is especially true if you feel your patron deities are no longer responding to your praise or requests. They may be testing your resolve to continue along your oath, or they may be telling you that you need to make some changes. To quote a phrase, "You're barking up the wrong tree," or, in this case, climbing up the wrong branch of the tree.

Another reason for your feelings of desolation or discontent may be that you're rushing your studies. You've stopped enjoying the process for what it is, and you have replaced that pleasure of process with a desire to reach an end that may never come.

Don't expect your Dark Night of the Soul ritual (see page 266) to end leaving you feeling perfectly in balance. Your energies may feel less scattered and you may feel a sense of calm you did not feel before the ritual began, but you're far from ready to leap into the routine of an average day. You will be tired in body, mind, and soul, and will need sleep and a good meal before you return to your mundane routine, much less resume your Craft work.

Don't try to do everything at once. Remember that learning and seeking the divine is a long process, one which you must take in small steps as you climb the tree of life. As French philosopher Voltaire wrote, "Perfection is attained by slow degree; it requires the hand of time."

Tarot Reading Prior to Ritual

Witches are used to doing divination before magickal spells, but don't often do them before rituals, especially those that seem routine. The Dark Night of the Soul is anything but routine, and you should use some divination device before you embark upon it.

There are many interpretations for almost any tarot card, and even more interpretations depending upon the deck you choose. This is because each design was created for a different spiritual tradition or path, and is the reason why one deck may be more attractive or work better for you than another.

One interpretation of the major arcana is that it represents the ubiquitous "hero's journey" as codified by famed mythologist Joseph Campbell in his many books and his critically acclaimed television series *The Power of Myth*. We start with the Fool—the face of the first card of the tarot's major arcana—walking heedlessly toward a cliff. Then we find a Magician and a Priestess who can tell the Fool that the power to change and grow is within. With this call to adventure, the seeker begins the climb toward the top of the deck, to the whole world of the universe in which divinity dwells. Along the way are many obstacles, tricksters, temptations, friends, allies, tests, and challenges.

Most Witches are used to performing divinations before enacting a spell for the following reasons:

- To make sure all the components are in place.

- To make sure the outcome will harm none.

- To see the possible outcome based on current energies
  that the Witch has placed in motion.

Because the Dark Night of the Soul ritual is rigorous and demanding, and can affect beings in other worlds, including your other selves, it is important to do a pre-ritual divination. Before undergoing a Dark Night of the Soul ritual you should look at your divinations for signs of how your ritual may affect or change you *and* all the other yous in all the worlds around you. Use it:

- To tell you if the ritual is needed at this time.

- To tell you if the ritual is appropriate at this time.

- To tell you if you should postpone or cancel your ritual plans.

- To make sure all the components of the ritual you plan are in place.

- To know if the two coworkers you've selected (if there are to be any)
  are the right people into whom you can place your trust.

- To make sure the outcome will harm none in any realm.

- To decide if all your selves want this ritual as much as your physical
  or primary self.

- To see the possible outcome based on current energies that you have
  placed in motion at this time.

You may use any divination device you choose for this, but my preference is for the rich symbolism of the tarot cards. Most Witches have at least one deck they like and find easy to use. I use the *Robin Wood Tarot* because of its Pagan orientation, but no deck is right or wrong if it's one you are comfortable with and have confidence in.

Shuffle your deck as usual while focusing on the ritual to come. Stop shuffling and fan the cards out in front of you facedown once you feel the cards are lined up the way they ought to be.

From these, randomly select your first card of the five you will be choosing. We use five because in each tarot suit there are ten cards, excluding court cards such as queens and kings. Five is the midpoint, the point in any progression where it's just as long a trip back to where you began as it is to where you want to go. This is the perfect time to assess what you have more strength for—going back a step or two or forging onward.

Place that first card in an upright position slightly to your left. Then choose your second card and place it upright to the right of the first card. Keep doing this until all five cards are selected and are upright in front of you. They will be read as they were drawn, from left to right.

Card 1: Shows the normal state of your progression to unity with the divine.

Card 2: Shows the current, present time state of your unity with the divine. It may even help to point out any particular area of your spirituality which makes you feel doubtful or in crisis. Study this card carefully for any sign that there may be a better way to handle your spiritual crisis other than a Dark Night of the Soul ritual.

Card 3: This gives an indication of your need for a Dark Night of the Soul ritual at this time. It will show if your crisis is ready to be healed by a long night's journey into light, or if you need to look to other methods for healing your doubts or crises. Compare the symbolism and concepts in this card with card 2 to decide if you're being led into or away from the ritual.

Card 4: This gives an indication if any Dark Night of the Soul ritual you perform in the immediate future will progress or not. You may be warned to wait or told to enact the ritual as soon as possible. If you sense a warning from the cards, compare this one with cards 2 and 3.

Card 5: Shows the spiritual outcomes of the Dark Night of the Soul ritual should it be done at this time. It may tell if you will feel rejuvenated in your faith, be healed of doubt, or if your spiritual crisis needs some other form of therapy.

If the cards aren't clear about your need for this ritual or don't seem to indicate the outcome you desire, you may wish to put the card away and wait a day or two and try again. You may just need to rethink some of your ritual ideas, or you may need to try another solution to your problem.

We'll go through two examples of two separate card spreads to see what they tell us about the ritual.

The first thing you should do is glance over the cards to get an overall feel for their meanings. Note, too, how many cards from the major arcana are present. The more of these showing in any reading means that the ritual, spell, or other issue for which you are divining is out of your control. The more major arcana you see, the less control over this issue you have. This should be considered a warning that the deities wish you to hold off on the ritual at this time and, instead, to spend some time with them in prayer and meditation. Do another reading in a few days to see if this changes.

Also look for any eights, nines, and tens that appear. Eights and nines infer an organizing and pulling inward of our spirituality, allowing us to integrate it with other aspects of our respective being. Tens infer the completion of a cycle and suggest that a new one is about to begin or should be forced to begin. Tens do not mean you've achieved full unity with the creator, or even of any single aspect of it/her/him/them, but it can tell you that you're on the correct path to that penultimate unity with divinity. This is only because in our stage of human evolution the full power of the creator seems to be out of reach. This doesn't mean the ritual can't yield other riches or that all deities can't be united with at this time, however. Tens may also be a sign that a Dark Night of the Soul ritual is not needed at this time, especially if the ten appears in the third or fourth card position.

Not everyone undergoes a formal Dark Night of the Soul ritual in the Craft. For some it happens spontaneously, directed by your deities; for others, it takes the form of extreme challenges by both the deities and the threshold guardians.

Let's assume that your five cards drawn are in this configuration:

1) Ten of Wands

2) The Magician

3) Ace of Cups

4) Two of Cups

5) Five of Wands

The ten in this case appears in card 1. It often shows up in readings for people who take on too much responsibility. These are the people who don't know how to say no, and can always be counted on to do more than their share in any effort they undertake. If you're one of those, let me say that your giving of yourself is admirable, but that you have the right—even the duty—to also give to yourself. In order to grow spiritually you'll have to learn to say no to some things. These things you release can be magickal, spiritual, or mundane, but something has to go or you'll have no strength left to pursue spiritual matters as you should. It can also mean you're not enjoying the process of becoming, but are rushing to reach an end that does not exist in your incarnate form.

The Magician is a card of the major arcana, usually the one appearing right after the Fool. It tells the Witch that she has the power within her to take all the elements and energies around her and bend them to her will. This would not indicate a state of spiritual crisis, but perhaps should be taken as a suggestion to work toward more spiritual goals rather than seeking magick for physical wants and needs.

One of the areas of our lives governed by the suit of cups is our spiritual one. The ace indicates that a new beginning must be made if you want to grow further. By my interpretation this reading so far seems to indicate that no Dark Night of the Soul ritual is needed at this time because there are still basic concepts and practices that need to be addressed first. But let's continue on and look at the last two cards drawn.

The Two of Cups indicates friendship and balance. If a ritual is undertaken, this card tells us it should progress properly and that any chosen helpers are the right people for the job.

The Five of Wands indicates energies either coming together or falling apart. It should be read as an indication that you are only halfway to your spiritual goals and that much more work is needed.

Nothing in this reading indicates that a Dark Night of the Soul ritual is necessary. This Witch is currently on her correct path and holding a course that will eventually allow her to meet her spiritual goals. Continuing study and practice is indicated by the Ace of Cups, which will allow the energy of the Five of Wands to pull together rather than fall apart.

Now let's look at another hypothetical spread:

1) The Tower

2) Eight of Swords

3) Nine of Swords

4) Death or Change

5) The Sun

At first glance we notice that two of the five cards are from the twenty-two cards of the major arcana, indicating that the Witch has somehow gone off track in his spiritual progression and that correcting the course is going to be difficult. The Tower card in the first position indicates that this Witch's normal state of progression to the creator is always crumbling, leading to one failure after another. This Witch is likely frustrated and in doubt about the existence of the deities, or of his own abilities.

In position two we have an eight, showing us a gathering of energies, but are they the right energies? Probably not. This card usually shows a blindfolded and bound figure standing in the center of a circle of swords thrust into the sand dune upon which she stands. A closer examination of the card shows that her feet are not bound, and that a clear path of sand lies before her. In other words, this Witch needs to take a leap of faith and allow the deities to lead him out of his imagined constraints, the ones inhibiting his spiritual growth.

The Nine of Swords in the third position indicates a gathering of energy. It shows someone in crisis and doubt, unsure of which way to turn to get back on the spiritual path that once made him so happy.

At this point it seems that a Dark Night of the Soul ritual could help this person, but let's look at the last two cards.

The Death card is another from the major arcana and heralds profound change. Since the number four position indicates how a Dark Night of the Soul ritual would progress, this one seems to be saying it would be a night of deep spiritual changes during which new spiritual goals will be established and a new course to the deities plotted.

The last card drawn is the Sun, the archetype of triumph and control. If you ask the question, "Will the Dark Night of the Soul ritual heal my spiritual poverty?" the answer seems to be a resounding "yes."

In this case the Witch might be wise to use the information from the cards to make changes on his own and then do another reading in another month's time. If at that time the cards still show that he is off track, a Dark Night of the Soul ritual may be the solution he seeks.

What to Expect from a Dark Night of the Soul Ritual

A rigorous ritual such as Dark Night of the Soul should only be undertaken in any of the following circumstances. You may have more than one that fits, and this is to be taken as another sign that this ritual is approved for you at this point in your progression.

- When you start to doubt the existence of your deities.

- When you feel you have been abandoned by your deities.

- When all your spells fail and you feel as if your own magick or your magickal tools have turned against you.

- When you feel you've stagnated and have not made any spiritual progression for many months.

- When you continually astral project into the lower astral realms or into unpleasant and disturbing places.

- When you know you've taken a wrong turn somewhere and need help getting back on track, such as when you've become more interested in pouring your energy into personal magickal needs rather than worship of the divine.

- When you feel your many selves are out of sync with one another and you wish to have everyone on the same level, reaching for the same spiritual goal.

- When you doubt Witchcraft is the right spiritual path for you in this lifetime.

- When you feel too many beings have been coming to your aid and fear that some of them are trickster spirits whose purpose is to distract you from your spiritual goals.

- When you feel you are no closer to unity with the godhead or creator than you were when you first began your Craft studies.

It should be made clear that this is not the same unity with deity we seek when we work with invocations and evocations. This is a method of standing on the precipice of unity on the spiritual plane, one branch below actually uniting the godhead or creator on our climb up the tree of life.

The ritual will allow you to know how close you are to this goal and the crisis you face will direct you to correcting your course. Psychologist Carl Jung referred to these types of rituals as tapping into the cosmic consciousness (as opposed to his well-known term *collective unconsciousness,* from which he believed all information of things past, present, and future could be culled), a universal database of thoughtforms that have shaped past, present, and future. It correlates with the center of our being and our psychic selves from which answers to the ancient mysteries will open to the seeker.

Everyone experiences this consciousness in a different way as we lose our personal sense of self, or our ego, and allow our conscious mind to merge into that of the spiritual. In this way we become a vessel for the divine energies, similar to the way we do in invocation rituals. The difference is that we not only gain knowledge through the Dark Night of the Soul, but the multilevel experience of learning and working in harmony with our body, brain, mind, and soul erases some of our physical desires and lets us look at our physical needs.

Remember that the ultimate divine states, "I am that which is attained at the end of desire." Through being human there will always be things we want that are more attractive to us than those things we need, and this ritual will help illumine those desires and needs and show us which is most important at our current stage of development.

In some cases the physical need may be more important. For example, if you've lost a job through no fault of your own, or had your car totaled, your immediate need is for income and transportation to and from that source of income. This ritual may show you this rather than give you a glimpse of your next spiritual step.

This is the way the cosmic wheel turns. In the Dark Night of the Soul we hover between the world of spirit and form. English poet Lord Byron wrote, "Between two worlds life hovers like a star, twixt night and morn, upon the horizon's verge." The metaphor of the horizon is appropriate for a Dark Night of the Soul ritual because we are literally standing at the feet of the deities, our heads in the spiritual, our hearts in the emotional, and our feet planted firmly on Mother Earth. We are in all worlds at once, and it is not unusual in this ritual to have your shadow self or co-walker show up to keep you company and to make sure that all your selves are taking the same journey.

It does you little good to have a mystic experience if it isn't recorded or reflected in all worlds in which you reside. This is the purpose of meeting your shadow self and spirit self. You want them to work in harmony with one another as you strive toward spiritual growth. This is similar to the way in which you want to integrate your conscious, subconscious, and superconscious minds. We can even correlate the two:

Your Physical Self = Your Conscious Mind

Your Shadow Self = Your Subconscious Mind

Your Spirit Self = Your Superconscious Mind

As an intermediate student you probably were taught, or figured out on your own, that the mind and the brain are not always the same thing. The brain is the physical organ that runs all your bodily processes. The mind is more esoteric, that part of you that transcends analytic thought and connects you to your superconscious self, or what some occultists refer to as your Higher Self.

Another phenomena of the Dark Night of the Soul ritual is that you may experience visions of the deity or deities that range from the spectacular to the scary. This is another version of the terror of the threshold, only this time, instead of guarding the gate to the divine, it is the divine itself that blocks your path to test your worthiness and to stay you on your course.

There can be serious repercussions for not staying the course, no matter how frightened you feel. Remember that your trusted friends are nearby and will not allow anything to happen to you.

If during the ritual you find that you are being taken off the course you felt was correct, take this as a hint from your patrons that you need to go where they direct you. You may need to climb down a few limbs and relearn some old lessons or explore areas of metaphysical practice you have not yet tried or mastered.

Other spirits may appear outside of your ritual circle, the one in which you will remain from the beginning of the ritual, just prior to sundown, to its end at sunrise. A deceased relative, an angelic being, a spirit guide, an elemental guardian, a faery, or a daemon (not demon) may make their presence known. Most of these are there to support your efforts while others may come to taunt you, which is another test of your worthiness to step across the next threshold of spiritual growth.

The Dark Night of the Soul Ritual

It should be obvious by this point in your career that the event which will transpire during your Dark Night of the Soul ritual will be unlike any rite you've ever before experienced. You may never do one, or you may decide to do only do one or two in your entire Craft career. And remember that with knowledge comes wisdom, which allows us to learn and grow, resetting our course toward the divine and reaffirming that commitment.

Even though you will perform the ritual within the confines of a cast circle and you may have visions and manifestations during this rite, they should never be confused with the average inner-world journey, shamanic journey, otherworld trip, *immrama* (epic otherworld journey), *aisling* (mythic dream), or vision quest. It's not something we do to seek answers, but to show us where we need to find ourselves and the deities who created us. In other words, the experience molds itself into what each individual needs to be told and shown so we may step over the edge of the next precipice and onto the next step in our growth.

There are some warnings that need to be heeded before you begin. The rigors of this ritual are not suitable for everyone, even when the tarot cards indicate a good outcome. The ritual is to begin just prior to sundown and will not end until sunrise. If you have any health condition that makes staying awake until dawn a danger to you, then you should not do the ritual. You also should not use stimulants, such as caffeine, to help you stay awake. That would be defeating your purpose.

For the hours of the ritual, you will be allowed no food or drink and are not to leave the confines of your circle for any reason. Again, be aware that there are many health conditions in which going even a few hours without food or water is contraindicated. For example, diabetics should not allow themselves to go into insulin shock just for a ritual. Either the rite should not be enacted or one of your chosen two helpers, often referred to as handmaidens or courtier men, should monitor your progress from start to finish.

Even though we think of this as a "dark" ritual, I recommend doing it as near to the summer solstice as possible. This makes the ritual much shorter, depending on latitude. This isn't a ritual of self-punishment, but one meant to enlighten. Pushing yourself through a long, unpleasant night is counterproductive for most Witches. Take the easy way out and perform the ritual when the nights are the shortest rather than attempting them during the dark half of the year.

Because the ritual combines lack of sleep with suggestions for where your thoughts should be directed, it is not uncommon to witness a myriad of visions. It will be up to the Witch to decide what are trickster manifestations, dissertations, and which ones contain genuine spiritual guidance.

I suggest you do this not only as close to the summer solstice as possible, when the days are longest and the nights the shortest, but that you have no other obligations on the day of the night you perform the ritual or the day after. On the day of, take a nap in the afternoon. If you find you can't sleep, then take some slow, deep breaths and meditate to relax. When you awaken, eat a light meal that is free from salts that will ground you and hinder your ritual goal, then drink eight ounces of water.

About an hour before sunset, take a relaxing bath or shower. You may want to use an herbal soap that has relaxing properties, such as lavender. Or you may want to use incense if your bathroom is large enough or is well ventilated.

Dress in your ritual robe if possible. Being nude for this many hours may make you too cold. You may, however, be nude for the hour that marks the high point of the ritual, which peaks at three o'clock in the morning.

If you are having handmaidens or courtier men assisting you, you must decide in advance when they will arrive. You may wish to give them a key to your home and have them come in around 2:30, or you may want them there for the entire ritual, especially if you have a health concerns such as diabetes. Having two assistants is traditional, but one will work.

Another serious note of caution is that this ritual calls for the use of lighted candles at times when the Witch will not be in any condition to monitor them. If you do not have reliable assistants then do not light the candles. The candles may be present but should not be lighted unless someone is awake and able to keep an eye on them at all times. The same goes for incense or anything else that has the potential to spark a fire that is out of your control.

Your assistants are not to enter your ritual space at any time during your rite unless there is an emergency, in which case they will immediately ground your circle as take care of your physical needs.

Atmosphere is everything in this ritual, and you may want to consider prerecorded music that will help set the mood. It's best if you record on a cassette that automatically repeats itself or use compact disks that are set to play continually.

You may want to choose pieces that have never had any lyrics associated with them. Many New Age collections are made for meditation and can give you a feeling of floating free, or you can use a drumming beat. Be warned that the pounding will make you crazy after about an hour; music is more soothing.

If you do choose music that is associated with lyrics or that has lyrics, make sure in advance that nothing in it is in conflict with your goal. It should contain words of hope and inspiration, never of failure. Some suggestions for music include:

"You'll Never Walk Alone." From the musical *Carousel* by Richard Rodgers and Oscar Hammerstein II.

"Night on Bald Mountain." Instrumental by Modest Mussorgsky, performed by Rimsky-Korsakov; music evokes chaos dispelled by the coming of dawn on a sacred day.

"Midnight on Olive's Brow." A Christian hymn that sings the praise of Jesus' success during his Dark Night of the Soul; use without lyric.

"Somewhere In Time." Instrumental version of the theme from the movie of the same name.

"Climb Every Mountain." From the musical *The Sound of Music* by Richard Rodgers and Oscar Hammerstein II.

"The Best of Times." From the musical *La Cage Aux Folles* by Jerry Herman and Harvey Fierstein.

"In the Hall of the Mountain King." Instrumental by Norwegian composer Edvard Grieg.

"The New World Symphony, Main Theme." Instrumental by Anton Dvorak.

"The Rose." Written for the movie of the same name; by Amanda McBroom.

"Ascension to The All That Is." Cadence-free instrumental by Robert Slap, produced by Valley of the Sun.

"Someone to Watch Over Me." From the musical *Oh Kay* by George and Ira Gershwin.

"The Wind Beneath My Wings." Written for the movie *Beaches*, recorded by various artists; by Larry Henley and Jeff Silbar.

These are just a few musical pieces that came to mind. There are hundreds more selections you could make, maybe thousands. Choose yours with care to meet your needs, picking those which give you comfort in times of despair.

As the last rays of the setting sun step down beyond the horizon, cast your circle in your usual manner. You may choose to have your ritual tools with you, but in most cases it's best to leave them out. You are seeking spiritual advancement and, in time, you want to leave behind your dependence on tools.

You may sit, stand, pace, or lie down as you desire, but you are to remain awake and focused on your spiritual needs. Praying is helpful for some. During this time many spirits may appear just outside your circle. They may tempt you, taunt you, or assist you. You may listen to them, verbally interact with them, or ignore them, as you see fit.

You may have a single candle lit to help you focus, but only if you're sure you can stay awake to keep an eye on it. A glass-enclosed or thick-based candle is best as it tends not to topple as easy, especially if you're on carpet, as most of us will be.

Around 2:30 in the morning your assistants should arrive, if they have not been there the entire time. When they arrive you, should lie facedown in your circle with your head pointing to the direction in which you or your tradition believes is the home of the deities. Fan your arms and legs out to make a pentagram.

Even if you have been robed for the first part of this ritual, you may choose to be sky-clad, or nude, for the the next hour. This is said to show the deities that you do not harbor hatred for the vessel in which your soul currently resides, that you are created in their beautiful image, and that you are like a newborn child, naked and fresh from the womb of the Mother Goddess.

Just outside your circle, your assistants will light a black or white candle of spirit; at your right hand, they will light a candle of blue, white, or yellow to represent the element of air. At your right foot, a candle of the fire element will be lit. This is usually red, orange, or gold. At your left foot is the earth candle of green, brown, or yellow; and at your left hand is a water candle of blue, silver, or violet. Small votives in glass containers are best to use. They are more stable than tapers and the glass still allows their light to show even as they melt down.

You are now approaching the apex of the ritual.

Three o'clock in the morning has long been known as "the soul's midnight." The origin of this term is hazy. Some say it was so named because it was a popular time to die. Others, like American author F. Scott Fitzgerald, called three o'clock "the crack up," and wrote, "In a real dark night of the soul it is always three o'clock in the morning."

Your assistants may offer words of encouragement or play devil's advocate. They may guide your mind toward specific thoughts or problems in your spiritual life if you've made them aware of these. You may choose to respond to them or not, but at no time is idle chatter to be indulged.

When it is three o'clock, they will let you know in some way. I suggest having them say:

> The midnight of the soul is here at last,
> A time of spirits present and past;
> Desolation and despair may be healed this night,
> Keep your heart and your will on divinity's light.

At this point your assistants should become silent as you seek your own inner transformation. All they should be doing now is sitting quietly, keeping an eye on the candles.

Around 3:30 they should extinguish all candles and either leave the house, or at least go into another room.

At this point you may sit up, stand, pace, or do whatever you wish within your circle. Most important of all, you should be aware of any change of feelings you have for your spiritual path. Examine any visions that came to you. You may even want your Book of Shadows or magickal diary in your circle with you so you don't lose any important information.

As the sun starts to rise you may thank your deities and any other helpful spirits for their assistance, then ground your circle.

Go to a nearby window and throw back the drapes. Robe yourself and go outdoors if you can and greet the rising sun. Welcome it as a sign that you have passed the challenge of the Dark Night of the Soul and you are ready to move back into the light that will illumine your path to your goal, which has been made clear by your long night's trial.

After that, take another soothing bath or shower and go to bed and sleep. Don't be surprised if you dream of visions from your ritual. This is natural and common and may be the deities' way of emphasizing a part of your growth they feel is important for you to follow and keep in the forefront of your conscious mind as you continue your spiritual journey.

At the end of each night is a new sunrise. Nothing lasts forever, but this is one thing scientists tell us we can count on for a few million more years. No matter how trying our Dark Night of the Soul, eventually the dawn heralds its ending, and we all come through our dark ordeals changed, for the better—we hope.

Assessing Your Progress

In the beginning of this book you were asked to write a definition of advanced Witchcraft or an advanced Witch. Without looking back at your original concept, take a moment to write your current definition. If you need time to think about it, close this book and take all the time you like to contemplate your response, but please do try to comment.

DATE OF ENTRY: _____

_____

_____

_____

_____

_____

_____

_____

_____

_____

_____

_____

Has your answer changed much, if at all? Why or why not? Is the change, or lack of it, good or bad? Are you comfortable with the change? Are you comfortable with the lack of change? Has your definition expanded, contracted, remained consistent?

What else do you want to know and do as an advanced practitioner? Where are you now and how have you come here? Where do you want to go and how will you get there? Do you feel compelled to take your practice in a new direction? An old one? What do you still seek? How will you find it? Do you have some new patron deities? Has your relationship with your old patrons remained the same? How do you feel your old patrons look upon your new ones?

As we pass from threshold to threshold time and time again, new challenges will face us. We may not always know what we want, or even what we don't want. But as Witches we keep seeking, sifting from the sands of all that is, was, or ever will be the tiny golden nuggets of wisdom only the tenacious seeker will find.

The endless seeker is the advanced Witch. Like the Hermit of the tarot who walks to the edge of the precipice and lifts his lamp high to peer out into the vast unknown, the cycle of seeking, the opening of the closed door, and the quest for the divine all begin again.

Resources &
References

Where our work continues

Afterword

. . . and the Ending

Another cycle ends and a new one begins. This is the foundation of the life of a Witch; an endless circle of endings and rebirthings where the learning never stops and the opportunity to grow is always present. Always our spirits strive to stay the course homeward toward their points of origin in the womb of the great Mother Goddess.

I hope you're not disappointed that I didn't give you three hundred pages of so-called advanced spells. That was not my purpose, and it would have been an injustice to you—an insult even to the truly advanced. I don't want to tell you what to think, but hope to stimulate your curiosity so you are forced to think for yourself. If you've reached this point in this book and do not like all I've written between the covers, I consider that a good thing. Spiritually healthy, in fact. It means you've not lost your ability to think critically. Critical thinking and self-responsibility are two characteristics that make the finest Witches. So if you are not happy with all you've read, then please take only what was valuable to you and discard the rest, or just internalize it to analyze against the next book on advanced Craft work you read.

As I stated in the preface, advancing in the Craft is like trying to work your way from the ground to the top point of a huge tree. The higher you climb, the more divergent and numerous the available pathways become. Many sights, sounds, and smells will dazzle and distract you. Some tangential branches can provide valuable lessons, others are a waste of time, and some are just there for fun. Almost all of them will get you where you want to go eventually, but each choice you make on the pathway is unique to your experience. Your ascent will change knowledge into wisdom. We won't all climb the tree the same way. Every branch will not suit every Witch. Also, there's no law that says if you bypassed something interesting a few limbs below, that you cannot go back and explore it further before continuing your ascent.

As an advanced Witch you may see that those branches not taken lead you to study an esoteric art that you have not yet mastered, or one that you once had to leave behind while making the choice to pursue another. As was established earlier, we cannot all be advanced in every art that makes up the full spectrum of the Witch's Craft, no matter how much we wish we could. That's just more than one lifetime will allow. So we pick and choose and hope we're doing the right things. For most of us there just isn't time for everything we want to do with our lives or our Craft. Some will compensate for this by developing only those areas for which an inborn talent is displayed. Others add elements from other paths, syncretic religion being an old and accepted practice virtually everywhere on the planet.

A Witch who reaches the advanced levels of the Craft is living an advanced life. She knows that the hungry soul must always be fed with knowledge if it is to continue to grow. Knowledge can be turned to wisdom, and wisdom into spiritual advancement.

And that segues very well into my comments upon my choice of works cited in the bibliography.

A book of this scope and size bellowed to have a bibliography attached to it, yet it was difficult for me to compile. Those of you who've been in the Craft even for as little as five years know there is no way you could ever offer thanks and acknowledgment to everyone or everything that helped shape your thinking and practice. Even after one year it can seem as if *everything* shaped your magickal worldview. Not that this is a bad thing; in fact, it's wonderful to actually live by the spiritual path you've chosen, which includes keeping an open mind.

I found it unavoidable that after over twenty years of living with Witchcraft that any bibliography can hope to encompass every book, movie, television show, teacher, student, acquaintance, novel, poem, tradition, myth, legend, workshop, pantheon, friend, magician, mystic, gnostic, New Ager, novice, sage, elder, crone, virgin, mother, dream, vision, fellow coven member, other coven members, ritual, spell, musician, artist, author, editor, article, publication, or website that has contributed to the sum of what I embrace and practice today. Many non-Craft events and experiences have contributed to my spiritual growth as well.

The result is a "select bibliography" exclusively made up of books. The books chosen are the ones I feel have had the most profound influence on me and, ultimately, to the material presented in this book. Even paired down to the book-only level, making selections was not an easy task. For every entry I put in, I took another out, then changed it again the next day, and then fretted for another night about my choice.

I'm still not wholly satisfied with the outcome, but I offer my best summary of some of the high points of the book phase of my spiritual education.

The same holds true for the acknowledgments in the front of this book. Some of those people listed are newcomers to the Craft. These are the ones who ask the questions that make me think the hardest and keep my mind open. Many of the others are longtime Witches, some are fellow writers, and a few others are both. Some are editors, others are activists, some are priestesses. Two are no longer inhabiting the earth plane, but their love and teachings made up a big part of who I am, and I could see no reason to exclude them by virtue of the fact that they are not here. Corporeal or not, they still live within my heart and on a plane in which I will someday join them.

To each of you trodding your special path through the Craft of the Wise, whatever your present level of skill or your long-term ambitions, I thank you for being one of us. You make our web stronger just by being who you are. I hope we all continue to share and grow as a community and in our collective spiritual strength as we seek union with the divinity from which we were created. Eventually we'll all get where we're going and will meet in the great otherworld cauldron of life, death, and life renewed.

If you feel so moved, please drop me an e-mail at edainmccoy@yahoo.com or visit my website at http://www.edainmccoy.com and let me know what you feel is advanced and what's not, what worked for you in this book and what did not. There can always be a Volume II. I'm not infallible, so corrections and contrary observations are welcome as well. Your ideas may not be in sync with my own, but I have other Witch writer friends who may love your concepts.

All feedback and insights are welcome and I try to respond to all my e-mail messages, but please be aware that my queue of unanswered mail can trail back for months at a time (even longer for snail mail).

I leave you now with my own version of the Witches' Rede, or Wiccan Rede, and a sound reminder of the Law of Threefold Return, whose responsibility we bear each time we attempt a spell or ritual:

The highest law I now shall teach,
Mind well your actions, thoughts, and speech;
Many beings can hear and spirits know
The wickedness you seek not to show.
So turns the wheel from year to year,
Live in Their love and have no fear;
This ancient wisdom to you I tell,
As it harms none, do what you will.
Take caution of the next law too,
For all you do comes back to you;
The wheel keeps turning, three times three,
As you will, so mote it be.

Here's wishing you the best on the newest branch of your spiritual journey.

Brightest blessings!

Edain McCoy

Resources

By the time one reaches the threshold of the advanced Craft, it's a good bet they already know where to find the tools and support they want. In case you don't, or if you've jumped way ahead of yourself and are reading this book as a beginner just to see what the future may hold, I include this appendix as a leaping-off point for finding what you need.

Common courtesy dictates that local occult supply shops should be checked into first for finding magickal accouterments before out-of-area resources. This not only helps support other members of your Craft community, but these shops are also good places to find local networking forums.

Every attempt has been made to make this appendix accurate at the time of publication, but remember that addresses can change suddenly, businesses can fail, and periodicals can cease publication. Sometimes free catalogs find they must charge for subscription or must raise prices to stay competitive. If you are reading this book a year or more from its publication date, you would be wise to query business contacts with return postage to check on prices and the availability of goods and services. Always remember to enclose an SASE (self-addressed stamped envelope) whenever making inquiries to businesses within your own country, or an IRC (international reply coupon) when querying elsewhere. This is not only a matter of courtesy, but is often the only way to ensure a reply.

Many organizations, publications, and businesses have found their way into cyberspace. Be sure to check the search engines on your Web browser for links to these and many other resources.

Herbs, Oils, Tools, and Other Accouterments

Aroma Vera
5901 Rodeo Road
Los Angeles, CA 90016
Write for catalog price for essential oils, floral waters, dried products, aromatherapy oils, and incense censors.

Azure Green
P.O. Box 48
Middlefield, MA 01243-0048
413-623-2155
http://www.azuregreen.com
Azure Green has almost everything, including stellar customer service. Request free catalog or order via their website.

Balefire
6504 Vista Ave.
Wauwatosa, WI 53213
This mail-order company carries a large stock of brews, oils, and incenses designed for specific Pagan needs such as scrying, spirit contact, and spellwork. Write for catalog.

Branwen's Cauldron
Dreaming Spirit
P.O. Box 4263
Danbury, CT 06813-4263
http://www.branwenscauldron.com
Natural, homemade incenses and resins, oils, and tools for using them. Dreaming Spirit welcomes queries about custom blends of incenses or oils. The $2 for their catalog is refundable with your first order.

Earth Scents by Marah
Box 948
Madison, NJ 07940
Sellers of herbs, incenses, books, oil blends and other tools. Catalog, $1.

General Bottle Supply
1930 E. 51st Street
Los Angeles, CA 90058
Write for free catalog of herb, oil, and salt bottles.

Gypsy Heaven
115 S. Main St.
New Hope, PA 18938
215-862-5251
Request catalog of magickal supplies. Currently catalog is being offered free, but it doesn't hurt to check this information.

Halcyon Herb Company
Box 7153 L
Halcyon, CA 93421
Sells not only magickal herbs but also staffs, brooms, cloaks, drums, and other items of interest to Pagan folk. Current catalog, $5.

Indiana Botanic Gardens
2401 W. 37th Avenue
Hobart, IN 46342
http://www.botanichealth.com
Sells herbal health products, dried herbs, and essential oils.

Isis Metaphysical
http://www.isisbooks.com
A popular Denver networking, classroom, bookstore, and supply shop.

Just Wingin' It
P.O. Box 7029
Riverside, CA 92513-7029
http://www.jwi.com
Jewelry, incense, bottles, and other magickal items both wholesale and retail.

Lavender Folk Herbal
P.O. Box 1261, Dept. SW
Boulder, CO 80306
Medicinal and magickal tea blends, herbs, and herbal crafts. $2 catalog is refundable with first order.

Leydet Oils
P.O. Box 2354
Fair Oaks, CA 95628
Sellers of fine essential oils. Price list $2.

Light and Shadows
Catalog Consumer Service
2215-R Market St., Box 801
San Francisco, CA 94114-1612
Write for their free metaphysical supply catalog.

MagiCrafts
http://www.magicrafts.com

Moon Scents
P.O. Box 1588-C
Cambridge, MA 02238
603-356-3666
http://www.moonscents.com
Large collection of magickal paraphernalia and books. May offer free catalog.

The Mystic Merchant
http://www.mysticmerchant.com

Natural Impulse Handmade Soap and Sundries
P.O. Box 94441
Birmingham, AL 35220
http://www.naturalimpulse.com
Sells readymade soaps made of natural oils by a company openly committed to protecting the environment.

Nimue's Garden
Body Au Natural
P.O. Box 224
Havelock, NC 28532
252-259-1227
http://www.nimuesgarden.com
Homemade ritual soaps, body lotions, and other magickal beauty products for both men and women. A $2 charge for their most recent catalog will be refunded with your first order.

Pagan Pretties
http://www.paganpretties.com
Jewelry and other odds and ends.

POTO
1223 Wilshire Blvd. # 925
Santa Monica, CA 90403
310-451-9166
http://www.poto.com
POTO is short for "Procurer of the Obscure." POTO specializes in stocking or locating rare and hard-to-find occult items. My experience with them is that they are fast and thorough.

Sacred Spirit Products
P.O. Box 8163
Salem, MA 01971-8163
Sellers of books, magickal tools, herbs, incense, and other occult items. Catalog, $3.

Sunburst Bottle Company
5710 Auburn Blvd., Suite 7
Sacramento, CA 95841
Bottle and container provider whose current catalog is $2. Write or call for current price.

Triple Moon Witchware
http://www.witchware.com
Lots of jewelry and other items.

Witch's Brew
http://www.witchs-brew.com

Valley of the Sun
P.O. Box 38
Malibu, CA 90265
http://www.sutphenpublishing.com
This is Dick Sutphen's company. Website has articles and information, as well as fine New Age videos and CDs.

General Pagan Publications

Accord
Council of the Magickal Arts, Inc.
P.O. Box 890526
Houston, TX 77289
Published by a well-known Texas-based networking organization. As of this writing, sample issues are $4.50.

Blessed Bee
P.O. Box 641
Port Arena, CA   95468
707-882-2052
info@blessedbee.com
Publication for Pagan families with younger children. Call or e-mail for rates.

Circle Magazine
P.O. Box 9
Barneveld, WI 53507
http://www.circlesanctuary.org
A popular, professional journal for Pagan news and gatherings, contacts and seasonal celebration information. Sample copy, $5. Write for other subscription information.

The Green Egg
P.O. Box 1542
Ukiah, CA 95482
http://www.caw.org.green-egg
This very popular magazine has been around for a long time. Professionally formatted and always controversial. Contains beautiful artwork. Write or see website for current rates.

Hecate's Loom
Box 5206, Station B
Victoria, BC
Canada V8R 6N4
Another professional quality journal. Focus on Pagan arts. Write for rates. United States residents should include an IRC to ensure a reply.

PanGaia
Blessed Bee, Inc.
P.O. Box 641
Point Arena, CA   95468-0099
http://www.pangaia.com
Earth-focused general Pagan publication. Professional format and artwork.

Stones of Avalon
11643 Pavilion
Pierrefonds, Quebec
Canada H8Y 2Y3
514-685-5828
E-Mail: stonesofavalon@hotmail.com
National Canadian Pagan journal published eight times a year. Publisher Rhiannon Hawthorn says they strive to be "new and different." Would like to be a force in uniting the Canadian Pagan community and welcomes feedback.

Online Networking

The Internet has exploded with Pagan and Wiccan information in proportion to booming interest. Local libraries or public universities often have connections you can use if you're not online at home. Even without a computer, Internet hookups are available through your television with relatively little expense through such devices as Web TV. The resources listed here are national or international in scope, but hundreds of viable regional, state/provincial, local, and campus organizations have been formed. Use your web server's search engine to find these.

BeliefNet
http://www.beliefnet.com
This unique site examines and connects people of all beliefs. Features articles from upcoming publications and offers challenging ideas for the exchange of ideas. It includes a large section on "earth-based" religions, including a detailed listing of open covens and groups and those that are forming. Nasty recent rumors are that this site will soon be shutting down. Let's hope these are not true.

British Pagan Circle
http://www.geocities.com/RainForest/canopy/7046

The Church of All Worlds
http://www.caw.org
This is the group that sponsors the well-known and controversial magazine *Green Egg*. They have Nests, or hive groups, around the world. If there is not one in your area, they can help you start one.

Circle Guide to Groups and Resources
http://www.circlesanctuary.org/publications
This biennial publication lists open groups, stores, forums, and other places to network.

The Council of Magickal Arts
http://www.houston-pno.org
Networking organization based in Texas. Produces excellent journal and is expanding its horizons all the time.

Covenant of the Goddess (COG)
http://www.cog.org
Perhaps the largest Pagan networking organization. If there is not a group near you, they can help guide you through their program.

Covenant of Unitarian Universalist Pagans (CUUPs)
http://www.cuups.org
If you live in or near a large city, it's likely you have a Unitarian Universalist Church near you. If they do not already have a CUUPs group, talk to someone there about what is needed to form one.

Advanced Paganism
http://groups.yahoo.com/groups/Advanced_Paganism
A forum for the discussion of advanced magickal and Craft topics.

The Fellowship of Isis
http://www.fellowshipofisis.com
A networking and teaching organization with lots of non-European members.

Magickal Education Convocation
http://www.convocation.org

New Age Information Network
http://www.newageinfo.com/res/wicca

Online Pagan Networks
http://www.candledark.net

Pagan Awareness Network, Australia
http://www.paganawareness.net.au

Pagan Education Network (PEN)
http://www.bloomington.in.us/~pen

PagaNet News
http://www.paganet.org

The Pagan Federation, Canada
http://www.pfpc.ca
The Pagan Federation, England
http://paganfed.demon.co.uk

The Pagan Federation, Scotland
http://www.vscotland.org.uk

The Pagan Federation, South Africa
http://www.pfsa.org

Pagan Ireland
http://www.paganireland.com

Pagan Network Webring
http://www.paganprofiles.com/webring

Pagan Paths IRC Chat Network
http://www.paganpaths.org

The Witches' Voice
http://www.witchvox.com
Excellent and beautifully maintained site for the latest news and information affecting the Pagan world. Educations, unity, and networking are the focus. Witches' Voice maintains a huge database of open circles, covens who teach or are open to new members, and Pagan gatherings at the local level.

Witches Against Religious Discrimination (WARD)
http://www.ward-hg.org
Most states and provinces now have their own organizations and welcome your involvement. Modeled on the effective work of the Jewish Anti-Discrimination League.

Witches' League for Public Awareness
http://www.celticcrow.com
First organized in the 1980s by Salem Witch, author, and activist Laurie Cabot to educate the public on Witchcraft. Like WARD, this organization has branches throughout North America.

Youth Wiccans and Pagans of Canada
http://www.OypcO.cjb.net

A Request to Other Advanced Practitioners

The number of advanced practitioners of various Craft traditions has blossomed in proportion to the amazing growth we've seen in our religion in the past decade. Some of you still maintain active leadership and teaching roles within your community. Many of us do not. Where once we looked forward to sharing and teaching and learning with others, as we approach or attained elderhood many of us turn inward, preferring to practice with significant others, our families, with one or two close friends, or as a solitary. Famous elders who helped found many of our traditions and share their knowledge with us throughout most of the last century, such as the esteemed "Grand Old Man of the Craft" (and one of my personal heroes) Raymond Buckland, and the Lady Janet Farrar, no longer head covens or organize teaching groups.

I'm not sure what causes this turning inward. Perhaps with age and wisdom comes the impulse to spend time with our many selves, living the life of soul peace for which we've striven for so long and so hard. Many of our advanced practitioners have worked hard in and with the Craft for most of their lives and have earned their sabbatical.

I would never ask you to give up your well-deserved retirement from public life, only that you make yourselves available to answer the occasional question from a sincere newcomer.

I receive a great many letters, both via e-mail and snail mail, showing me that many people want to turn to the Craft, not as a spiritual path or a religion but as a cure for their chaotic, troubled lives. I'm not a lawyer, a doctor, or an accountant, and don't even know where to begin answering some of the mail I get.

Just yesterday I opened a package of letters forwarded from my publisher. There were seventeen. Two letter writers told me they were possessed by evil entities and wished me to remove them. Another was being harassed by an astral being that would not leave her alone, but she informed me that if I were a real Witch I'd know who it was and be able to do something about it. Another was a twelve-year-old boy who was determined to be a "warlock" with or without my help. (Where do you begin dispelling all the misconceptions that go with that one?) One writer said he saw my book *Bewitchments* in a store but couldn't afford to buy it right now; would I please tell him about everything that was in it? From another envelope fell a huge hunk of dark hair, and from another some nail clippings. There was a request to work manipulative magick on a girlfriend who'd left a relationship to pursue other interests, and another who felt demons were coming to him at night and picking at him with tiny pitchforks. One woman wanted magick to create an entire new life in which her old one would not be remembered by either her or anyone else. Some admitted to having been raised in strict fundamental Christian households, and that background showed in their attitudes toward the various tortures they described or feared. Naturally, only one of the seventeen contained an SASE, and that one was from a bright teenager who asked good questions and whose letter I will be delighted to answer. Someday he will be a fine full member of our web and, hopefully, pass his knowledge and strength on to others.

Some letters are even worse and scare me to the core of my spirit. I fear for the health, safety, and future of these people who are suffering terrible trials as they try to get through each day of their lives in one piece. I wish I could do more than return a letter months later recommending books or professional help, but no religion, especially not one as self-responsible as Witchcraft, can be the cure-all these people seek.

My request to those of you who are advanced practitioners is to make yourself available to these needy people inasmuch as you are able without sacrificing your privacy, safety, or sanity. Perhaps giving a post office box number to a local occult store saying you'd be glad to counsel the occasional someone by mail or phone would be all you'd need to do to help someone over their hurdle, or send them on to the next religion that appears as a panacea.

I'm not asking you to make Witches of all these people, but to help those of us being crushed under bags full of mail that would be the envy of Santa Claus. Consider it a community service, one an elder should be proud to do, even if it's just getting one toenail wet in the pool of those who are drowning.

In most of the mainstream religions this approach of tell the priest/ess and s/he will fix it for you could work. A minister, Sunday school teacher, rabbi, priest, cantor, or other elder would take such sad cases under their proverbial wing and attempt to solve their life's difficulties for them, often by using their religion as a carrot to dangle in front of these starving rabbits.

This approach does not work in Witchcraft. Again I repeat what we all know, that Witchcraft is a path of self-responsibility, and before one can successfully undertake its demanding lessons, they have to have their personal life in some semblance of order. American psychologist Harold Maslow's *Maslow's Hierarchy of Human Needs* lists "order" and "beauty" among its top seven requirements necessary for happy and balanced living.

While "order" may mean different things to different people—some people can maintain well-ordered clutter—it is a necessity for our psyches, especially in the Craft where so many choices are left to us alone. Yet I'll bet if it's known in the community that you're a priest, priestess, elder, or other advanced practitioner that you have been bombarded with bizarre requests to help people whom you know cannot and will not be helped.

There has to be a better way and I see that as all of us taking the time to answer the queries of one or two people each month, sending the sincere seekers in the right direction and dissuading those not yet ready for all the Craft demands us to handle. In no way am I asking anyone to mentor someone or to continue to waste valuable hours of their time on people who have an unending litany of problems to solve.

In metaphysics we label these people "psychic vampires." They can leach the energy from an individual or coven in a matter of weeks. They live in a state of permanent turmoil and chaos. A few truly want the madness to end, in which case they need to be seen by a therapist or doctor; not a Witch, unless, of course, one of these happens to be your normal occupation. It's sad but true that many people love their personal world of chaos. It keeps attention focused on them and keeps someone else worrying about their problems. In some cases you'll succeed in giving real help and, with luck and some assistance from the deities, you may uncover a new Witch who can take his or her experience and help others.

It should go without saying that you should not work with minors unless you wish to be sued, and you should never dispense medical, legal, or financial advice unless you're licensed to do so. All most of us can do is answer some questions, then send people off to seek their own answers, which is the way the Craft of the Wise is intended to be learned.

To do this the seeker must first be urged to look within; a very hard task. This is why it's always easier to see how someone else should solve their problems than it is to see how to fix your own.

As you are all too aware, a great many people come to Witchcraft expecting us to have the same "take charge" attitude they got at the local Rescue Mission or Outreach Center. Even an intermediate level Witch knows this doesn't work.

One of the first books on the Craft I read—actually it was the second—was the late Sybil Leek's *The Complete Art of Witchcraft* (New York: Harper and Row, 1971). She wrote that a Witch could not be made from a life in constant turmoil. She used a term I cannot quote with accuracy, but which has always remained in the forefront of my mind: "See to your own house first."

No one's life is free from ups and downs, but we learn to use the magick of our inner selves to bring those into balance and harmony with the world around us. This isn't always easy, and sometimes our efforts fail, but at least we're not running in unknown directions demanding that someone handle the problem for us. On the path of the self-responsible one must first have some "order and beauty," a sense of soul peace, before our faith can be practiced with success. This doesn't mean we have to know what we want and need; those things will come later. This doesn't mean our lives are perfect; such a miracle is not likely to occur any time soon. It requires knowing only one thing, but it's the hardest of all things to find and to incorporate into our wholeness of being.

The works of Jacobian playwright William Shakespeare are full of metaphysical wisdom if one is willing to look for them. One of his most famous and oft-quoted lines is from his play *Hamlet*. If you live by it, the tenets of the Pagan Rede will follow as spring follows winter: "To thine own self be true." If you remain true to yourself and your ethics, you will never cause harm to yourself or others. Best of all, you will be living an honest life in harmony with the whole universe. And since magick takes the path of least resistance, you benefit yourself by becoming a conduit of positive power.

Another famous oracle, the one at Delphi, Greece, taught seekers of spiritual knowledge this same basic truth. Witchcraft cannot be a panacea for all ills, but it is a powerful working tool for those practicing in courage, conviction, and faith. It stands as a universal tenet for all of us who look for solutions and answers. The Delphic Oracle of ancient Greece told us the greatest truth of all if we seek to live in balance and harmony with all their ever was, is, or will be: *know thyself.*

Bibliography

Aburrow, Yvonne. *Auguries and Omens: The Magical Lore of Birds*. Cheiveley, Berks, UK: Capall Bann, 1994.

Adler, Margot. *Drawing Down the Moon*. Boston: Beacon Press, 1986. Revised and expanded edition.

Alexander, Jane. *Sacred Rituals at Home*. New York: Sterling Publishing Co., 2000.

Amber, Reuben. *Color Therapy*. Santa Fe: Aurora Press, 1983.

Andrews, Ted. *Animal-Speak: The Spiritual and Magical Powers of Creatures Great and Small*. St. Paul: Llewellyn, 1993.

Arrowsmith, Nancy, and George Moorse. *A Field Guide to the Little People*. New York: Hill and Wang, 1977.

Ashcroft-Nowicki, Dolores. *The Initiate's Book of Pathworkings*. York Beach, ME: Samuel Weiser, Inc., 1999.

———, and J. H. Brennan. *The Magical Use of Thought Forms*. St. Paul: Llewellyn, 2001.

Ashe, Geoffrey. *The Ancient Wisdom*. London: MacMillan, 1977.

———. *The Discovery of King Arthur*. New York: H. Holt, 1987.

———. *Mythology of the British Isles*. North Pomfret, VT: Trafalgar Square Publishers, 1990.

———. *The Virgin*. London: Routledge and Kegan Paul, 1976.

Ashlag, Yehudah. *An Entrance to the Tree of Life*. Jerusalem and New York: Research Centre of Kabbalah, 1977.

Asimov, Isaac. *The Clock We Live On*. New York: Abelard-Schuman, 1959.

Auerbach, Lloyd. *Mind Over Matter*. New York: Kensington, 1996.

Barksdale, E. C. *Enchanted Paths and Magic Words: The Quantum Mind and Time Travel in Science and in Literary Myth*. New York: Peter Lang, 1998.

Beck, Peggy V., and Anna L. Walters. *The Sacred*. Tsaile, AZ: Navajo Community College Press, 1988.

Berger, Pamela. *The Goddess Obscured: Transformation of the Grain Protectress from Goddess to Saint*. Boston: Beacon Press, 1985.

Bettelheim, Bruno. *The Uses of Enchantment: The Meaning and Importance of Fairy Tales*. New York: Vintage Books, 1977.

Bharati, Swami Krishna Tirtha. *Vedic Metaphysics*. Delhi, India: Motilal Barnarsidass, 1988.

Blamires, Steve. *Celtic Tree Mysteries*. St. Paul: Llewellyn, 1997.

———. *Glamoury: Magic of the Celtic Green World*. St. Paul: Llewellyn, 1995.

———. *The Irish Celtic Magical Tradition*. London: Aquarian Press, 1992.

Bonewits, Isaac. *Real Magic*. York Beach, ME: Samuel Weiser, 1989.

Bonnet, James. *Stealing Fire from the Gods: A Dynamic New Story Model for Writers and Filmmakers*. Studio City, CA: Michael Wiese Productions, 1999.

Bonwick, James. *Irish Druids and Old Irish Religions*. Dorset Press, 1986.

Bord, Janet. *Fairies: Real Encounters with Little People*. New York: Dell, 1997.

Born, Max. *Einstein's Theory of Relativity*. Mineola, NY: Dover Publications, 1969.

Brennan, J. H. *Astral Doorways*, revised edition. Wellingborough, Northamptonshire, England: Aquarian Press, 1986. First published in 1971.

———. *Time Travel: A New Perspective*. St. Paul: Llewellyn, 1997.

Briggs, Katherine. T*he Vanishing People: Fairy Lore and Legends*. New York: Pantheon Books, 1978.

Brunaux, Jean Louis. *The Celtic Gauls: Gods, Rites and Sanctuaries*. London: Seaby Ltd., 1988.

Brunvand, Jan H. *The Study of American Folklore: An Introduction*, third edition. New York: W. W. Norton, Co., 1986.

Burchenal, Elizabeth. *Folk-Dances from Old Homelands*. New York: G. Schirmer, 1922.

Burt, Kathleen. *Archetypes of the Zodiac*. St. Paul: Llewellyn, 1988.

Buckland, Raymond. *Advanced Candle Burning*. St. Paul: Llewellyn, 1994.

———. *Buckland's Complete Book of Witchcraft*. St. Paul: Llewellyn, 1987.

———. *Doors to Other Worlds: A Practical Guide to Communicating with Spirits*. St. Paul: Llewellyn, 1993.

———. *Practical Color Magic*. St. Paul: Llewellyn, 1986.

Budapest, Zsuzsanna E. *The Grandmother of Time*. San Francisco: Harper and Row, Publishers, 1989.

———. *Grandmother Moon*. San Francisco: HarperCollins, 1991.

Budge, E. A. Wallis. *The Egyptian Book of the Dead*. Mineola, NY: Dover Publications, 1967.

Butler, W. E. *Magic: Its Ritual Power and Purpose*. York Beach, ME: Samuel Weiser, 1971.

Byrne, Patrick F., editor. *Tales of the Banshee*. Dublin: Mercier Press, 1987.

Cabot, Laurie. *The Power of the Witch*. New York: Delta Books, 1989.

Calder, George, editor. *The Book of Leinster*, bilingual edition. Edinburgh: John Grant, 1917.

Campanelli, Pauline, and Dan Campanelli. *Ancient Ways*. St. Paul: Llewellyn, 1991.

———. *Circles, Groves and Sanctuaries*. St. Paul: Llewellyn, 1992.

———. *Rites of Passage*. St. Paul: Llewellyn, 1994.

———. *Wheel of the Year*. St. Paul: Llewellyn, 1989.

Campbell, Joseph. *The Hero with a Thousand Faces*. Princeton, NJ: Princeton University Press, 1973.

———. *The Masks of God*: Primitive Mythology. New York: Viking Press, 1959.

———. *The Mythic Image*. Princeton, NJ: Princeton University Press, 1974.

———. *The Transformation of Myth Through Time*. New York: Harper and Row, 1990.

Carmichael, Alexander. *Carmina Gadelica*, vols. I and II. Edinburgh: Oliver and Boyd, 1928.

Caro Baroja, Julio. *Las Brujas y Su Mundo*. Madrid: Alianza, 1973.

Carrion, Jorge. *Mitos y Magia del Mexicano*. Mexico D. F.: Porrua y Obregon, 1952.

Casteneda, Carlos. *A Separate Reality*. New York: Pocket Books, 1976.

Chernin, Kim. *Sex and Other Sacred Games*. New York: Times Books, 1989.

Chia, Mantak, and Maneewan Chia. *Healing Love Through the Tao: Cultivating Female Sexual Energy*. Huntington, NY: Healing Tao Books, 1986.

Clodd, Edward. *Magic in Names and Other Things*. New York: Dutton, 1921.

Cockrell, Robert. *The Study and Practice of Astral Projection*. New Hyde Park, NY: University Press, 1966.

Coleman, Martin. *Communing with Spirits*. York Beach, ME: Samuel Weiser, Inc., 1998.

Collins, Terah Kathryn. *The Western Guide to Feng Shui: Room by Room*. Carlsbad, CA: Hay House, Inc., 1999.

Cooper, Jason D. *Esoteric Rune Magic.* St. Paul: Llewellyn, 1994.

Conway, D. J. *Advanced Celtic Shamanism.* Freedom, CA: The Crossing Press, 2000.

———. *By Oak, Ash and Thorn: Modern Celtic Shamanism.* St. Paul: Llewellyn, 1995.

———. *Falcon Feather and Valkryie Sword: Feminine Shamanism, Witchcraft and Magick.* St. Paul: Llewellyn, 1995.

———. *Moon Magick.* St. Paul: Llewellyn, 1995.

Cowan, Tom. *The Book of Séance: How to Reach Out to the Next World.* Chicago: Contemporary Books, 1994.

———. *Fire in the Head: Shamanism and the Celtic Spirit.* San Francisco: HarperCollins, 1992.

Crandall, Joanne. *Self-Transformation Through Music.* Wheaton, IL: The Theosophical Publishing House, 1986.

Crowley, Aleister. *Liber 777*, revised edition. York Beach, ME: Samuel Weiser, 1986.

Crowley, Vivianne. *The Phoenix from the Flame.* Longmeade, UK: Aquarian, 1994.

Cuchulain, Kerr. *The Wiccan Warrior.* St. Paul: Llewellyn, 1997.

Cunningham, Scott. *The Complete Book of Incense, Oils and Brews.* St. Paul: Llewellyn, 1989.

———. *Cunningham's Encyclopedia of Magical Herbs.* St. Paul: Llewellyn, 1985.

———. *Cunningham's Encyclopedia of Crystal, Gem and Metal Magic.* St. Paul: Llewellyn, 1988.

———. *Earth, Air, Fire and Water: More Techniques of Natural Magic.* St. Paul: Llewellyn, 1991.

———. *Earth Power: Techniques of Natural Magic.* St. Paul: Llewellyn, 1987.

———. *Magical Herbalism.* St. Paul: Llewellyn, 1982.

———. *Wicca: A Guide for the Solitary Practitioner.* St. Paul: Llewellyn, 1988.

David-Neel, *Madame Alexandra. Magic and Mystery in Tibet.* Mineola, NY: Dover Publications, 1971.

Davies, Marion. *Lore of the Sacred Horse.* Cheiveley, Berkshire, UK: Capall Bann, 1995.

Davidson, H. R. Ellis. *The Lost Beliefs of Northern Europe.* London: Routledge and Kegan Paul, 1993.

———. *Myths and Symbols in Pagan Europe.* Syracuse, NY: The University of Syracuse Press, 1988.

Davis, Rod. *American Voudou: Journey Into a Hidden World*. Denton, TX: University of North Texas Press, 1999.

de Givry, Grillot. *Witchcraft, Magic and Alchemy*. New York: Dover Publications, Inc., 1971. Originally published in France in 1931.

Denning, Melita, and Osborne Phillips. *Psychic Self-Defense and Well Being*. St. Paul: Llewellyn, 1980.

Diaz, Adrian. *Freeing the Creative Spirit: Drawing on the Power of Art to Tap the Magic and Wisdom Within*. San Francisco: HarperSanFrancisco: 1992.

Dillon, Myles. *Cycles of the Irish Kings*. Oxford: Oxford University Press, 1946.

———. *Early Irish Literature*. Chicago: The University of Chicago Press, 1972.

Dillon, Myles, and N. Chadwick. *The Celtic Realms*. New York: Weidenfeld and Nicolson, 1976.

Dodd, Penelope Reed. *The Idea of the Labyrinth*. Ithaca, NY: Cornell University Press, 1990.

Dolfyn. *Shamanic Wisdom: Nature Spirituality, Sacred Power and Earth Ecstasy*. Oakland, CA: Earthspirit, Inc., 1990.

Dorson, Richard M. *Folklore and Folklife: An Introduction*. Chicago: The University of Chicago Press, 1972.

Eisler, Riane Tennenhaus. *Sacred Pleasure: Sex, Myth, and the Politics of the Body*. San Francisco: HarperSanFrancisco, 1996.

Eliade, Mircea. *Occultism, Witchcraft, and Cultural Fashions: Essays in Comparative Religions*. Chicago: University of Chicago Press, 1976.

———. *Rites and Symbols of Initiation*. New York: Harper and Row, 1965.

———. *Shamanism: Archaic Techniques of Ecstasy*. Princeton, NJ: Princeton University Press, 1964.

Ellis, Thomas E., Psy.D., and Cory F. Newman, Ph.D. *Choosing to Live*. Oakland, CA: New Harbinger Publications, 1996.

Erdoes, Richard, and Alfonso Ortiz, editors. *American Indian Myths and Legends*. New York: Pantheon Books, 1984.

Evans, J. Gwenogryn, editor. *The Black Book of Caermarthen*. Llanbedrog, N. Wales: Pwllheli, 1906.

Evans-Wentz, W. Y. *The Fairy Faith in Celtic Countries*. New York: University Books, 1966. First published in 1911 as The Fairy Mythology.

Evola, Julius. *The Metaphysics of Sex.* New York: Inner Traditions International, 1983. Originally published in Italy in 1969.

Farrar, Janet and Stewart. *Eight Sabbats for Witches.* Custer, WA: Phoenix Publishing, 1981.

———. *The Witches' God.* Custer, WA: Phoenix Publishing, Inc., 1989.

———. *The Witches' Goddess.* Custer, WA: Phoenix Publishing, 1987.

———. *What Witches Do: A Modern Coven Revealed.* Custer, WA: Phoenix Publishing, 1972.

Flint, Valerie I. J. *The Rise of Magic in Early Medieval Europe.* Princeton: Princeton University Press, 1991.

Fortune, Dion. *Applied Magic.* York Beach, ME: Samuel Weiser, Inc., 1982. Compiled from articles written in the 1930s–1950s.

Frankfort, H. *Ancient Egyptian Religion: An Interpretation.* New York: Harper and Row, 1961.

Franklin, Eric. *Dance Imagery for Technique and Performance.* Champaign, IL: Human Kenetics, 1996.

Franklyn, Julian. *Death by Enchantment: An Examination of Ancient and Modern Witchcraft.* London: Hamilton, 1971.

Frazer, Sir James. *The New Golden Bough*, abridged edition. New York: Criterion Books, 1959. First published in 1890 in twelve volumes.

Gager, John G., editor. *Curse Tablets and Binding Spells from the Ancient World.* London and New York: Oxford University Press, 1999.

Galenorn, Yasmine. *Trancing the Witch's Wheel.* St. Paul: Llewellyn, 1997.

———. *Tarot Journeys.* St. Paul: Llewellyn, 1999.

Gardner, Adelaide. *Meditation: A Practical Study.* Wheaton, IL: Quest Books, 1968.

Gauqueline, Michael. *The Scientific Basis of Astrology.* New York: Stein and Day, 1970.

Gawain, Shakti. *Creative Visualization.* Berkeley: Whatever Publishing, 1975. First published in 1955.

Gawr, Rhuddlwn, and Merridwin Gawr. *The Way: The Discovery of the Grail of Immortality.* Litha Springs, GA: New Leaf, 1998. Part 2 of the Quest trilogy.

———. *The Word: The Greater Mysteries of Welsh Witchcraft.* Litha Springs, GA: New Leaf, 1998. Part 3 of the Quest trilogy.

George, Demetra. *Mysteries of the Dark Moon.* San Francisco: HarperCollins, 1992.

George, Llewellyn. *The A to Z Horoscope Maker and Delineator,* revised and expanded twelfth edition, fifty-ninth printing. St. Paul: Llewellyn, 1989.

Gimbutas, Marija. *Goddesses and Gods of Old Europe.* Berkeley: University of California Press, 1982.

Ginzburg, Carlo. *Ecstacies: Deciphering the Witches' Sabbat.* Translated by Raymond Rosenthal. New York: Penguin, 1993.

———. *The Night Battles: Witchcraft and Agrarian Cults in the Sixteenth and Seventeenth Centuries.* Translated by Anne Tedeschi. New York: Penguin, 1992.

Glass-Koentop, Pattalee. *Year of Moons, Season of Trees.* St. Paul: Llewellyn, 1991.

González-Wippler, Migene. *The Complete Book of Spells, Ceremonies and Magic.* St. Paul: Llewellyn, 1988.

———. *Santería: The Religion.* St. Paul: Llewellyn, 1989.

Gray, John, Ph.D. *Men, Women and Relationships.* New York: HarperPaperbacks, 1993.

Gray, William G. *Evoking the Primal Goddess.* St. Paul: Llewellyn, 1989.

———. *Magical Ritual Methods.* Cheltenham, UK: Helios Book Service, 1969.

Graves, Robert. The White Goddess. New York: Farrar, Straus and Giroux, 1973. First published in 1953.

Green, Marian. *Elements of Natural Magic.* Longmeade, Dorset: Element Books, 1989.

———. *The Path Through the Labyrinth: The Quest for Initiation into the Western Mystery Tradition.* Shaftesbury, Dorset, UK: Element Books, 1988.

Green, Miranda J. *Animals In Celtic Life and Myth.* London: Routledge and Kegan Paul, 1992.

———. *Celtic Goddesses: Warriors, Virgins and Mothers.* London: British Museum Press, 1995.

———. *Symbol and Image in Celtic Religious Art.* London: Routledge and Kegan Paul, 1992.

Greene, Rosalyn. *The Magic of Shapeshifting.* York Beach, ME: Samuel Weiser, Inc., 2000.

Gregory, Laneta, and Geoffrey Treissman. *Handbook of the Aura.* Norwich, UK: Pilgrim Book Services, 1985.

Grimassi, Raven. *Hereditary Witchcraft.* St. Paul: Llewellyn, 1999.

———. *Wiccan Magick.* St. Paul: Llewellyn, 1998.

———. *The Wiccan Mysteries.* St. Paul: Llewellyn, 1997.

Guerber, H. A. *Legends of the Rhine*, fourth edition. New York: A. S. Barnes and Company, 1895.

Gundarsson, Kveldulf. *Teutonic Magic*. St. Paul: Llewellyn, 1990.

———. *Teutonic Religion*. St. Paul: Llewellyn, 1993.

Halprin, Anna. *Dance As a Healing Art*. Mendocino, CA: Life Rhythm, 2000.

Harner, Michael. *The Way of the Shaman*, tenth anniversary edition. San Francisco: HarperSanFrancisco, 1990.

Hazlitt, W. Carew. *Faiths and Folklore of the British Isles*, vol. I and II. New York: Benjamin Blom, 1965.

Herm, Gerhard. *The Celts: The People Who Came Out of the Darkness*. New York: St. Martin's Press, 1975.

Hitchcock, Ethan Allen. *Alchemy and the Alchemists*. Los Angeles: Philosophical Research Society, 1976. Originally published in 1850.

Hoch-Smith, Judith, and Anita Spring. *Women in Ritual and Symbolic Roles*. New York: Plenum Press, 1978.

Hughes, Russell M. *Total Education in Ethnic Dance*. New York: M. Dekker, 1977. Originally published in 1928.

Hunt, Robert. *Cornish Folk-Lore*. Penryn, Cornwall: Tor Mark Press, 1988.

———. *Cornish Legends*. Penryn, Cornwall: Tor Mark Press, 1990.

Hunter, Dale, Anne Bailey, and Bill Taylor. *The Art of Facilitation: How to Create Group Synergy*. Tucson, AZ: Fisher Books, 1995.

Hurdy, John Major. *American Indian Religions*. Los Angeles: Sherbourne Press, Inc., 1970.

Huson, Paul. *Mastering the Craft*. New Work: Pedigree, 1980.

Hutchens, Alma R. *Indian Herbalogy of North America*, fifteenth edition. Windsor, ON: Merco, 1989.

Hutton, Ronald. *The Pagan Religions of the Ancient British Isles*. Oxford: Blackwell Press, 1991.

———. *The Stations of the Sun: A History of the Ritual Year in Britain*. Oxford, England: Oxford University Press, 1996.

Irwin, Harvey J. *Flight of Mind: A Psychological Study of the Out-Of-Body Experience*. Metuchen, NJ: Scarecrow Press, 1985.

Jones, Gwyn, and Thomas Jones, translators. *The Mabinogion*, revised edition. London: Everyman, 1993.

Judith, Anodea. *Wheels of Life: A User's Guide to the Chakra System*. St. Paul: Llewellyn, 1986.

Jung, Carl G. *The Archetypes and the Collective Unconscious*, vol. 1–9. Edited by Herbert Read. Princeton, NJ: Princeton University Press, 1981.

———. *Man and His Symbols*. New York: Doubleday, 1964.

———. *The Undiscovered Self.* Princeton, NJ: Princeton University Press, 1990. Originally published in 1957.

Kaplan, Aryeh. *Innerspace: Introduction to Kabbalah, Meditation and Prophecy*. Jerusalem: Moznaim, 1990.

Keane, Patrick J. *Terrible Beauty: Yeats, Joyce, Ireland, and the Myth of the Devouring Female*. Columbia, MO: The University of Missouri Press, 1988.

Keightley, Thomas. *The World Guide to Gnomes, Fairies, Elves and Other Little People*. New York: Avenel Books, 1978. Originally published in 1880 as The Fairy Mythology.

Kieckhefer, Richard. *Magic in the Middle Ages*. Cambridge, UK: Cambridge University Press, 2000.

King, Francis, and Stephen Skinner. *Techniques of High Magic*. New York: Warner-Destiny Books, 1976.

King, Serge Kahili, Ph.D. *Urban Shaman*. New York: Simon and Schuster, Inc., A Fireside Books Imprint, 1990.

Knight, Gareth. *Occult Exercises and Practices*. York Beach, ME: Samuel Weiser, 1976.

Knightly, Charles. *Customs and Ceremonies of Britain*. London: Thames and Hudson, 1986.

Kondratiev, Alexei. *The Apple Branch: A Path to Celtic Ritual*. County Cork, Ireland, 1998.

Kraig, Donald Michael. *Modern Magick: Eleven Lessons in the High Magickal Arts*. St. Paul: Llewellyn, 1988.

LaBerge, Stephen, Ph.D. *Lucid Dreaming*. New York: Ballantine Books, 1986.

Lachapelle, Dolores. *Sacred Land, Sacred Sex*. New York: Kivaki Press, 1992.

Larrington, Carolyne, ed. *The Feminist Companion to Mythology*. Hammersmith, London: Pandora Press, 1992.

Leek, Sybil. *The Complete Art of Witchcraft*. New York: Harper and Row, 1971.

Lehner, Ernst. *Folklore and Symbolism of Flowers, Plants and Trees*. New York: Tudor Publishing Co., 1960.

Lehner, Ernst, and Johanna Lehner. *Picture Book of Devils, Demons and Witchcraft*. New York: Dover Publications, Inc., 1971.

Lévi, Eliphas. *A History of Magic: Including a Clear and Precise Exposition of Its Procedure, Its Rites and Its Mysteries*. London: Rider, 1969. First published in France in 1860.

Levox, Irena. *Ancient Egyptian Dances*. Mineola, NY: Dover Publications, 2000.

Lincoln, Bruce. *Priests, Warriors, Cattle*. Berkeley, CA: The University of California Press, 1981.

Linn, Denise. *Sacred Space: Clearing and Enhancing the Energy of Your Home*. New York: Ballantine Wellspring, 1995.

Littleton, Scott C. *The New Comparative Mythology*. Berkeley, CA: The University of California Press, 1982.

Llewellyn's Magical Almanac. Edited by Cynthia Ahlquist and Michael Fallon. St. Paul: Llewellyn, 1992 through present. Annual publication.

Loomis, Roger Sherman. *The Grail: From Celtic Myth to Christian Symbol*. Princeton, NJ: Princeton University Press, 1991.

Lorler, Marie-Lu. *Shamanic Healing*. Translated from German by Matt Schultz and Winter Laite. Albuquerque, NM: Brotherhood of Life, 1986, 1989.

Lonsdale, Steven H. *Dance and Ritual Play in Greek Religion*. Baltimore: Johns Hopkins University Press, 1993.

Lowe, J. E. *Magic in Greek and Latin Literature*. Oxford, UK: Oxford University Press, 1929.

Ludzia, Leo F. *The Space/Time Connection*. St. Paul: Llewellyn, 1989.

MacCulloch, John A. *The Celtic and Scandinavian Religions*. London and New York: Hutchinson's University Library, 1948.

MacDonald, Margaret Read, editor. *The Folklore of World Holidays*. Detroit: Gale Research, 1992.

MacKenzie, D. A. *Scottish Folk Lore and Folk Life*. Edinburgh: Blackie and Sons, 1935.

MacLean, Adam. *The Triple Goddess*. Grand Rapids, MI: Phanes Press, 1989.

MacLellen, Gordon. *Sacred Animals*. Cheiveley, Berkshire, UK: Capall Bann, 1997.

MacManthuna, Seamus. *Immram Bran: Bran's Journey to the Land of Women*. Tubingen, Wales: Neimeyer, 1985.

MacManus, Dermot. *The Middle Kingdom: The Faerie World of Ireland*. Gerrards Cross, Buckinghamshire: Smythe, 1973.

Macvey, John W. *Time Travel: A Guide to Journeys in the Fourth Dimension*. Chelsea, MI: Scarborough House, 1990.

Malbrough, Ray T. *Charms, Spells and Formulas*. St. Paul: Llewellyn, 1989.

Markale, Jean. *Celtic Civilization*. Translation of *Les Celtes et la Civilisation Celtique*. London: Gordon and Cremonesi, 1978.

———. *Merlin: Priest of Nature*. Translation of *Merlin L'Enchanteur*. Rochester, VT: Inner Traditions, 1981, 1995.

———. *Women of the Celts*. Translation of *La Femme Celts*. Rochester, VT: Inner Traditions International, Ltd., 1972.

Marshall, Peter H. *The Philosopher's Stone: A Quest for the Secrets of Alchemy*. London: MacMillan, 2001.

Matthews, Caitlín. *The Celtic Book of the Dead*. New York: St. Martin's Press, 1992.

———. *The Elements of the Celtic Tradition*. Longmeade, Shaftesbury, Dorset: Element Books, 1989.

———. *The Elements of the Goddess*. Longmeade, Shaftesbury, Dorset: Element Books, 1989.

———. *Mabon and the Mysteries of Britain*. London: Arkana, 1987.

Matthews, John. *The Celtic Shaman*. Shaftesbury, Dorset: Element Books, 1992.

———. *The Elements of the Arthurian Tradition*. Longmeade, Shaftesbury, Dorset: Element Books, 1989.

———. *The Elements of the Grail Tradition*. Longmeade, Shaftesbury, Dorset: Element Books, 1990.

———. *Taliesin: Shamanism and the Bardic Mysteries in Britain and Ireland*. London: Aquarian Press, 1991.

Matthews, John, and Caitlin Matthews. *The Encyclopaedia of Celtic Wisdom*. Shaftesbury, Dorset: Element Books, 1994.

———. *Ladies of the Lake*. Hammersmith, London: The Aquarian Press, 1992.

Matthews, William Henry. *Mazes and Labyrinths: Their History and Development*. Mineola, NY: Dover Publications, 1985.

McClain, Florence Wagner. *A Practical Guide to Past Life Regression*. St. Paul: Llewellyn, 1987.

McConnell, R. A. *Psychology and Self-Deception in Science*. Pittsburgh, PA: R. A. McConnell, 1983.

Mella, Dorothee L. *Stone Power*. New York: Warner Books, 1988.

Mercatante, Anthony S. *The Magic Garden: The Myth and Folklore of Flowers, Plants, Trees and Herbs*. San Francisco: Harper and Row, 1976.

Miller, Richard Alan. *The Magical and Ritual Use of Herbs*. New York: Destiny Books, 1983.

———, and Iona Miller. *The Magical and Ritual Use of Perfumes*. Rochester, VT: Destiny Books, 1990.

Monaghan, Patricia. *The New Book of Goddesses and Heroines*, third edition. St. Paul: Llewellyn, 1997.

———. *O Mother Sun*. Watsonville, CA: The Crossing Press, 1994.

Monroe, Douglas. *The 21 Lessons of Merlyn: A Study in Druid Magic and Lore*. St. Paul: Llewellyn, 1992.

Morwyn. *Secrets of a Witches' Coven*. West Chester, PA: Whitford Press, 1998.

Mumford, John. *Sexual Occultism*. St. Paul: Llewellyn, 1975.

Murray, Margaret A. *The God of the Witches*. London: Faber and Faber, Ltd., 1952. Originally published in 1931.

Nahmad, Claire, and Camilla Charnock. *Garden Spells: The Magic of Herbs, Trees and Flowers*. New York: Gramercy, 1999.

Newall, Venetia, ed. *The Witch Figure: Folklore Essays by a Group of Scholars in England Honoring the 75th Birthday of Katherine M. Briggs*. London: Routledge and Kegan Paul, 1973.

Nichols, Ross. *The Book of Druidry: History, Sites and Wisdom*. Yorkshire, UK: Thorsons Publications, 1992.

Ophiel. *The Art and Practice of Talismanic Magic*. York Beach, ME: Samuel Weiser, 1979.

Pachter, Henry Maximilian. *Paracelsus: Magic Into Science*. New York: Schuman Publishers, 1951.

Peerce, Donna, and Jackie Allen. *Dream Messages: How to Make the Connection Between Heaven and Earth*. Philadelphia: Nova Science Publishers, 1999.

Pelton, Robert W. *Voodoo Charms and Talismans*. New York: Drake, 1973.

Pennick, Nigel. *Celtic Sacred Landscapes*. London: Thames and Hudson, 1996.

Pentikainen, Juha. *Kalevala Mythology*, expanded edition. Translated by Ritva Poom. Bloomington, IN: Indiana University Press, 1999.

Pettis, Chuck. *Secrets of Sacred Space*. St. Paul: Llewellyn, 1999.

Perkins, John. *PsychoNavigation: Techniques for Travel Beyond Time*. Rochester, VT: Destiny Books, 1990.

Pinch, Geraldine. *Magic in Ancient Egypt*. London: British Museum Press, 1994.

Qualls-Corbett, Nancy. *The Sacred Prostitute: Eternal Aspect of the Feminine*. Detroit: InnerCity Books, 1988.

RavenWolf, Silver. *To Stir a Magick Cauldron*. St. Paul: Llewellyn, 1996.

Reed, Ellen Cannon. *The Witches Qabala*. (Revised Edition) York Beach, ME: Samuel Weiser, Inc., 1997.

Rees, Alwyn, and Brinley Rees. *Celtic Heritage: Ancient Tradition in Ireland and Wales*. New York: Thames and Hudson, 1961.

Regardie, Israel. *The Golden Dawn*, fifth edition. St. Paul: Llewellyn, 1986.

Reichenbach, Hans. *The Direction of Time*. Mineola, NY: Dover Publications, 1995.

Rhea, Lady Maeve. *Summoning Forth Wiccan Gods and Goddesses: The Magick of Invocation and Evocation*. New York: Citadel Press, 1999.

Rhea, Maeve, and Barbara E. Vordenbrueggen. *Summoning Forth the Wiccan Gods and Goddesses: The Magick of Invocation and Evocation*. New York: Citadel Press, 1999.

Rhys, Sir John. *Celtic Folklore: Welsh and Manx*, vol. 2. Oxford: Clarendon Press, 1901.

Richardson, Alan. *Earth God Rising: The Return of the Male Mysteries*. St. Paul: Llewellyn, 1992.

———. *Gate to the Moon: Mythical and Magical Doorways to the Otherworld*. Wellingborough, UK: Aquarian Press, 1984.

Ritchie, James N. Graham. *Scotland: Archaeology and Early History*. London: Thames and Hudson, 1981.

Roderick, Timothy. *Dark Moon Mysteries*. St. Paul: Llewellyn, 1992.

Rogo, Scott. *Parapsychology: A Century of Inquiry*. New York: Taplinger, 1975.

Rolleston, T. W. *Celtic Myths and Legends*. New York: Avenel Books, 1986.

Rosen, Barbara. *Witchcraft in England, 1558–1618*. Amherst, MA: University of Massachusetts Press, 1991.

Rosenfeld, Albert, ed. *Mind and Supermind*. New York: Holt, Rinehart and Winston, 1977.

Rudhyar, D. *The Magic of Tone and the Art of Music*. Boulder, CO: University of Colorado Press, 1982.

Ruffing, Janet K. *Mysticism and Social Transformation*. Syracuse, NY: Syracuse University Press, 2001.

Sabrina, Lady. *Reclaiming the Power*. St. Paul: Llewellyn, 1992.

St. Clair, David. *Pagans, Priests, and Prophets*. Englewood Cliffs, NJ: Prentice-Hall, Inc., 1976.

Sands, Helen Raphael. *The Healing Labyrinth: Finding Your Path to Inner Peace*. Hauppauge, NY: Barrons, 2001.

Savage, Candace. *Witch: The Wild Ride from Wicked to Wicca*. Vancouver, BC: Grey Stone Books, 2000.

Scholem, Gershom. *On the Kabbalah and Its Symbolism*. New York: Schocken Books, 1965.

Schuler, Gerald J. *Enochian Magic: A Practical Manual*. St. Paul: Llewellyn, 1985.

Scott, Allan, and Michael Scott Rohan. *Fantastic People: Magical Races of Myth and Legend*. New York: Galahad Books, 1980.

Scullard, H. H. *Festivals and Ceremonies of the Roman Republic*. Ithaca, NY: Cornell University Press, 1981.

Seleneicthon. *Daemonic Magick*. Los Angeles: International Imports, 1994.

Serith, Ceisiwr. *The Pagan Family*. St. Paul: Llewellyn, 1994.

Shuttle, Penelope, and Peter Redgrove. *The Wise Wound: Myths, Realities, and Meanings of Menstruation*, revised edition. New York: Bantam Books, 1990. Originally published in 1978.

Simms, Maria Kay. *A Time for Magic: Planetary Hours for Rituals and Spells*. St. Paul: Llewellyn, 2001.

Skelton, Robin. *Talismanic Magic*. York Beach, ME: Samuel Weiser, 1985.

Skene, William F. *The Four Ancient Books of Wales*. Edinburgh: Edmonston and Douglas, 1868.

Spence, Lewis. *Legends and Romances of Brittany*. London: Frederick A. Stokes Co., 1917.

———. *The Magic Arts in Celtic Britain*. New York: Dorset Press, 1992. Reprint of an edition that appeared in Britain in the 1950s.

———. *The Magic Arts in Celtic Britain*. New York: Dorset Press, 1992. Reprint of an earlier edition, original publication date not given.

Spencer, John, and Anne Spencer. *The Encyclopedia of Ghosts and Spirits*. London: Headline Books, 1992.

Sheba, Lady. *The Grimoire of Lady Sheba*. St. Paul: Llewellyn, 1972.

Squire, Charles. *Celtic Myth and Legend, Poetry and Romance*. New York: Bell Publishing Co., 1979. Originally published in 1905 as *The Mythology of the British Islands*.

Starhawk. *The Spiral Dance*. San Francisco: Harper and Row, 1979.

Steiger, Brad. *Astral Projection*. West Chester, PA: ParaResearch, 1982.

Stepanich, Kisma K. *The Gaia Tradition: Celebrating the Earth in Her Seasons*. St. Paul: Llewellyn, 1991.

———. *Sister Moon Lodge*. St. Paul: Llewellyn, 1993.

Stevens, Jose, Ph.D., and Lena S. Stevens. *Secrets of Shamanism: Tapping the Spirit Power Within You*. New York: Avon, 1988.

Stewart, Iris J. *Sacred Woman, Sacred Dance: Awakening Spirituality Through Movement and Ritual*. Rochester, VT: Inner Traditions, 2000.

Stewart, R. J. *Advanced Magickal Arts*. Shaftesbury, Dorset, UK: Element Books, 1988.

———. *Earth Light: Rediscovery of the Wisdom of Celtic Faery Lore*. Shaftesbury, Dorset: Element Books, 1992.

———. *The Power Within the Land*. Shaftesbury, Dorset: Element Books, 1991.

———. *The Spiritual Dimension of Music*. Rochester, VT: Destiny Books, 1987, 1990.

———. *The Underworld Initiation: A Journey Towards Psychic Transformation*. Wellingborough, England: Aquarian, 1985.

Stone, Merlin. *When God Was a Woman*. New York: Dorset Press, 1976.

Stutley, Margaret. *Ancient Indian Magic and Folklore*. London: Routledge and Kegan Paul, 1980.

Sutphen, Dick. *Finding Your Answers Within*. New York: Pocket Books, 1989.

———. *Past-Life Therapy in Action*. Malibu, CA: Valley of the Sun, 1983, 1987.

Telesco, Patricia. *A Kitchen Witch's Cookbook*. St. Paul: Llewellyn, 1994.

Thorsson, Edred. *The Book of Ogham*. St. Paul: Llewellyn, 1992.

———. *Futhark: A Handbook of Rune Magick*. York Beach, ME: Samuel Weiser, 1984.

———. *Northern Magic: Mysteries of the Norse, Germans and English*. St. Paul: Llewellyn, 1992.

Tyson, Donald. *Ritual Magic*. St. Paul: Llewellyn, 1992.

———, ed. *Three Books of Occult Philosophy*. St. Paul: Llewellyn, 1995. From the collected writings of occultist Henry Cornelius Agrippa, originally published in 1531.

Underhill, Evelyn. *Mysticism: A Study in the Nature and Development of Man's Spiritual Consciousness*. London: Methuen, 1949. Available as a reprint from Dover Publications as *Practical Mysticism*.

Valiente, Doreen. *Natural Magic*. Custer, WA: Phoenix, 1980.

———. *The Rebirth of Witchcraft*. Custer, WA: Phoenix, 1989.

———. *Witchcraft for Tomorrow*. Custer, WA: Phoenix, 1978.

Vigfusson, Gudbrand, and F. York Powell, translators. *Norse Mythology*. Hamden, CT: Archon Books, 1974.

VonFranz, Marie-Louise. *Creation Myths*. Boston: Shambhala Publications, Inc., 1995. Originally published in 1972.

Walker, Barbara G. *The Crone: Woman of Age, Wisdom and Power*. San Francisco: Harper-Collins, 1990.

Webb, Don. *Uncle Setnakt's Essential Guide to the Left Land Path*. Smithville, TX: Runa-Raven Press, 1999.

Webster, Richard. *Feng Shui for Beginners*. St. Paul: Llewellyn, 2000.

Weinstein, Marion. *Earth Magic: A Dianic Book of Shadows*. Custer, WA: Phoenix, 1986.

———. *Positive Magic*. Custer, WA: Phoenix, 1980.

Wendell, Leilah. *The Necromantic Ritual Book*. New Orleans, LA: Westgate Press, 1993.

Whitmont, Edward C. *The Symbolic Quest*. New York: G. P. Putnam's Sons (for the C. G. Jung Foundation for Analytical Psychology), 1969.

Williams, Selma R. *Riding the Nightmare: Women and Witchcraft from the Old World to Colonial Salem*. San Francisco: HarperPerrenial, 1992. First published in 1972.

Wilson, Colin. *Beyond the Occult: A Twenty Year Investigation Into the Paranormal*. New York: Carroll and Graf Publishers, Inc., 1988.

Wilson, David. *Anglo-Saxon Paganism*. London: Routledge, 1992.

Wold, Astri Heen. *Decoding Oral Language*. London and New York: Academic Press (with cooperation of the European Association of Experimental Social Psychology), 1978.

Woolley, Benjamin. *The Queen's Conjurer: The Science and Magic of Dr. John Dee, Advisor to Queen Elizabeth I*. New York: Henry Holt, 2001.

Wright, Elbee. *The Book of Legendary Spells*. Minneapolis: Marlar Publishing Co, 1974.

Zotti, Carlos Liberio del. *Brujería y Magia en America*. Barcelona: Plaza y Janes, 1974.

Zweig, Connie, and Jeremiah Abrams, eds. *Meeting the Shadow: The Hidden Power of the Dark Side of Human Nature*. New York: Penguin Putnam, 1991.

A Witch's World of Magick

Expanding Your Practice with Techniques &
Traditions from Diverse Cultures

MELANIE MARQUIS

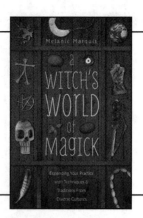

This sparkling, in-depth examination of theories and techniques from around the world will help you reach higher levels of magickal insight and success. Each chapter features examples of tried-and-true magickal techniques gathered from the annals of folk magick around the world. By becoming more familiar with these classic "magickal moves," you'll have a solid starting point for designing your own mystical innovations.

Melanie Marquis, author of *The Witch's Bag of Tricks*, helps you explore the ins and outs of magickal skills and concepts from an eclectic perspective, providing a deeper understanding of spellwork and a greater appreciation for our magickal world. From Wiccan spells to Chaos magick, magick without tools to potion-making, discover love spells, word charms, curse-breaking, potion-making, contemporary spellwork, and more.

978-0-7387-3660-0
240 pp., 6 x 9 $16.99

Buckland's Complete Book of Witchcraft

RAYMOND BUCKLAND

The most complete resource to the study and practice of Wicca

Never before has so much information on the Craft of the Wise been collected in one place. Traditionally, there are three degrees of advancement in most Wiccan traditions. When you have completed studying this book, you will be the equivalent of a Third-Degree Witch. Even those who have practiced Wicca for years find useful information in this book, and many covens are using this for their textbook. If you want to become a Witch, or if you merely want to find out what Witchcraft is really about, you will find no better book than this.

978-0-87542-050-9
368 pp., 8½ x 11, illus.

$21.99

To order, call 1-877-NEW-WORLD
Prices subject to change without notice
Order at llewellyn.com 24 hours a day, 7 days a week!

To Write to the Author

If you wish to contact the author or would like more information about this book, please write to the author in care of Llewellyn Worldwide and we will forward your request. Both the author and publisher appreciate hearing from you and learning of your enjoyment of this book and how it has helped you. Llewellyn Worldwide cannot guarantee that every letter written to the author can be answered, but all will be forwarded. Please write to:

Edain McCoy
⅝ Llewellyn Worldwide
2143 Wooddale Drive
Woodbury, MN 55125-2989
Please enclose a self-addressed stamped envelope for reply,
or $1.00 to cover costs. If outside U.S.A., enclose
international postal reply coupon.

Many of Llewellyn's authors have websites
with additional information and resources.
For more information, please visit our website at
www.llewellyn.com